Contemporary Issues in Caribbean and Latin American Relations

Contemporary Issues in Caribbean and Latin American Relations

Edited by
Raymond Mark Kirton and Marlon Anatol

LEXINGTON BOOKS
Lanham • Boulder • New York • London

Published by Lexington Books
An imprint of The Rowman & Littlefield Publishing Group, Inc.
4501 Forbes Boulevard, Suite 200, Lanham, Maryland 20706
www.rowman.com

6 Tinworth Street, London SE11 5AL, United Kingdom

Copyright © 2021 The Rowman & Littlefield Publishing Group, Inc.

British Library Cataloguing in Publication Information Available

Library of Congress Cataloging-in-Publication Data

Names: Kirton, R. Mark (Raymond Mark), 1951- editor. | Anatol, Marlon, editor.
Title: Contemporary issues in Caribbean and Latin American relations / edited by
    Raymond Mark Kirton, and Marlon Anatol.
Description: Lanham : Lexington Books, [2021] | Includes bibliographical references
    and index.
Identifiers: LCCN 2021031463 (print) | LCCN 2021031464 (ebook) |
    ISBN 9781793655783 (hardback) | ISBN 9781793655790 (epub)
    ISBN 9781793655806 (pbk)
Subjects: LCSH: Caribbean Area—Foreign relations—Latin America. |
    Latin America—Foreign relations—Caribbean Area. |
    Latin America—Foreign relations—1980- | Caribbean Area—Foreign
    relations—1945-
Classification: LCC F2177 .C66 2021 (print) | LCC F2177 (ebook) |
    DDC 327.72908—dc23
LC record available at https://lccn.loc.gov/2021031463
LC ebook record available at https://lccn.loc.gov/2021031464

Contents

Introduction

Contemporary Issues in Caribbean and Latin American Relations

Raymond Mark Kirton and Marlon Anatol

ABOUT THE CARIBBEAN

This region has been a part of the world economy since it was "discovered" over 500 years ago. From that time to the present, the region has existed in a non-reciprocal relationship with its colonial masters. While economic and other support was freely given to the region as a strategy for increasing the exploitation of the natural resources and the creation of markets for excess goods from the metropole, the situation has changed drastically in the last few decades. This is characterized by reduced financial aid, deteriorating terms of trade, loss of geopolitical significance to the metropoles, among others. Coupled with this loss of significance to the metropoles, countries in the region, particularly the Caribbean states, have also been plagued with issues of smallness, vulnerability, sustainability, and survival. Smallness matters as the individual nations are insignificant in the global system.

The states are also vulnerable, not just to shock in the economic and financial system, but also to natural phenomenon/disasters such as hurricanes, floods, and landslides, all of which leaves them devastated. The issues of sustainability arise when one recognizes that due to the limited landmass and population, the economic activities need to be conducted in a sustainable manner so that the future generations will not suffer from the productive methods/decisions made today. Survival is also a crucial issue for the developing states in the Caribbean and Latin America, as in many cases they have faced political instability, rising rates of internal crime and violence, falling demand for their exports, foreign exchange shortages, rising external debt, economic collapse, increased social unrest and insecurity, as well as new challenges including climate change and ecological and environmental degradation.

Understanding the issues that plague the region now necessitates a re-conceptualization of the approach that needs to be taken to tackle the problems and ensure the survival of the countries. Further, it involves a re-prioritizing of the issues that plague the region and a developmental approach that is sustainable and achievable in the countries. While there are limited resources, issues of collaboration and cooperation should be high on the agenda for the development of the region, particularly at a time when the external realities are in flux, and the future of these states is unsure.

To be sure the countries of the region are intricately linked to the rest of the world, regardless of their small size and limited power in the international arena. Globalization has ensured that the link to the system is constant, and one needs to be able to leverage this fact in order to increase the chances of survival. Notwithstanding issues such as weak institutions and governance structures, lack of internal and regional infrastructure, lack of adequate shipping lines and routes, risk-averse banking systems and weak legislatures; these states have to adapt and exist in the changing world, and as such need to be flexible and adaptive in their approaches to development. The process of globalization has been asymmetrical and the region has not benefited from the expansion in communication and transport, but may be viewed as being relegated to an irrelevant space in the system, which does not make it a direct or primary actor, but simply exists and is a recipient of the actions of other actors in the system.

This publication highlights and interrogates many of the issues that plague the Caribbean and Latin American states, and provides the foundation for a new approach to development, taking into account the global realities and the rights of the citizens, seeking to produce the best policy alternatives for sustainable development in the region. Policy implementation and coordination has always been areas of contention in the region, and this publication suggests that in light of the changing international environment and the position of these states therein, policy development, implementation, and coordination are critical for survival.

The COVID-19 pandemic has also served to highlight the fragility of the system, with increasing crises and insecurities (inclusive of security, health, migration, and economic) being bought to the forefront of the international narrative. These occurrences in the system suggest that some attention and academic consideration needs to be given to the processes within, in the aim of attaining a better understanding of possible approaches to counteract the negative consequences.

This publication delivers scholarly perspectives and approaches for dealing with some of the issues that are affecting the region, and makes a significant contribution to the discourse, in many cases highlighting country-specific studies. The chapters present fresh perspectives on political, economic, and social issues which confront the Caribbean and Latin American states in the changing global environment. The critical analysis presented by the authors will allow generation of serious discussion and debate and will spread interest for the topic both regionally and internationally.

Chapter 1

The Guyana Shield in a Changing Regional Environment

Challenges and Opportunities

Raymond Mark Kirton

INTRODUCTION

The view has been advanced that, in spite of its increasing significance in the region, scholarly attention has not been directed to issues related to the Northern tier of South America, and the Guiana Shield in particular. This chapter seeks to interrogate the current sociopolitical and economic environment, and the challenges and opportunities related to the relations among the countries of the Guiana Shield.

In order to place the Guiana Shield in context, it is noted that, according to the United Nations Development Programme (UNDP), the Guiana Shield can be defined as "an eco-region of regional and global significance."[1]

The Guiana Shield covers an area of 270 million hectares and consists of varied and various ecosystems that house keystone species of biodiversity, store globally significant amounts of carbon and water, and provide livelihoods for many human cultures. All or part of six countries—Brazil, Colombia, French Guiana, Guyana, Suriname, and Venezuela—share this unique area. The Guiana Shield is also described as one of the last remaining blocks of pristine rainforest, with approximately 20 percent of the world's remaining freshwater reserves, which allows it to capture significant quantities of carbon dioxide. It has also been recognized that the biodiversity of the Guiana Shield provides ecosystem services such as food, freshwater, and medicinal products as well as an environmental support in areas such as water quality and pollination. According to Lewis (2017), as part of a global resource pool, "the Guiana Shield has been recognized for its potential for expanded hydro-energy production, agricultural development, mainly in the

1

coastal area near the Atlantic Ocean and the promotion of sustainable eco-tourism." One can therefore support the view posited by former President David Granger of Guyana that the Guiana Shield is "essential to enriching and replenishing the world's biodiversity and consequently the Guiana Shield is essential to the survival of Planet Earth."[2]

It is against this background that this chapter includes an assessment of the current status of the efforts at collaboration in the Guiana Shield and an analysis of the challenges and opportunities for greater interaction and integration among the countries in the subregion. It must be noted, however, that given its status as a French overseas department or "DOM," and its current relative isolation in the Guianas, with limited political space to engage the Guiana Shield arena, the chapter will, to a large extent focus on the two independent states—Guyana and Suriname, and other Guiana Shield countries. It must however be clearly noted that the increasing potential for cooperation among states of the Guiana Shield has received the attention of the government of France. Indeed, in 2017, during a visit to French Guiana in 2017, the French President highlighted the significant benefits which could accrue from increased cooperation in the subregion, and it is envisaged that strenuous efforts will be made by France to engage the countries of the Guiana Shield in the short and medium term.

Traditionally, small states of the Caribbean and the Guianas were first viewed as being under the British or Dutch control or later as part of the United States' "backyard" or sphere of influence and this led to a largely asymmetrical relationship marked by the significant disparity in power relations, as suggested by the realist perspective in international relations. In these circumstances, the possibility for alternative pathways to enhance regional collaboration to be chosen by these states, like Guyana and Suriname, was severely constrained.

As a result, the discourse with respect to the relations between the small states of the Guiana Shield, especially the relatively newly independent Guyana and Suriname, and countries of Latin America generally, has traditionally centered around the sense of "separateness" and the economic and cultural "distance" which have constrained the emergence of strong and sustained linkages, especially between them and the larger states of the subregion—Brazil, Venezuela, and Colombia. Several arguments have been advanced, including the view that the impact of colonial bilateralism, which included political, social, and economic dimensions, as well as linguistic and cultural differences, served to limit the development of sustained linkages between the three Guianas—Guyana, Suriname, and French Guiana—and their Spanish and Portuguese-speaking neighbors in the Guyana Shield. One must consider that Guyana was a colony of Great Britain until 1966, Suriname was a colony of the Netherlands until 1975, and French Guiana currently remains an Overseas Department of France. It is also noteworthy that territorial controversies between Guyana and Suriname and Suriname and France in relation to its boundary with French Guiana have at times led to strained relations.

It has also been observed that the political history of French Guiana included its incorporation into the French colonial system and as a department of France in 1946. As Grant (2007) noted, "in the course of its assimilation, French Guiana has acquired not only a French, but a European identity to the extent that it is primarily of relevance to France and the European Community as a showcase of European scientific advance,"[3] and this has accounted, in part, for its limited relations with countries of the Guiana Shield.

In recent times, however, the imperatives of geographical proximity, moves toward new forms of regional collaboration in South America, widening areas of South–South cooperation and new regional and global issues which have emerged, influenced a growing convergence of interests among countries of the Guiana Shield, and presented the prospect for a sustained relationship. There are lingering concerns which still remain among the Guianas, including continued consciousness about their small size and the potential fragility of their national identities, especially in the case of Guyana and Suriname, in the wider Guiana Shield environment of larger states and emerging powers.

The view has also been advanced that levels of development, differences in physical and population size, natural resource endowments, and the presence and influence of strong extra-regional cultural influences have constrained the growth of a sustained relationship in the Guiana Shield region. Indeed, these complex sets of factors have contributed to the development of strongly rooted negative perceptions on all sides, which have influenced not only popular attitudes but also the formal relations not only among governments and states of the Guiana Shield but also among the wider Caribbean Community (CARICOM) states and Latin America.

It has been noted[4] that especially in the Caribbean and the Guianas, the lengthy periods of political and economic relationship with Europe, the extreme dependence of the small countries on these relationships for their viability, and the cultural and educational impact of the relationship have not traditionally disposed the people of these countries to think of themselves as being part of the American Continental Zone. Further, Gill (1995) has advanced the view that the Caribbean (including the Guianas) and Latin America appeared to constitute "two separate worlds which took no notice of each other in spite of their proximity. Separately they organized their national existence, having as axis, a preferential relationship with the countries that fulfilled a hegemonic function with respect to them" (Maira, 1983). These factors therefore also contributed to the low levels of interaction between the Guianas and the other states of the Guiana Shield.

It is also noted that since the Latin American states, including those of the Guiana Shield, enjoyed political sovereignty since the early nineteenth century, their attitudes and orientations were significantly different to those of the Caribbean including the Guianas, which were only beginning to achieve independence in the 1960s and 1970s. These explanations demonstrate, therefore, that there have been important constraints to the emergence of a structured and comprehensive set of relationships in the Guiana Shield until recently.

As the small states, Guyana and Suriname, gained their independence, there was a cautious approach toward the Latin American region in general with little difference in their approach to the Guiana Shield countries. It must be reiterated that these small states at that time were forced to operate in a geographical and international relations environment dominated by the United States and in the midst of a bipolar Cold War U.S.–USSR conflict, which limited their attempts to secure new international linkages.

However, though small in size, the emergence of these new states brought new political orientations and cultural backgrounds to the interplay of relations between states in the Guiana Shield and added a new dynamic to the regional mosaic. Further, Guyana with a predominant African and East Indian-descended population, was governed by adaptations of the Westminster model of governance, while Suriname, a small multiethnic society had a unique constitutional arrangement which led to a consociational political and governance structure. Both of these constitutional structures were sufficiently distinct from the political model of the other Guiana Shield states (Brazil, Colombia, and Venezuela) and introduced a new dimension to the practice of politics and international relations in the region in general and in the Guiana Shield in particular.

Additionally, it was observed that in the early postindependence period, Caribbean states and those of the Guianas did not find ready political acceptance with Latin American governments generally, and the diplomatic response by these states to Latin America in the 1960s was selective and on a "stop-and-go basis" and was derived from perceptions of countries of the Latin American region as a source of serious threats to the territorial integrity of two Caribbean states, Guyana and Belize. Undoubtedly, the Venezuelan claim to nearly two-thirds of Guyana was considered a serious dysfunctionality, which affected the conduct of relations between the CARICOM states and Latin America, especially Venezuela, a Guiana Shield state. Additionally, a border controversy between Guyana and Suriname also slowed the pace of interaction among countries in the Guiana Shield, in the midst of an era of serious mistrust and suspicion, alongside gradual moves to establish a "modus vivendi" among the states. Further, one can also support the view that being new entrants to the hemispheric international relations system, countries such as Guyana and Suriname ranked low on the major South American countries "hierarchy of concern" and this further limited the early development of a solid and well-defined relationship in the Guiana Shield region.

The decade of the 1970s, however, brought with it the gradual development of linkages between the small states of the region, including Guyana and Suriname, and their Latin neighbors. This era coincided with the promotion of Third World and collective solidarity among developing states and an emphasis on South–South cooperation which facilitated a change in the pattern of the relations between the small states and their larger Guiana Shield neighbors. By 1975, the establishment of the Latin American Economic System (SELA), which was intended to introduce new economic linkages between Latin America and the Caribbean, as well as the creation of the regional maritime transport network (NAMUCAR), the Latin American and Caribbean Sugar Producer's Association (GEPLACEA), and participation in forums such as the Inter-American Development Bank (IDB), the Organization of American States (OAS), the United Nations Economic Commission for Latin America and the Caribbean (UNECLAC), and the Group on Latin American and the Caribbean (GRULAC) at the United Nations, set the stage for the phased emergence of structured linkages between the two sets of states. These initiatives also provided the basis for new windows of opportunity for cooperation among countries of the Guiana Shield.

Further, the participation of Guyana and Suriname, as signatories to the Treaty for Amazonian Cooperation, initiated by Brazil in 1978 and with the participation of all of the countries of the Guiana Shield, also provided important forums to develop new patterns of collaboration between countries in the Guiana Shield. The Treaty came at a time when Brazil was seeking to carve a new space for itself in South American international relations, and as a potential leader in South America, it was important to structure and articulate a functional relationship with its Amazonian neighbors in the Guiana Shield, including the small states of the Guiana Shield—Guyana and Suriname.

The Treaty also promoted joint action in the areas of technological and scientific research, and the implementation of measures to develop economic cooperation and the promotion of greater contact among the citizenry of the participating states. Some analysts have argued that the Treaty was an effort by Brazil to reduce the mistrust and suspicion of its neighbors, especially Guiana Shield states, which at that time expressed some concerns about Brazil's expansionist projections. Indeed, for Guyana and Suriname, this initiative was the first multilateral cooperation effort initiated by Brazil and it engaged the two small states and provided them with the first institutional opportunity, as countries in the Guiana Shield, to become more engaged with the rest of the countries of the subregion.

In the 1980s, however, the challenges of the external debt crisis which negatively impacted Latin American, Caribbean, and Guiana Shield states brought about a retreat from the positive push for closer collaboration which was aimed at developing sustainable cross-border programs for mutual benefit. Additionally, in the 1980s, differences in foreign policy positions, the domestic and international demands for the shift from authoritarian rule to democratic governance in Latin America, and the deepening economic crisis in the wider region also contributed to a decline in the development in closer collaboration among Guiana Shield states.

It can be argued, however, that as global and hemispheric changes occurred in the early 1990s, these new developments influenced a convergence of interests between CARICOM states and Latin America and a new impetus for collaboration in the Guiana Shield.

Critical issues of mutual concern such as the impact of globalization on developing countries, the debilitating consequences of increasing poverty and inequality on the region's citizenry, a renewed awareness of the vital role of economic cooperation, as well as common health challenges such as the HIV/AIDS pandemic, environmental and security concerns, among others, served to promote active collaboration to be sought in Caribbean–Latin American relations in general and among countries of the Guiana Shield in particular. Of equal significance was the report of the West Indian Commission, which was established by the CARICOM Heads of Government in 1989, in the context of the recognition of the changing global environment and its potential impact on CARICOM states. In that report "Time for Action," one of the major recommendations was that "CARICOM bridge the divide between its Member States and other states and territories of the Caribbean and Latin America, recognizing the advent of an increasingly wider regional approach to international negotiations and development issues, as well as changes within and among Latin American countries."[5]

This was perceived by states like Guyana and Suriname, to be a new opportunity to transform geographical proximity in the Guiana Shield into a new level of networking and collaboration in both the economic and political arenas. This period also marked the establishment of the Association of Caribbean States (ACS) in 1994, arising out of a CARICOM initiative, and its membership including all the Guiana Shield countries, except Brazil. It has been argued elsewhere that the omission of Brazil from the ACS was a tactical and strategic error since this initiative could have prompted with greater momentum and facilitated enhanced cooperation among the states of the Guiana Shield since Brazil had already signaled its intention to engage the subregion and the wider Caribbean region as a priority.

At the same time, the end of the Cold War brought with it the emergence of "new" regionalism, which can be described as a multidimensional form of integration which included economic, political, social, and cultural aspects. The adoption of "new regionalism" in Latin America introduced an important dimension to interregional cooperation, including the consolidation of democracy, regional security, and political dialogue and cooperation. This period also coincided with the revitalization and reconfiguration of previous integration initiatives in the region, including the Rio Group, the Amazonian Cooperation Treaty Organization, as well as the establishment of MERCOSUR, which generated significant interest among Guiana Shield states, including Guyana and Suriname, due to the recognition of growing interdependence in the changing regional environment. At the same time, Latin American states were seeking to extend cooperation across the region, and to develop trade and functional cooperation with the CARICOM states, especially in the context of global changes which were taking place and the interest which developed in the small states of the Guiana Shield was significant at that time.

The first decade of the twenty-first century undoubtedly brought with it an increase in the momentum in collaborative activity in the region, with serious attention being given to the Guiana Shield. At the same time, there was the emergence of the South American Community of Nations (SACN) in 2004, inspired by Brazil and which included Guyana and Suriname among its membership. Further, its successor institution, The Union of South American Nations (UNASUR) in 2008, developed an economic and development agenda in the region which targeted energy, physical, social, financial, and institutional integration as its major focus points. As a result, new initiatives emerged which aimed to foster development in the Guiana Shield, aimed at improving physical infrastructure, increase productivity, and competitiveness in the areas of transportation, energy, and telecommunications. The Initiative for the Integration of Regional Infrastructure in South America (IIRSA) also sought to implement projects which included the construction of a bridge which links Brazil and Guyana, along with roads and bridges which was envisaged to enhance the surface communication linkage among Brazil, Venezuela, Guyana, Suriname, and French Guiana and positively impact the economic and social relations among the states of the Guiana Shield.

It is interesting to note that, with an activist regional policy initiated by the Lula administration in Brazil, in 2008, the first Latin American and Caribbean Summit on Integration and Development was convened. This was an historic event for Guyana and Suriname, since it was the first time that heads of state and government of Latin America and the Caribbean, among them the countries of the Guiana Shield, convened a meeting with their own agenda and without the influence and presence of the major global and hemispheric powers. For the small states of the Guianas, this event demonstrated the political will of the regional leaders to create a new space for dialogue and cooperation. It is also important to note that the momentum built around this historic event prepared the ground for the establishment of the Community of Latin American and Caribbean States (CELAC) which was formally established in 2011, and this mechanism created a new space for the development of mutually beneficial political and economic relations. Undoubtedly, the current economic and political environment has served to slow the pace of CELAC initiatives but the initiatives established by CELAC have provided the impetus especially in the Guiana Shield for the development of closer collaborative linkages. There are still challenges and concerns which remain and which must be addressed by countries in the Guiana Shield, in order to move toward sustained collaboration. In the first place, there are concerns with respect to the sustainability of the initiatives, given the remaining levels of mistrust that still limit the linkages among the countries of the Guiana Shield.

The argument has been advanced that there has, as yet, not been the emergence of a common development strategy, especially in the Guiana Shield. There are concerns that inadequate contact and communications continue to constrain the pursuit of stronger linkages and as Sanders (2005) contends "in short, the small Caribbean states and the larger Latin American territories share very little more than the same geographical region of the world, and their relationship is not mutually supportive." One can posit that a robust strategy for collaboration, initiated by the states of the Guiana Shield, can change that perception.

Additionally, while there has been expressed concern with respect to the challenges related to the potential "swamping" of the small states of the Guiana Shield, Latin America has generally in the past shown little concern for the potential calamitous effects on their economies as a result of loss of preferential markets for important foreign exchange and employment-generating exports including sugar and other primary products from small states including Guyana and Suriname. While these concerns linger, there is a pressing need for a sustained level of engagement among countries of the Guiana Shield, especially given the recent emergence of new oil and gas sectors in the economies of Guyana and Suriname. These new sectors present the opportunity for closer collaboration and the sharing of experience, especially by Brazil, the largest Guiana Shield state.

There are also other significant security and political challenges facing states in the Guiana Shield which demand the construction of sustainable strategic alliances. In the security sector, the Guiana Shield states, especially the small states, Guyana and Suriname, continue to suffer from the increasing levels of transnational organized crime, including drug trafficking, trafficking in persons, the illicit trade in firearms and other criminal activity, with interregional criminal networks developing rapidly. Further, the porous borders of Guyana and Suriname represent strong potential threats to the sovereignty and territorial integrity of these small countries and provide ample opportunity for higher levels of transnational criminal penetration. In addition, both human and financial resource constraints, along with limited defense and security capabilities, have left the Guianas vulnerable to threats from terrorism. The larger Guiana Shield states, like Brazil on the other hand, have since the 1990s become involved in developing defense and security networks, including the establishment of the Amazonian Surveillance System (SIVAM).

The extensive networks of borders in the Guianas undoubtedly bring challenges and the states' ability to monitor and control them, especially in sparsely populated areas. The porous frontiers and the complex problems associated with their security, coupled with a lack of law enforcement, manpower and deterrence capability, as well as the absence of technological assets of small states of the Guiana Shield, has left them exposed and vulnerable.

According to Cope (2016), in 1985,[6] recognizing the need to effectively secure its strategic Northern locations and borders, Brazil initiated the Calha Norte (North Corridor) program aimed at "augmenting the military and government presence in the zone, creating clearly demarcated international borders through surveying and physical markers, increasing bilateral relations (in terms of commerce and technical and infrastructural cooperation) and defining an appropriate policy for indigenous groups in the corridor." Of equal significance to the Guianas, was the establishment of the System for the Surveillance of Amazonia (SIVAM) in 1992, which became fully operational in 2004 and now involves environmental surveillance, the processing of meteorological information, air traffic control and emergency search, and rescue operations. Alongside the operations of SIVAM, the overarching system, the System for the Protection of Amazonia (SIPAM) is responsible for the coordination and oversight of these activities.

The limited human and financial resources of the small states of the Guiana Shield, especially Guyana and Suriname, and their potential vulnerability require urgent attention as potential threats to their territorial integrity increase and as a joint security initiative, SIVAM can be extended to include these countries so that effective monitoring and control of the Guiana Shield could become part of a collaborative arrangement. A structured and institutionalized plan across the Guiana Shield can therefore provide all states with early indicators related to security concerns and provide the states with increased capacity to confront criminal networks. One can therefore posit that a mutual security agreement among the Guiana Shield states could be established, and can serve to increase the levels of confidence and security among the citizens of the subregion.

It has also been established that traditionally there have been limited trade and commercial linkages between the small states of the Guiana Shield and their larger counterparts. The constraints have included inadequate maritime and air links, underdeveloped surface communication, language and cultural constraints, and limited knowledge of market demands, among others. Guiana Shield states therefore must address these challenges which will require the engagement of both the public and private sectors, in efforts to improve infrastructure, develop networks, and provide the enabling environment to exploit the significant potential for the integration of production among the states. Undoubtedly, opportunities exist for the exploitation of new economic complementarities in areas including multi-destination ecotourism, wood processing, aluminum product manufacturing, jewelry production, agroindustrial processing and the development of the creative arts, music and cultural industries, among others. The private sectors in the Guiana Shield states must therefore play a leading role to initiate and sustain joint venture partnerships and devise creative frameworks for mutually beneficial trade and commercial activities.

It has also been recognized that cooperation in energy generation and distribution among Guiana Shield states could serve to guarantee supply, minimize the environmental effects and impact, and improve the productivity in industries, among other potential positive outcomes. As the InterAmereican Development Bank report "Arco Norte Electrical Interconnection Study" (Larrea, 2017),[7] "the electrical interconnection of the region would improve the regional electrical system, allowing electricity trading among these countries." In addition, the study added, "this would allow for an optimal power generation expansion plan, under which the region could use the most efficient sources of electricity, minimizing cost and environmental and social impacts." Undoubtedly, a structured and well-defined Guiana Shield interconnected power system could facilitate the emergence of new and clean energy sources, including hydropower, solar power and wind and serve to expand transmission networks into currently underserved or unserved areas and areas of economic development.

While challenges remain, the prudent development of linkages among the Guiana Shield states have a positive impact on the development of countries, especially the small states of Guyana and Suriname. There must be, however, well-coordinated cross-border efforts engaging all the stakeholders, both public and private sectors as well as civil society organizations. At the technical level, every effort must be made to protect the biodiversity of the region and it has been noted that in 2016, President Granger of Guyana at the 4th International Congress on Biodiversity proposed a three-tiered approach to facilitate the effective protection and preservation of the Guiana Shield. The approach contemplates the establishment of a scientific research institute, the formulation and implementation of strong mechanisms for data and information sharing, and the provision of adequate investment funding to facilitate economic growth. As President Granger noted "the Guiana Shield is essential to enriching and replenishing the world's biodiversity, and consequently the Guiana Shield is essential for the survival of planet earth" (Thompson, 2016).

It has been noted that French Guiana, as an Overseas Department of France, has traditionally focused its trade and commercial linkages with Europe. As a new era of cooperation is envisaged, the development of linkages among Guiana Shield states that especially Guyana and Suriname, with French Guiana, will require the creation of programs and policies aimed at providing the environment for the strengthening of economic relations, which have the greatest potential for mutual benefit. Guiana Shield states must also swiftly pursue joint action in areas of water, wind, and solar power to reduce energy costs which can redound to the benefit of the industrial sectors and the wider citizenry of the region. The movement toward increased levels of collaboration between French Guiana and the other Guiana Shield states can provide an opening for France and the European Union to occupy more economic and commercial space in the larger Guiana Shield states, as well as the South American Common Market (MERCOSUR) and create new opportunities for economic activity in the subregion.

In order to facilitate sustained collaboration, one can contend that the Guiana Shield must become a zone of peace in order to ensure the safety and security of its citizenry. Unfortunately, there are still unresolved border controversies, most significantly Venezuela's claim to two-thirds of Guyana's territory. After an international Arbitral Tribunal in 1899 gave a full, perfect, and final settlement in 1962, Venezuela denounced the Arbitral Award and has continued to promote this claim since then, at times with acts of aggression. It has been noted that the United Nations Secretary General Ban Ki Moon and his successor Antonio Gutteres made the decision in keeping with a 1966 Agreement between Venezuela and Great Britain (acting on behalf of its then-colony British Guiana) that, if by 2017, there had been no significant progress made toward arriving at a full agreement for the settlement of the controversy, the International Court of Justice (ICJ) would be the means chosen to determine a peaceful settlement, unless Guyana and Venezuela jointly requested another mechanism.

In 2020, the ICJ after an oral hearing in the case against Venezuela, determined that the ICJ has jurisdiction over the case which was filed by Guyana in March 2018 in which that country seeks to obtain from the court, a final and binding judgment "that the 1899 Arbitral Award which established the location of the land boundary between them—British Guiana and Venezuela—remains valid and binding, and that Guyana's Essequibo region belongs to Guyana and not Venezuela."[8] The ICJ in its ruling concluded that "it has jurisdiction to entertain Guyana's claim concerning the 1899 Award . . . and the related question of the definitive settlement of the land boundary dispute between the territory of the parties."

In March 2021, the ICJ fixed time limits for written submissions by both parties on the merits of the views expressed by Venezuela in relation to its disagreement with the ICJ decision on its jurisdiction.

While there are unresolved border controversies which involve all the countries of the Guiana Shield except Brazil, the most recent escalation of tensions and serious acts of aggression have occurred in pursuit of Venezuela's claim to Guyana's territory. Guiana Shield citizens can positively contribute to the de-escalation of these tensions, as the ICJ process unfolds, through greater contact and dialogue in order to reduce mistrust and suspicion, utilizing "second track" or "track two" diplomacy. This diplomatic effort which can involve nongovernmental organizations (NGOs), academic institutions, humanitarian agencies, among others, can create new initiatives to promote greater understanding through unofficial and informal interaction.

In the case of the lingering tensions between Guyana and Suriname, in 2016, in a round of Presidential diplomacy, the two heads of state indicated that "the two countries are looking for ways to ensure that the legacy of the Netherlands and Britain does not jeopardize the future of Guyana and Suriname."[9] As former President Granger of Guyana observed, "we are convinced that there are possibilities to address the border issues without considering the river as something that separates us, but rather be seen as something that unites us."[10] Since then, even with changes in government in both countries, significant efforts at closer collaboration have been launched and it is envisaged that there will be joint venture activities, at both the public and private sector levels, which can redound to the benefit of both states as well as those of the Guiana Shield.

A recent challenge that has emerged in the small states of the Guiana Shield—Guyana and Suriname—has been the emergence of an ever-increasing presence of Venezuelan migrants as a result of the political and economic crises facing that state. In Guyana, data indicate that by February 2019, Guyana hosted approximately 36, 400 Venezuelan migrants.[11] For small countries the social service systems including public health care and education have been stretched and strained as a result of the influx of the migrants and this movement of migrants has also led to increased risk of sexual exploitation and human trafficking which impact both the immigrant and the receiving countries. It is therefore recommended that a structured and organized approach to the Venezuelan migrant issue be established among the Guiana Shield states which can serve to provide a unified, institutional engagement through the pooling of resources and the sharing of information for mutual benefit.

It has been established that the indigenous people of the Guiana Shield, the original inhabitants of the area, who have long been considered stewards of the space, have witnessed the rapidly deteriorating environmental, social, and economic conditions of their geographic space. Recent economic activity including forest degradation, the severe negative impact of the operations of the extractive industries, environmental pollution, and the lack of capacity demonstrated by the various environmental monitoring agencies to effectively oversee these activities have led to unsustainable livelihoods and health and social challenges in the indigenous communities. The establishment of sustainable participatory processes, inclusive community-based initiatives, capacity-building programs, and economic empowerment of the indigenous communities must be priorities in the design of the development planning activities and strategies for the development of the Guiana Shield.

Most recently, the coronavirus, COVID-19 pandemic has negatively impacted all the states of the Guiana Shield. The Brazilian states in the Guiana Shield, Roraima, Amazonas, Amapa, and Para have registered among the highest number of cases and death rates in the world and particularly rural and hinterland communities in the Guiana Shield states, with limited medical facilities, small numbers of health professionals, and limited access to prevention, testing, and care have seen unprecedented suffering and an uncertain future. While at times there have been curfews, "lockdowns," border closures, social distancing, quarantine, isolation of patients, and other medical protocols in Guiana Shield states, political denial of the crisis, as well as slow and ambiguous action and responses by governments have contributed to increasing numbers of positive cases and spiraling death rates. Greater regional collaboration, comparative data analysis, the sharing of new initiatives, and approaches and the establishment of a regional plan, involving all the stakeholders in the Guiana Shield can assist in the construction of a comprehensive response to the crisis.

In conclusion, it has been noted that the recent convulsions in Brazil's political and economic environment, the ongoing crisis in Venezuela, the sluggish economies of some Guiana Shield states, the general reduction in momentum in regional integration efforts across the region, as well as the leadership changes in several Guiana Shield countries have also contributed to the deceleration in the collaborative arrangements which were emerging in the subregion. Further, it is recognized that the states of the region must demonstrate greater political will to accelerate the process and pace of collaboration, especially in the context of a COVID-19 impacted environment. According to UNCTAD (2020),[12] the spread of the virus has unleashed a global economic shock and has shaken the trade and development landscape and the pandemic has created social and economic disruption on an unprecedented scale, creating a "new normal." These challenges must be addressed by Guiana Shield states and there must be an increased focus on capacity building, joint investment in strategic sectors of the economy, including manufacturing and agro-processing. Strategic planning in the post-pandemic environment in the Guyana Shield must also focus on reducing the potential vulnerability to a food crisis in the region through increased production in basic food items which can be easily transported across borders in Guiana Shield states through the creation of reliable transport networks. This subregional initiative can contribute to food security and influence joint investment in processing, storage and distribution centers. In order to ensure a resilient and sustainable future, the small independent States in the Guianas—Guyana and Suriname—will have to effectively use their geographical proximity for sustained engagement with larger Guiana Shield states for mutual economic and social benefit and move from the "distant cousin" relationship to a reliable neighborly engagement in a new and sustainable partnership.

NOTES

1. http://guianashield.org/index.php/publications-home/cat_view/89-publications, November 18, 2014.

2. Guyana, Ministry of the Presidency, 2016.

3. Cedric Grant 2007 "The three Guianas: their external relations." In Kenneth Hall and Myrtle Chuck-a-sang, Miami, Ian Randle publishers.

4. D.O. Mills, and V. Lewis (1982) *Caribbean/Latin American Relations.* Trinidad, ECLAC.

5. Shridath Ramphal, *Time for Action: Report of the West Indian Commission.* The Press, UWI, Mona. Jamaica 1993. OR West Indian Commission Report (1992) Time for Action; Black Rock, Barbados.

6. John Cope, "Frontier Security: The Case of Brazil." Institute for National Strategic Studies: Strategic Perspectives 20. National Defense University Press, Washington, DC, August 2016.

7. Sylvia Larrea (2017) Arco Norte Electrical Interconnection Study, IDB Washington, DC.

8. Ministry of Foreign Affairs, Guyana. www.minfor.gov.gy.

9. https://www.kaieteurnewsonline.com July 5, 2016.

10. https://www.kaieteurnewsonline.com July 6, 2016.

11. Guyana Chronicle, June 30, 2019.

12. UNCTAD—2020 "The impact of the COVID-19 pandemic on trade and development: Transitioning to a new normal."

REFERENCES

Gill, Henry. (1995) "Association of Caribbean States: Prospects for a Quantum Leap." North—South Agenda Paper 11, Florida, North-South Center Press.

Guyana Chronicle E-paper 06-07-2019, Published on Jun 6, 2019 (http://guianashield. org/index.php/publications-home/cat_view/89-publications), November 18, 2014.

Joseph, Cedric. "A persistent threat to Guyana's territorial" Guyana News and Information, http://www.guyana.org/features/territorial_integrity.html (http://www .guyana.org).

Maira, Luis. (1983) "Caribbean State Systems and Middle-States Power," in P. Henry and C. Stone (eds.), *The Newer Caribbean: Decolonization, Democracy and Development*. Philadelphia: Institute for the Study of Human Issues.

Ministry of Foreign Affairs, Guyana. www.minfor.gov.gy.

Sanders, Ronald. (2005) *Crumbled Small. The Commonwealth Caribbean in World Politics*. London: Hansib Press.

Thompson, Akola. "The Guiana Shield, the 'greenhouse of the world." Mongabay Series (2016) https://news.mongabay.com/2016/10/experts-warn-more-monitoring -neededfor-the-guiana-shield-the-greenhouse-of-the-world/ on October 19, 2016.

Remarks by His Excellency Brigadier David Granger at the opening of the Fourth International Congress on the Guiana Shield Biodiversity, at the Arthur Chung Convention Centre, Liliendaal August 8, 2016. https://motp.gov.gy/index .php/2015-07-20-18-49-38/201507-20-18-50-58/1875remarks-by-his-excellency-brigadier-david-granger-at-theopening-of-the-fourthinternational-congress-on-the-guiana-shield-biodiversity-at-the-arthur-chungconvention-centre-liliendaal-8th-august-2016.

Chapter 2

The Impact of Venezuelan Immigrants on Crime in Trinidad and Tobago

A Critical Evaluation

Marlon Anatol, Amanda Anatol,
and Sacha Joseph-Mathews

INTRODUCTION

The Republic of Trinidad and Tobago is the Caribbean's southernmost island, and the country since its independence, has experienced sustained periods of both internal and external migration, with many of the nationals migrating to the United States, Canada, and Europe, while it hosts migrants primarily from many other Caribbean countries. Since independence, it has been observed that the migratory trends have intensified, leaving the country as an origin, transit, and destination country for migrants in the region.

Trinidad and Tobago is the fifth largest country in the West Indies and has an area of 4,768 square kilometers (1,841 square miles) . It also has a unique location geographically as the closest of all Caribbean islands to the South American mainland, and this factor plays a large part in migration patterns, particularly of late, with the large numbers of Venezuelan migrants arriving to its shores.

Further, the historical economic dominance of Trinidad and Tobago has been due to its abundance of fossil fuels (oil and natural gas) and this has served as a major 'pull' factor for many Caribbean nationals who seek employment, educational opportunities, and residence there. This has translated into Trinidad and Tobago's status as a major transit point for migrants from the smaller Caribbean islands, as well as for extra-regional migrants, such as Venezuelans who seek to gain access to North America and other destinations.

Since the end of the Second World War, the country has been part of the international migratory process. There exists a need to increase the documentation of immigrants locally, as the dearth of such information makes data-driven immigration policy problematic.

This is most evident in the case of the large immigration flows into Trinidad and Tobago from neighboring Venezuela as a result of its economic and political crisis. This has brought a new dimension to the migration debate in Trinidad and Tobago. Research on migration in Trinidad and Tobago[1] advocates that nationals of the country have historically been accepting of and tolerant toward immigrants; and in 2013, this research indicated that 56 percent of the nationals presented the view that migration has a positive effect on the local economy.

While this has been documented, it is also significant to note that there has been to some extent, a reversal of this position in recent times, if one is to believe the national media houses. It has been postulated that this phenomenon can be attributed to the downturn of the local economy, the fall in the prices of oil and natural gas, the major contributors to the national economy, rising level of unemployment, and the social and economic strains created by the advent of the COVID-19 pandemic.

From a historical point of view, the most noticeable groups of migrants to Trinidad and Tobago other than from Guyana, are from the Hispanophone countries of Colombia and the Bolivarian Republic of Venezuela. These trends have been attributed to the close geographical proximity, as well as mutual interests in energy initiatives and cultural similarities. Notwithstanding, it is predictable, even with the uncertainly of the political and economic future of Venezuela, that some degree of migration will shift form Trinidad and Tobago toward Guyana due to its recent oil finds, as many Venezuelan migrants may have expertise in that sector or may find it more attractive than the waning economic situation in Trinidad.

The Bolivarian Republic of Venezuela is geographically located at the northern end of South America. To the north, Venezuela is bounded by the Caribbean Sea and the Atlantic Ocean; to the south, by Brazil: to the east, by Guyana; and to the southwest and west, by Colombia. Venezuela's population has been estimated at approximately 30.6 million people and the country occupies a landmass of 352,144 square mi (912,050 square km). Further, Venezuela administers several Caribbean islands and archipelagos, inclusive of Margarita Island, La Blanquilla, La Tortuga, Los Roques, and Los Monjes.

Geopolitically, since the early nineteenth century Venezuela has claimed jurisdiction over Guyanese territory west of the Essequibo River totalling some 53,000 square miles (137,000 square km), representing approximately two-thirds of the land area of Guyana. Venezuela is also in dispute with Colombia over the delimitation of maritime boundaries in the Gulf of Venezuela and around the archipelago of Los Monjes.

Due to the political and economic crises in Venezuela one author[2] has cited soaring crime rates, hyperinflation, food and medicine shortages in the country and states that these occurrences account for the mass migration from the country to neighboring states, by whatever means necessary. While there is no official agreement on the rate of emigration from Venezuela[3] in part due to the inability of the national institutions to map the movement of their nationals and the high number of illegal/undocumented departures; it is generally agreed upon that the exodus has been exacerbated by the lack of basic amenities and high levels of crime and violence,[4] poverty and hunger, political persecution, and the overall demise of the society.

MIGRATION AND CRIME

One of the issues consuming immigration policy is whether, or to what extent, immigrants increase crime rates in the host countries. This debate has consumed some quarters in recent times, particularly as the pace and rates of globalization and migration have been increasing significantly. As such, policy makers have been consumed with a number of issues including migration policy, nationalism, security policies, and the like. Due to the political and economic crisis in Venezuela, Trinidad and Tobago has seen a marked increase in Venezuelan immigrants over the past two years. While it is generally accepted that the concern about immigrants being involved in criminal activities is as old as migration itself, there are new data and research that add critical insights into the debate.

While old reports[5] and investigations[6] suggested that permitting immigration was tantamount to increasing crime rates, more recently, this view that the migrants all have criminal intent has been challenged by many authors. An example of the challenge to the old view is exemplified in Mariani's paper entitled "Migration and Crime" presented at the Paris School of Economics (IRES, Université Catholique de Louvain). Investigating the propensity of immigrants to commit crimes, the author states, "just to give a few examples, Bianchi et al. (2008), Plecas (2002), Butcher and Morrison Piehl (1998, 2005), Albrecht (1997) and Francis (1981) find that immigrants are less involved than natives in criminal activities, in Italy, Canada, US, Germany, and Australia, respectively."[7] Alternatively, as other work have argued in more recent times, this perception about immigrants increasing significantly has survived in the OECD.[8]

This chapter addresses the issue of the perspectives related to migrants increasing the rates of crime in the host country, namely Trinidad and

Tobago. It also supports the view that there exists a dearth of data in illegal and undocumented immigrants in most countries in the world and this is also true for Trinidad and Tobago, and as such one needs to be weary of information that is published from non-data driven sources, as much of the analysis is based on subjectivity and anecdotal evidence.

Recent research suggests[9,10] that there is no causal connection between immigration and crime, even though anecdotally, many people believe that illegal immigrants contribute to increased levels of crime in host countries.[11] Based on the limitation in the data, it is suggested that there needs to be more complicated approaches to determining the extent to which migrants contribute to crime in the host countries. This may include examining the crime data (without identifying the perpetrators) then comparing those figures with the trends in migration into the target area, and this can be further stratified by types of crime. This will give a more balanced interpretation of the actual contribution of the native and immigrant populations to crime in the particular area, while also identifying the types of crime in which each group is more likely to be involved. This of course does not take into account the sociological cultural or psychological reasons for involvement in crime.

Notwithstanding, this negative view of immigrants as they relate to crime has persisted, and the lack of data and information to dissuade this view is to a large extent still forthcoming. One view suggests that immigrants tend to be prone to crime due to their poor economic situation, while another suggests that they offer economic and cultural benefits to the host countries, as most come to find employment or are fleeing from some form of persecution and do not have the intent of engaging in criminal activity.

A cursory glance of articles in the local media suggests that the general sentiment in Trinidad and Tobago is that the Venezuelan immigrants have significantly contributed to increasing crime locally, notwithstanding the fact that Trinidad and Tobago has one of the highest crime rates in the region (in excess of Colombia, Mexico, and Brazil) and internationally, even before the Venezuelan arrivals.

Some studies have found that in some cases migrants form gangs,[12] possibly due to culture (gang members migrate) or simply as a means of survival. However, this has not been substantiated in the Trinidad and Tobago/ Venezuela context. Recent data has shown that there has been some gang infiltration partly because of the inability of Trinidad and Tobago's authorities to identify Venezuelan gang members as they lack the cultural and other competencies to make such identifications. This was evident when amnesty was given to the Venezuelan immigrants, including gang members without the knowledge of the authorities.

In terms of the number of Venezuelan immigrants that reside in Trinidad and Tobago, government official figures differ from international agencies and NGOs, due in part to the large number of undocumented immigrants; however, some estimates put that figure of in excess of 70,000 individuals.

To be sure, the mass exodus from Venezuela was a result of the political and social meltdown of that economy, which left Venezuelans seeking to make a better life elsewhere, and as logic will serve, they will seek refuge with their closest neighbors, including Trinidad and Tobago. This phenomenon is not new to the populace of Trinidad and Tobago, as this country has seen waves of emigration since the end of the Second World War to England, the United States, and Europe.[13]

In many cases the Venezuelan immigrants may be highly educated or skilled, and this can have a long-term positive effect on the local economy in Trinidad and Tobago; which may have the spillover effect of benefitting the region due to high levels of intraregional travel of skilled professionals that exists. While the proximity between the two states is a crucial factor, it is also clear that in the long run a portion of these immigrants may find themselves leaving Trinidad and Tobago in search of a better life in other countries, regionally and internationally. Labour market dynamics and mechanisms based on the laws of demand and supply suggest that Venezuelan migration to Trinidad and Tobago is likely to decline in the long run.[14]

While the local media may portray the illegal immigrant from Venezuela as a criminal and increase sentiments of xenophobia in many cases, the empirical evidence in the literature is indeterminate with regards to the direct and clear nexus between immigration and crime.

Many of the migrants that arrive on the shores of Trinidad and Tobago, legally or otherwise, hope to find opportunities for better living, are escaping from persecution, poverty, and crime, and as such have little interest or intention in committing crimes in this country. While at the same time, one must recognize that some of the immigrants do indeed have criminal backgrounds, belong to gangs, or are willing to capitalize on the apparent crime spree in Trinidad and Tobago; this group does not appear to represent the majority of immigrants who are clearly exploiting the labour market opportunities that exist locally.

Acknowledging the plethora of issues surrounding the immigration–crime nexus, this chapter restricts itself to the general issues of immigration and to what extent it contributes to crime in Trinidad and Tobago. This chapter seeks to fill some of the gaps in the literature about the contribution of the Venezuelan immigrant to the rising crime rates in Trinidad and Tobago, taking into account several theories that speak to the issue of migration and crime in the literature.

THEORETICAL CONSIDERATIONS

While there are numerous approaches to migration theory, the structural approach focuses on the macroeconomic processes of migration. This approach argues that socio-spatial inequalities cause international migration and affects the life chances of individuals and members of specific social classes in particular places.[15] To these theorists, migration is a result of socio-spatial inequalities that are systematically reproduced within the national and global economies. As such, crises such as those experienced in Venezuela serve to create and sustain spatial inequalities among the Venezuelan nationals and the host countries, thus accounting for these Venezuelan nationals seeking to create better lives for themselves and increase their standards of living in the host countries.

Further, the dual-labour market theory can also shed some light on the migration pattern that is evident in the region due to the Venezuelan crisis. It assumes from the onset, that there exists a demand for the skills of the Venezuelan workers to fill the gap required for economic development in the host countries (inclusive of Trinidad and Tobago). As the argument goes, while acknowledging the existence of both a relatively stable high-income market and a coexisting sub-economy with low incomes and job security, this new migrant labour from Venezuela is fundamentally a defining characteristic of the sub-economy with low incomes and low levels of job security.[16] This sub-economy is often characterized by avoidance by the locals as it offers low income and low job security, and this presents an opportunity for the migrants to secure labour in the host economies. Further, it has been argued that immigrants increase crime in the host countries as they are fleeing from poverty and persecution and as such, have less to lose by committing crimes; as opposed to the natives.[17] This is not to say that it is the immigrant profile or status that increases the odds of being noncompliant to the laws of the land, but the propensity to commit crimes is more reliant on the fact that they are economically disenfranchised and have fewer legitimate opportunities[18] to earn income and improve their standards of living.[19] Another consideration is the fact that the immigrant may be less compelled to commit crimes in the host country because, under normal circumstances, they fear that they will be deported to their country of origin and be unable to return to the host country to improve their life chances and earn levels of income unavailable to them at home.[20]

There is a discourse claiming that the immigration–crime nexus is more evident when dealing with large groups of immigrants entering into small countries/economies, such as the case with Venezuelan immigrants in Trinidad and Tobago. In such cases, "many citizens, community groups, and policymakers believe that illegal aliens are disproportionately responsible for crime and disorder and for placing a strain on jails, prisons, and law enforcement."[21] Even with high levels of suspicion, objection, and distrust between the native and migrant populations, it should be noted that economic theory is unable to quantify the amount of crime to expect in relation to migration. This is exacerbated in cases where immigrants may indeed reduce the natives' access to legitimate employment, increasing the incidences of them engaging in illegal activities to secure money, while blaming the immigrants for their situation as a justification. Another issue in relation to the immigration–crime nexus is that some theorists[22] argue immigrants are less likely to commit crimes in host countries based on the fact that they perceive themselves to be profiled, and their punishment to be harsher than the natives, particularly as they may suffer the fate of deportation.

These theoretical considerations are necessary, as the data that is necessary to make definitive statements are not available, and the rhetoric spewed may be due to misinformation, miseducation, high levels of mistrust and suspicion, a declining economy, and negative portrayal of the immigrants in the media.

ECONOMIC MODEL OF CRIME

Like all other issues in a country, crime has to be relegated to a certain 'corner' and all issues related to it have to be debated based on social, economic, and political positions. While this chapter does not intend to deal with the political issue directly, the economic and social issues are necessary to interrogate for this analysis.

Following on the economic model by Becker,[23] which assumed that individuals choose between legal and criminal activities by deciding on the net benefit from each activity; we move to a position that is nonjudgemental and seeks to let the official data guide theory and policy. The old models assumed that the migrant makes a conscious and rational decision between engaging in illegal and legal activities, while being able to determine or at least conceptualize the outcomes and consequences. This position assumed that migrants with low/poor labour market opportunities are more likely to be involved in criminal activities in the host country.

In order to evaluate this position, one has to look at international trends in the migration and crime debate. Many studies including Bell et al.[24] and Bianchi et al.[25] have found that the impact of migrant crime in Italy is negligible and approaching zero. While there seems to be some link with immigrants and property crime, in general, the authors found that there was no evidence of a causal link between migrants and violent crime.

A view of the criminology literature identifies associations between immigration and crime that in reality reflects relative deprivation and unemployment rather than direct immigration effects.[26]

As a consequence of the rise of immigration over the last two decades, there is an obvious increase in the number of economic studies dedicated to the impact of migration on crime in countries that have become destinations for migrants. There is evidence indicating that relative labor market opportunities have, to some extent, an effect on criminal activity,[27] due to the fact that as the economy slows down there is heightened competition for employment which at times may lead to increases in nonviolent crimes, whether committed by immigrants or nationals.

The findings suggest that when rationally behaving immigrants have access to a legal income through normal labour market opportunities, they indeed commit less crime, as the opportunity cost of crime is increased.[28] Some studies, such as that by Alonso-Borrego et al. (2012),[29] while using longitudinal studies, found a positive correlation between immigration and crime; while at the same time they are quick to caution that this does not suggest a causal effect. As such, there is a need for further research to determine the extent to which the economic effects of migration impact rising crime levels.

In the case of the Venezuelan immigrant that arrives on the shores of Trinidad and Tobago, whether documented or otherwise, it is argued that if the individual has marketable skills and some degree of education, it can be postulated that this individual will be less likely to engage in criminal activity,[30] as opposed to an unskilled and uneducated immigrant. Similarly, it is conceivable that the documented immigrant will be less likely to get involved in criminal activities as the opportunities for employment will be greater; which in turn leads to the issues of justifying such assumptions as the lack of data on these migrants make such justifications problematic.

Other theorists have posited that when the legal status allows immigrants to find employment more easily in the formal employment sector, this increases the labor supply locally, thus making it more difficult for the less skilled and educated immigrants who may as a result have less economic opportunities to resort to criminal activity to earn a living.[31]

OTHER THEORETICAL CONSIDERATIONS

In support of some policy positions on the immigration–crime nexus, social disorganization theory[32,33,34] states that higher inflows of immigrants will produce higher crime rates, thus, with the increases in immigration one can expect a corresponding increase in crime rates. This theory speaks to the cultural assimilation of the immigrant into the host country's culture. It postulates that with high rates of immigration, the individual does not get the necessary time and contact with any particular group of nationals to assimilate their culture and understand, at the cultural level, what is acceptable behavior. These immigrants usually come seeking employment and find themselves in the inner cities where work is most abundant, and as they progress; they will naturally move out of these areas into some affluent areas, thus from generation to generation may not share the value of any one group of national. To these theorists, this also explains why crime rates are higher in the inner cities than in the suburbs, because of the high traffic/turnover of immigrants, while as one moves away from the inner city, the communities are more established and have more coherent and identifiable culture with shared values and norms.

Similarly, cultural theories[35,36] suggest that one can expect increased criminal activity from immigrants because they reside in areas that are characterized by adverse economic conditions, such as is present in the inner cities, as cited by Social Disorganization theories. In these areas, the emergence and persistence of delinquent, antisocial, and criminal behaviors are simply an adaptation strategy for survival. While this theory seems to support the Social Disorganization theory, caution must be taken as research and empirical data to confirm its arguments has been inconclusive at best. The social strain[37,38] and opportunity theories[39] also presuppose that individuals are more likely to engage in illegitimate activities to achieve their social goals when their predicament does not allow them the opportunity (real or perceived) to find meaningful employment.

CAUSAL RELATIONSHIP: THE NEXUS

While there is a plethora of research dedicated to finding the link between immigration and crime, and seeking to make a determination about the strength of this link, taking into consideration economic opportunities and culture; one must be mindful of the rhetoric that suggests that immigrants cause or increase crime in the host destinations.[40] It has been argued that by simply using the term 'immigrant; that there is an implicit bias on the part of the state as it seeks to discriminate or separate different categories of residents which will in turn affect state-determined policies.'[41] This approach suggests that the authorities believe that the immigrant "disturbs the mythical purity or perfection of [the national] order,"[42] and as such the state-based view of the immigrant, as potentially upsetting the national order,[43] then becomes the framework for the public debates and perceptions about immigrants and their activities.

Following this argument, the Venezuelan immigrant in Trinidad and Tobago is seen as an 'outsider' and viewed with suspicion in many cases and this translates to being intrinsically delinquent by virtue of their displaced status, and this view is further supported when they are convicted of a crime; as they have for some reason broken the 'unwritten law' of how foreigner/immigrants are supposed to behave. One may be tempted to argue, with some level of justification or impunity, that the national perception of the Venezuelan immigrant as inherently criminal or delinquent is a form of structural violence that can easily manifest in institutional discrimination and violence. This violence linking the immigrant to crime manifests into a set of legal, social, and other considerations which serve to stigmatize the migrants and allocate their place within the social hierarchy.[44]

While Trinidad and Tobago has undoubtedly been grappling with increased crime and a marked slowing down of the economy due to reduced levels of productivity and falling prices of its major export (fossil fuels), the issues of increased crime that may be caused by Venezuelan immigrants[45] have been given national attention. The events of late have highlighted the fact that based on the situation in Venezuela, many skilled migrants are leaving their homes and devaluing their skills in an attempt to secure employment in Trinidad and Tobago to attain a better standard of living for themselves and their families; and as such, may not have the predetermined intent of committing crimes.[46]

Alternatively, some commentators[47] have presented the view that the Venezuelan immigrant has increased crime in Trinidad and Tobago and that many of them arrived on these shores with criminal backgrounds and intent. They cite the fact that while Trinidad and Tobago is a transhipment point for drugs, many of these drugs come through the Venezuelan connection or pipeline and are supported by gang activities.[48] This view has been largely supported by authorities in Trinidad and Tobago[49] where statements have been made suggesting that much of the crime locally can find its genesis in Venezuela, inclusive of human trafficking gang activity, drug trafficking, other such activities, and some even go so far to accuse the immigrants of recruitment activities locally to increase their operations.

CONCLUSIONS AND RECOMMENDATIONS— POLICY CONSIDERATIONS

While this chapter acknowledges that the current research on the immigration–crime nexus in Trinidad and Tobago is almost nonexistent, one must be mindful of the policy implications of the strategies developed to address this issue with the absence of such data. As with other receiving states, Trinidad and Tobago needs to evaluate the existing immigration policy to and its effectiveness in preventing and discouraging the admission of criminals into society.

In the attempt to reduce the incidence of 'importing' criminals, local policymakers may seek to identify and target some immigrants with the aim of controlling and reducing the level of crime locally.

More resources are necessary to ensure the collection of reliable and accurate data on immigrants, their statuses, and their involvement in criminal and antisocial behavior once in-country; without this data it will be difficult to craft appropriate policy responses.[50] It is recommended that the government of Trinidad and Tobago engage in a national pre-immigration and post-immigration exercise to determine the prevalence and incidence rates for various types of crimes within the national borders.

It has been also argued that in order to effectively control the dissemination of information and the views given to the public, the government needs to engage in sensitization and education programmes specifically targeting the national media as these actors usually lack the factual data and theoretical understanding of the causes of crime and, more importantly, of the debate about the immigrant–crime nexus.[51] Based on this acknowledgement, the media may be seen as an agent of perpetration and disseminating options and "information" that either purposefully or inadvertently fuels the public's paranoia about immigrants, thereby increasing xenophobia.[52]

Based on the aforementioned comments, it may be useful for the government of Trinidad and Tobago to identity the subpopulation of immigrants who are most at risk of becoming involved in antisocial and criminal activities. Thereafter, they will be in a position to more effectively craft strategies and interventions for these groups that will take into consideration the specific risk factors and socioeconomic conditions that pre-suppose them to said behaviours.

Another approach[53] posits that a critical evaluation needs to be made in relation to migration and criminal laws in the aim of being more effective for immigration law to expand into the realm of criminal law rather than the other way around, as this will lead to a better fit in national approaches and policy.

Further, as a matter of government policy, some authors[54] have posited that language courses and job training can be useful for migrants and may help them adjust to the local environment, thus reducing their propensity to engage in antisocial and criminal activities. With this in mind, it is crucial that the distinction between migrants, asylum seekers, and refugees be acknowledged, as this has an impact on the resources required for the implementation of any integration assistance, policy, strategy, or legislation going forward. The government should also continue to work with international agencies such as the United Nations High Commissioner for Refugees (UNHCR) and the International Organisation for Migration (IOM), especially given the recently established regional refugee and migrant response plan which includes, *inter alia*, areas of intervention related to socioeconomic integration, and capacity-building for receiving states.

As a matter of policy, it is suggested that as per the official response to the large numbers of Venezuelan immigrants into the national economy of Trinidad and Tobago, the authorities need to develop targeted mechanisms to ensure the smooth transition of the immigrants, and this may involve the issuance of a range of instruments including temporary work permits, short-term-stay permits, that have the aim of increasing self-reliance through lawful employment, in the short run; to be complemented by longer-term strategies for the regularization of the Venezuelan immigrants.

It is also recommended that Trinidad and Tobago take a leadership role in CARICOM to lobby for more resources to support the humanitarian effort of accommodating the Venezuelan refugees in the region. Supporting this view is the fact that there is a need for the creation of more synergistic relationships between institutions, agencies and bodies, at the national, regional, and international levels.[55] To illustrate this point, in September 2018, Latin American countries formerly recognized the need for a coordinated regional approach to the crisis and its associated mass population displacement and have subsequently met on a number of occasions to address this issue; and this can be replicated among CARICOM states with Trinidad and Tobago taking a lead role.

The government of Trinidad and Tobago, in taking a leading role in the Venezuelan immigration issue, needs to lead the narrative in issues that include the legal vs illegal categorization of immigrants and the incorporation of migrants into the CARICOM economies; with more attention and resources allocated to the strengthening of border controls, and ensuring security, freedoms, and human rights of the migrants[56]. It has been posited that one of the central themes of international migration is the issue of motivation which dictates all forms of migration related to the legal and illegal migrant, whether permanent or temporary, skilled or unskilled, individual or family, voluntary or forced.[57]

To be sure, even a cursory glance at the discussion in this chapter, related to the issues related to the rising levels of crime in Trinidad and Tobago coupled with the increase in immigration from Venezuela, highlights the significance of understating the migration–crime nexus. This will allow a better understanding of the issues and direct the narrative of compromise and best practices in policy making in relation to the issues, based primarily on data-driven approaches.

NOTES

1. Marlon Anatol, Mark Kirton, and Nia Nanan (2013). *Becoming an Immigration Magnet: Migrants' Profiles and the Impact of Migration on Human Development in Trinidad and Tobago* (Report No. ACPBOS/2013/PUB15). Geneva: ACP Observatory on Migration. IOM.

2. Yohama Caraballo-Arias, and Jesús Madrid (2018 September). *Working in Venezuela: How the crisis has affected the labour conditions, annals of global health.* https://www.annalsofglobalhealth.org/articles/10.29024/aogh.2325/.

3. Tomas Páez (2017). Amid Economic Crisis and Political Turmoil, Venezuelans Form a New Exodus. *Migration Policy Institute.*

4. R. Evan Ellis (2017). The Collapse of Venezuela and Its Impact on the Region. *Military Review, July-August 2017,* Article 6, 1–13. https://www.armyupress.army.mil/Journals/MilitaryReview/English-Edition-Archives/July-August-2017/Ellis-Collapse-of-Venezuela/.

5. Edith Abbott (1931a). "The problem of crime and the foreign born," in National Commission on Law Observance and Enforcement: Report on crime and the foreign born, Washington, DC, United States Government Printing Office.

6. C.C. Van Vechten (1941). "The criminality of the foreign born." *Journal of Criminal Law and Criminology* 32, 139–147.

7. Fabio Mariani (2010). *Migration and Crime.* Paris School of Economics (IRES, Université Catholique de Louvain). IZA, Bonn.

8. Thomas Bauer, Magnus Lofstrom, and Klaus F. Zimmermann (2000). "Immigration policy, assimilation of immigrants, and natives' sentiments towards immigrants: evidence from 12 OECD countries." *Swedish Economic Policy Review* 7, 11–53

9. David Sklansky (2012). "Crime, immigration, and Ad hoc instrumentalism," *New Criminal Law Review: An International and Interdisciplinary Journal* 15(2), 157–223. https://doi.org/10.1525/nclr.2012.15.2.157.

10. Brian Bell and Stephen Machin (2011). *The Impact of Migration on Crime and Victimisation: A Report for the Migration Advisory Committee.* London: Centre for Economic Performance, LSE.

11. Jessica Retis and Jose Luis Benavides (2005). "Miradas hacia Latinoamérica: la representación discursiva de los inmigrantes latinoamericanos en la prensa española y estadounidense [Glances Toward Latin America: The Discursive Representation of Latin American Immigrants in the Spanish and American Press," *Temas de Portada* 8 (2): 93–114. https://www.redalyc.org/pdf/649/64901304.pdf.

12. Ramiro Martinez and Matthew Lee (2000). "On Immigration and Crime." *Criminal Justice 2000: The Nature of Crime—Continuity and Change* 1, 485–524.

13. Alejandro Portes (1981). "Modes of Structural Incorporation and Present Theories of Labour Immigration." In *Global Trends in Migration: Theory and Research on International Population Movements,* ed. Mary M. Kritz, Charles B. Keely, and Silvano M. Tomasi, pp. 279–297. Staten Island, NY: Center for Migration Studies.

14. Douglas Massey, Joaquin Arango, Graeme Huyo, Ali Kouaouci, Adela Pellegrino, and J. Edward Taylor (1998). *Worlds in Motion: Understanding International Migration at the End of the Millennium.* Oxford: Clarendon Press.

15. Khalid Koser and John Salt (1997). "The geography of highly skilled international migration." *Population, Space and Place* 3(4), 285–303.

16. Douglas Massey, Joaquin Arango, Graeme Huyo, Ali Kouaouci, Adela Pellegrino, and J. Edward Taylor (1993). "Theories of international migration: A review and appraisal." In *Population and Development Review*, pp. 431–466.

17. Robert LaLonde and Robert Topel (1991). "Immigrants in the American labor market: Quality, assimilation, and distributional effects," *American Economic Review* 81(2), 297–302.

18. Isaac Ehrlich (1996). "Crime, punishment, and the market for offenses." *Journal of Economic Perspectives* 10(1), 43–67.

19. Gary Becker (1968). "Crime and punishment: An economic approach." *Journal of Political Economy* 76(2), 169–217.

20. Kristen Butcher and Ann Morrison Piehl (2005). "Why are immigrants' incarceration rates so low? Evidence on selective immigration, deterrence, and deportation." Federal Reserve Bank of Chicago WP-05-19.

21. Charles Katz (2008). *The Connection between Illegal Immigrants and Crime.* Center for Violence Prevention and Community Safety, Arizona State University.

22. Thomas Miles and Adam Cox (2014). "Does Immigration Enforcement Reduce Crime? Evidence from Secure Communities." *The Journal of Law & Economics* 57(4), 937–973. https://doi.org/10.1086/680935.

23. Gary Becker (1968). "Crime and punishment: An economic approach." *Journal of Political Economy* 76(2), 169–217. https://doi.org/10.1086/259394.

24. Brian Bell, Francesco Fasani and Stephen Machin (Forthcoming 2013). "Crime and Immigration: Evidence from Large Immigrant Waves." *Review of Economics and Statistics.*

25. Milo Bianchi, Paolo Buonanno and Paolo Pinotti (2012). "Do Immigrants Cause Crime?" *Journal of the European Economic Association* 10, 1318–1347.

26. Tuba Bircan, and Marc Hooghe. (2011). "Immigration, diversity and crime: an analysis of Belgian national crime statistics, 2001–6." *European Journal of Criminology* 8(3), 198–212.

27. Eric Gould, Bruce Weinberg, and David Mustard (2002). "Crime rates and local labour market opportunities in the United States: 1979–697." *Review of Economics and Statistics* 84(1), 45–61. https://doi.org/10.1162/003465302317331919.

28. Giovanni Mastrobuoni, and Paolo Pinotti (July 21, 2011). Migration Restrictions and Criminal Behaviour: Evidence from a Natural Experiment. FEEM Working Paper No. 53.2011.

29. César Alonso-Borrego, Nuno Garoupa, and Pablo Vázquez (April 1, 2012). "Does immigration cause crime? Evidence from Spain." *American Law and Economics Review* 14(1), 165–191.

30. Brian Bell and Stephen Machin (2011). *The Impact of Migration on Crime and Victimisation: A report for the Migration Advisory Committee.* London: Centre for Economic Performance, LSE.

31. Luca Nunziata (2015). "Immigration and crime: evidence from victimisation data." *Journal of Population Economics* 28(3), 697–736. https://doi.org/10.1007/s 00148-015-0543-2.

32. Clifford Shaw, and Henry McKay (1942). *Juvenile Delinquency and Urban Areas.* Chicago: University of Chicago Press.

33. Robert Sampson, Stephen Raudenbush, and Felton Earls (1997). "Neighborhoods and violent crime: A multilevel study of collective efficacy." *Science* 277(5328), 918–924.

34. Charis Kubrin, and Ronald Weitzer (2003). "New directions in social disorganization theory." *Journal of Research in Crime and Delinquency* 40(4), 374–402.

35. Jeff Ferrell, and Clifton Sanders, eds. (1995). *Cultural Criminology.* Boston: Northeastern University Press.

36. Steve Redhead (1995). *Unpopular Cultures: The Birth of Law and Popular Culture.* Manchester, UK: Manchester University Press.

37. Robert Merton (1938). "Social structure and anomie." *American Sociological Review* 3(5), 672682.

38. Raymond Paternoster, and Paul Mazerolle (1994). "General strain theory and delinquency—a replication and extension." *Journal of Research in Crime and Delinquency* 31(3), 235–263.

39. Lance Hannon (2002). "Criminal opportunity theory and the relationship between poverty and property crime." *Sociological Spectrum* 22(3), 363–381, doi: 10.1080/02732170290062676.

40. Michael Tonry (1997). "Ethnicity, crime and immigration." *Crime and Justice* 21, 1–29.

41. Abdelmalek Sayad (2004). *The Suffering of the Immigrant.* Cambridge, UK: Polity.

42. Ibid, Pg. 280.

43. Loïc Wacquant (2005). "'Enemies of the Wholesome Part of the Nation': Postcolonial migrants in the prisons of Europe." *Sociologie* 1, 31–51.

44. Pierre Bourdieu (1998). *Practical Reason: On the Theory of Action.* Stanford, CA: Stanford University Press.

45. Loan Grillo, and Jorge Benezra (2016, May 20). "Venezuela's murder epidemic rages on amid state of emergency." Timeonline.

46. Nicholas Casey (2016, November 25). "Hungry Venezuelans Flee in Boats to Escape Economic Collapse." *New York Times.* Retrieved November 27, 2016.

47. "Gary Griffith points to non-nationals involved in criminal activities." *Loop.* (2019, April 15). http://www.looptt.com/content/griffith-points-non-nationals-involved-criminal-activities.

48. Mark Bassant (2019, April 15). "Notorious Venezuelans Infiltrate T&T Gangs." *Trinidad Guardian.* Retrieved from https://www.guardian.co.tt/news/notorious-venezuelans-infiltrate-tt-gangs-6.2.825577.970dd1facb.

49. Charles Kong Soo (2018, February 4). "Venezuela crisis fuels exploitation in T&T." *Trinidad Guardian.* http://www.classifieds.guardian.co.tt/news/2018-02-04/venezuela-crisis-fuelsexploitation-tt.

50. Carolyn Moehling, and Anne Morrison Piehl (2009). "Immigration, crime, and incarceration in early 20th Century America." *Demography* 46(4), 739–763. https://doi.org/10.1353/dem.0.0076.

51. William McDonald (1997). "Crime and illegal immigration: Emerging local, state, and federal partnerships." *National Institute of Justice Journal* (232), 2–10. https://www.ncjrs.gov/App/AbstractDB/AbstractDBDetails.aspx?id=184605.

52. Luca Nunziata (2015). "Immigration and crime: Evidence from victimisation data." *Journal of Population Economics* 28(3), 697–736. https://doi.org/10.1007/s00148-015-0543-2.

53. David Sklansky (2012). "Crime, immigration, and ad hoc instrumentalism." *New Criminal Law Review: An International and Interdisciplinary Journal* 15(2), 157–223. https://doi.org/10.1525/nclr.2012.15.2.157.

54. Brian Bell, Francesco Fasani, and Stephen Machin (2013). "Crime and immigration: Evidence from large immigrant waves." *The Review of Economics and Statistics* 95(4), 1278–1290. ISSN 0034-6535 DOI: 10.1162/REST_a_00337.

55. Marlon Anatol, Mark Kirton and Nia Nanan (2013). *Becoming an Immigration Magnet: Migrants' Profiles and the Impact of Migration on Human Development in Trinidad and Tobago* (Report No. ACPBOS/2013/PUB15). Geneva: ACP Observatory on Migration. IOM.

56. Didier Bigo (2006). "Internal and external aspects of security." *European Security* 15, 385–404. 10.1080/09662830701305831.

57. (2005). The Global Commission on International Migration. Migration in an interconnected world: New directions for action Report of the Global Commission on International Migration.

REFERENCES

Abbott, E. (1931a). "The problem of crime and the foreign born." In National Commission on Law Observance and Enforcement: Report on crime and the foreign born, Washington, D.C., United States Government Printing Office.

Albrecht, H.-J. (1997). "Ethnic minorities, crime, and criminal justice in Germany." *Crime and Justice* 21, 31–99.

Alonso-Borrego, César Nuno Garoupa Pablo Vázquez. (April 1, 2012). "Does immigration cause crime? Evidence from Spain." *American Law and Economics Review* 14(1), 165–191.

Anatol, M., Kirton, R.M., and Nanan, N. (2013). *Becoming an Immigration Magnet: Migrants' Profiles and the Impact of Migration on Human Development in Trinidad and Tobago.* (Report No. ACPBOS/2013/PUB15). Geneva: ACP Observatory on Migration. IOM.

Bassant, Mark. (April 15, 2019). "Notorious Venezuelans Infiltrate T&T Gangs." *Trinidad Guardian.* Retrieved from https://www.guardian.co.tt/news/notorious-venezuelans-infiltrate-tt-gangs-6.2.825577.970dd1facb.

Bauer, Thomas, Lofstrom, M. and Zimmermann, Klaus F. (2000). "Immigration policy, assimilation of immigrants, and natives' sentiments towards immigrants: evidence from 12 OECD countries." *Swedish Economic Policy Review* 7, 11–53 .

Becker, G. (1968). "Crime and punishment: An economic approach." *Journal of Political Economy* 76, 175–209.

Bell, B., Fasani, F., and Machin, S. (2013). "Crime and immigration: Evidence from large immigrant waves." *The Review of Economics and Statistics* 95(4), 1278–1290. https://doi.org/10.1162/REST_a_00337.

Bell, B., and Machin, S. (2011). *The Impact of Migration on Crime and Victimisation: A Report for the Migration Advisory Committee.* London: Centre for Economic Performance, LSE.

Bianchi, M., Buonanno, P., and Pinotti, P. (2012). "Do immigrants cause crime?" *Journal of the European Economic Association* 10(6), 1318–1347. https://doi.org /10.1111/j.1542-4774.2012.01085.x.

Bircan, Tuba and Hooghe, M. (2011). "Immigration, diversity and crime: An analysis of Belgian national crime statistics, 2001–6" *European Journal of Criminology* 8(3), 198–212.

Borjas, G.J., Grogger. J., and Hanson, G.H. (2010). "Immigration and the economic status of African American men." *Economica* 77(306), 255–282. https://doi.org/10 .1111/j.1468-0335.2009.00803.x.

Butcher, K.F. and Piehl, A. Morrison (1998). "Cross-city evidence on the relationship between immigration and crime." *Journal of Policy Analysis and Management* 17(3), 457–493. https://doi.org/10.1002/(SICI)1520-6688(199822)17:3<457::AI D-PAM4>3.0.CO;2-F.

Butcher, K. F. and Piehl, A. M. (2005). "Why are immigrants' incarceration rates so low? evidence on selective immigration, deterrence, and deportation." Federal Reserve Bank of Chicago WP-05-19.

Butcher, K., and Piehl A. M. (2007). "Why are immigrants' incarceration rates so low? Evidence on selective immigration, deterrence, and deportation." National Bureau of Economic Research, Working Paper 13229. http://www.nber.org/papers /w13229.

Camarota, S.A., and Vaughan, J.M. (2009). "Immigration and crime: Assessing a conflicted issue." *American Law and Economics Review* 16(1), 177–219. https://ci s.org/Report/Immigration-and-Crime.

Caraballo-Arias, Y., and Madrid, J. (2018 September). *Working in Venezuela: How the crisis has affectedthe labour conditions, annals of global health.* https://www .annalsofglobalhealth.org/articles/10.29024/aogh.2325/.

Casey, N. (2016, November 25). "Hungry Venezuelans Flee in boats to escape economic collapse." *New York Times.* Retrieved November 27, 2016.

Caviedes, A. (2015). "An emerging 'European' news portrayal of immigration?" *Journal of Ethnic and Migration Studies* 41(6), 897–917. https://doi.org/10.1080/1 369183X.2014.1002199.

Cox, A.B., and Posner, E.A. (2007). "The second-order structure of immigration law." *Stanford Law Review* 59(4), 809–856. https://papers.ssrn.com/sol3/papers .cfm?abstract_id=941730.

Ehrlich, I. (1996). "Crime, punishment, and the market for offenses." *Journal of Economic Perspectives* 10(1), 43–67.

Ellis, R. E. (2017). "The collapse of Venezuela and its impact on the region." *Military Review*, July-August 2017, Article 6, 1–13. https://www.armyupress.army.mil/

Journals/Military-Review/English-Edition-Archives/July-August-2017/Ellis-Collapse-of-Venezuela/.

Ferrell J., and Sanders C.R., eds. (1995). *Cultural Criminology*. Boston: Northeastern University Press.

Francis, R.D. (1981). *Migrant Crime in Australia*. St. Lucia: University of Queensland Press.

Freeman, R. B. (1999). "The economics of crime." In Orley C. A and Card, D. (Eds.), *Handbook of Labour Economics* (pp. 3529–3571). Elsevier.

Gedan, B. (2017). "Venezuela migration: Is the Western Hemisphere prepared for a refugee crisis?" *SAIS Review of International Affairs* 37(2), 57–64. https://doi.org/10.1353/sais.2017.0027.

Gould, E., Weinberg, B., and Mustard, D. (2002). "Crime rates and local labour market opportunities in the United States: 1979–97." *Review of Economics and Statistics* 84(1), 45–61. https://doi.org/10.1162/003465302317331919.

"Griffith points to non-nationals involved in criminal activities." *Loop*. (2019, April 15). http://www.looptt.com/content/griffith-points-non-nationals-involved-criminal-activities.

Grillo, L., and Benezra, J. (2016, May 20). "Venezuela's murder epidemic rages on amid state of emergency." Timeonline.

Hannon, Lance (2002). "Criminal opportunity theory and the relationship between poverty and property crime." *Sociological Spectrum* 22(3), 363–381, DOI: 10.1080/02732170290062676.

Katz, C. M. (2008). *The Connection between Illegal Immigrants and Crime*. Center for Violence Prevention and Community Safety, Arizona State University.

Kong Soo, Charles. (2018, February 4). "Venezuela crisis fuels exploitation in T&T." *Trinidad Guardian*. http://www.classifieds.guardian.co.tt/news/2018-02-04/venezuela-crisis-fuels-exploitation-tt.

Kubrin, C. E., and Weitzer, R. (2003). "New directions in social disorganization theory." *Journal of Research in Crime and Delinquency* 40(4), 374–402.

LaLonde, R. J. and Topel, R. H. (1991). "Immigrants in the american labor market: Quality, assimilation, and distributional effects." *American Economic Review* 81(2), 297–302.

Mariani. (2010). *Fabio: Migration and Crime*. IRES, Université Catholique de Louvain Paris School of Economics IZA, Bonn.

Massey, D. S., Arango, J., Hugo, G., Kouaouci, A., Pellegrino, A., and Taylor, J. E. (1993). "Theories of international migration: A review and appraisal." In *Population and Development Review* (pp. 431–466).

Mastrobuoni, Giovanni and Pinotti, Paolo. (July 21, 2011). "Migration restrictions and criminal behaviour: Evidence from a natural experiment." FEEM Working Paper No. 53.2011.

McDonald, W. F. (1997). "Crime and illegal immigration: Emerging local, state, and federal partnerships." *National Institute of Justice Journal* (232), 2–10. https://www.ncjrs.gov/App/AbstractDB/AbstractDBDetails.aspx?id=184605.

Miles T. J., and Cox, A. B. (2014). "Does immigration enforcement reduce crime? Evidence from secure communities." *The Journal of Law & Economics* 57(4), 937–973. https://doi.org/10.1086/680935.

Merton, R.K. (1938). "Social structure and anomie." *American Sociological Review* 3(5), 672–682.

Moehling, C. and Piehl, A.M. (2009). "Immigration, crime, and incarceration in early 20th Century America." *Demography* 46(4), 739–763. https://doi.org/10.1353/dem .0.0076.

Nunziata, L., (2015). Immigration and crime: Evidence from victimisation data. *Journal of Population Economics* 28(3), 697–736. https://doi.org/10.1007/s00148 -015-0543-2.

Páez, T., (2017). "Amid economic crisis and political turmoil, Venezuelans form a New Exodus." *Migration Policy Institute.*

Paternoster, R. and Mazerolle, P. (1994). "General strain theory and delinquency—A replication and extension." *Journal of Research in Crime and Delinquency* 31(3), 235–263.

Plecas, D., Evans, J. and Dandurand, Y. (2002). "Migration and crime: A Canadian per- spective," mimeo.

R4V Response for Venezuelans. (2020). *Situational Report: Trinidad and Tobago.* UNHCR The UN Refugee Agency. https://data2.unhcr.org/es/documents/download /75060.

Ragoonath, R. (2019, September 18). "Thousands of Venezuelans await registration cards." *Trinidad & Tobago Guardian.* http://www.guardian.co.tt/news/thousands -of-venezuelans-await-registration-cards-6.2.938780.ab44067cae.

Redhead, S. (1995). *Unpopular Cultures: The Birth of Law and Popular Culture.* Manchester, UK: Manchester University Press.

Reis, M. (2009). "Contemporary Venezuelan student emigration to Trinidad." In E. Thomas-Hope (Ed.), *Freedom and Constraint in Caribbean Migration and Diaspora* (pp. 36–51) Ian Randle.

Retis, J., and Benavides, J.L. (2005). "Miradas hacia Latinoamérica: la representación discursiva de los inmigrantes latinoamericanos en la prensa española y estadoun-idense" [Glances Toward Latin America: The Discursive Representation of Latin American Immigrants in the Spanish and American Press]. *Temas de Portada* 8(2), 93–114. https://www.redalyc.org/pdf/649/64901304.pdf.

Seepersad, R. (2016). *Crime and violence in Trinidad and Tobago (Technical Note No. IDB-TN-1062)* https://publications.iadb.org/publications/english/document/ Crime-and-Violence-in-Trinidad-and-Tobago-IDB-Series-on-Crime-and-Viol ence-in-the-Caribbean.pdf.

Shaw, C. and McKay, H. (1942). *Juvenile Delinquency and Urban Areas.* Chicago: University of Chicago Press.

Sklansky, D. (2012). "Crime, immigration, and Ad hoc instrumentalism." *New Criminal Law Review: An International and Interdisciplinary Journal* 15(2), 157–223. https://doi.org/10.1525/nclr.2012.15.2.157.

Smilde, D. (2017). "Crime and revolution in Venezuela." *NACLA Report on the Americas* 49(3), 303–308. https://doi.org/10.1080/10714839.2017.1373956.

UNHCR The UN Refugee Agency. (2018, March). *Venezuela situation: responding to the needs of people displaced from Venezuela.* http://reporting.unhcr.org/sites/default/files/UNHCR%20Venezuela%20Situation%202018%20Supplementary%20Appeal_0.pdf.

Upsurge in Crime from Venezuela's Delta. (2019, April 21). *Trinidad Guardian.* http://www.guardian.co.tt/news/upsurge-in-crime-from-venezuelas-delta-6.2.828729.5e6e43fd99.

Van Vechten, C.C. (1941). "The criminality of the foreign born." *Journal of Criminal Law and Criminology* 32, 139–147.

Chapter 3

Leveraging the Asylum System to Overcome Immigration Barriers in Small Island States

Ashaki L. Dore

INTRODUCTION

Islands play a significant role in migration studies and have become strategic locations as stepping-stones in the geopolitics of irregular migration by facilitating the clandestine movement of irregular migrants.[1] However, islands have also been defined as paradoxical spaces which lend themselves to being paradise and prison, heaven and hell.[2] In some instances islands are final destinations, and in other cases they are transitional spaces en route to other places, but people become stuck and unable to move on, and are yet unwilling to turn back to their country of origin.[3] While the most recent migration studies cite the Mediterranean Sea as the main geographic reference in the massive migratory movement between Africa and Europe, this chapter looks at the Caribbean Sea as it relates to movement from Latin America to the Caribbean, in particular, from Venezuela to Trinidad and Tobago.

Over the last ten years Trinidad and Tobago has received a number of asylum-seekers coming from over thirty countries, the second largest number of asylum-seekers in the region after Belize. These migrants are predominantly African, with smaller numbers originating from Asia, the Middle East, and other countries in the Americas.[4] However, political persecution, shortages in food and medicine, and a lack of access to social services have caused approximately three million Venezuelans to flee their country. This exodus constitutes a significant displacement crisis for a number of countries in the Latin American and Caribbean region which have been forced to absorb increasing numbers of arrivals. This has had a significant impact on small countries; particularly in the case of Trinidad and Tobago as a small island state with a population of 1.4 million people, where it is estimated that the country hosts over 60,000 Venezuelans.[5]

People who move in an irregular fashion leave their countries for the same reasons as other migrants: to seek work and a better life, and to flee persecution.[6] However, because of restrictive asylum and immigration policies, there are proportionately fewer legal opportunities for them to migrate. This chapter argues that the growth of asylum-seekers from Venezuela to Trinidad and Tobago is an unintended consequence of restrictive immigration policies. While the literature employs constructs such as abuse, contestation, and resistance against the asylum system,[7] this chapter discusses immigrant agency on the basis that there are some immigrants who are not in need of international protection and are instead economic migrants in disguise[8] who resort to asylum channels in the hope of gaining temporary or permanent stay in the host country,[9] thereby deliberately leveraging the asylum system to achieve their goal of migration.

According to the Refugee Convention (1951), a refugee is a person who is unable or unwilling to return to their country of origin owing to a well-founded fear of being persecuted for reasons of race, religion, nationality, membership of a particular social group, or political opinion (Article 1A.2).[10] Subsequently, the United Nations High Commissioner for Refugees (UNHCR) issued guidance as a result of the influx of Venezuelans, which advised that everyone coming out of Venezuela should be considered a refugee and granted refugee rights on the basis of the Cartagena Declaration, which expands the initial definition of a refugee to include instances of serious disturbance of public order, foreign aggression, and threats to society. The Cartagena Declaration identifies a threat as existing at the community and national levels, and this is what is said to be occurring in Venezuela, where armed groups have more power than the state, and where the government has its own armed group called the 'Colectivos," there is rampant crime, and access to food is dependent on political affiliation, making it a political issue.[11]

Trinidad and Tobago acceded to the 1951 convention and 1967 Protocol relating to the status of Refugees in 2000, and by acceding to these international instruments that govern the treatment of asylum-seekers and refugees, it acknowledged their vulnerability and the role of the international community in the protection of the rights of refugees.[12] However, most Caribbean states do not have laws on asylum;[13] with the exception of Belize's legislation for refugees in the Independent Commonwealth Caribbean, and while the government of Trinidad and Tobago adopted a National Policy to address Refugee and Asylum matters in June 2014, as did Jamaica,[14] to date, these have not been incorporated into domestic legislation and this has hindered the application of proper protection principles for refugees and asylum-seekers.[15]

Today, many signatories continue to fail in adequately supporting asylum-seekers, where policy responses in Europe, North America, and Australasia have been highly criticized as they appear to penalize asylum-seekers by obstructing their efforts to mobilize and find settlement.[16] As a result, asylum policies focus increasingly on control rather than on the protection of refugees, and this has become evident in immigration provisions which have proven to be detrimental for asylum-seekers and refugees.[17] This may be as a result of the way policy makers interpret the phenomenon of irregular migration and how these interpretations are institutionalized and implemented in the governance of irregular migration and the asylum system; guided by a set of beliefs, ideas, material circumstances, and processes.[18]

STIGMATIZATION OF IRREGULAR MIGRATION AND ITS IMPLICATIONS FOR MIGRANTS

Any attempt to define irregular migration that overlooks the complexity of contemporary flows would be misguided.[19] There are conceptual challenges involved in differentiating stocks from flows in migration studies,[20] where migration is usually defined as the movement of people from one place or country to another, for a significant period of time.[21] Recently, however, it has become somewhat difficult to distinguish asylum-seekers or refugees from aggregate statistics on irregular migration; this is further compounded by the realization that the legal status of immigrants can change quickly. Irregular migration is a complex phenomenon as it includes migrants who are in irregular situations for a range of different reasons, and for whom irregularity has different outcomes.

There are many routes to achieving irregular status which include irregular entry into the country through clandestine entry or the use of fraudulent documents. This can be followed by regularization obtained by applying for asylum or entering a regularization program. Regular entry can result in irregular status via obtaining employment without a work permit or overstaying a visa or work permit. Other routes entail sham marriages and fake adoptions. Asylum-seekers become irregular migrants when their application for asylum is rejected and they remain in the country of application without authority.[22] Irregular status can also result from a number of administrative obstacles such as changing immigration laws, the inability to obtain a passport, or failure to renew expired traveling documents because of a lack of material. Thus there are a number of intervening factors which can lead to an irregular status.[23]

Two other terms that are often used interchangeably in this context are "undocumented" and "'unauthorized." These terms do not apply to all irregular migrants, although "undocumented" is often used to cover them all.

Similarly, not all irregular migrants are necessarily unauthorized, and so this term too is often used incorrectly. The term "irregular" is considered conceptually problematic; yet it is preferable to the term "illegal."[24] It is used by most organizations with a competence in migration, including the Council of Europe, International Labour Organisation (ILO), International Organisation for Migration (IOM), the Organisation for Security and Cooperation in Europe (OSCE), and UNHCR. Indeed, the European Union (EU) is the only significant international actor that continues to use the term "illegal migration." The concept of illegality attached to migration has been criticized on the basis that it connotes criminality. Most irregular migrants are not criminals, and yet the term can be interpreted as denying their humanity, and the labeling of "illegal" for asylum-seekers who find themselves in an irregular situation may further jeopardize their asylum claims.[25]

A number of studies have explored the implications of mobilizing the illegal immigration classification in political and media discourses, where it has been employed to construct a negative "other" representation. The negative stereotypical connotations have been intrinsically linked to immigrant groups, and in some cases, illegality has been used as a metonym for Latin American immigrants. Moreover, it has also become difficult to distinguish between the mechanisms used for migration control and those used for refugee protection.[26] This is critical given that the way migrants are characterized, treated, and represented upon arrival, is guided by a perception of threat to society, rhetoric of fear, crisis and emergency in public opinion, and a view of irregular migration as a form of criminality, where immigrants are viewed as undesirable, unwanted, and unaccepted intruders.[27]

The contextualization of illegal immigration as a threat within discourses of "risk" and uncertainty by explicitly evoking associations of immigration with unlawfulness, have functioned to justify practices of immigrants' deportation.[28] These views have implications for how immigrants live, how they are treated, and how they socialize with others in society. Consequently, the line between irregular migrants and asylum-seekers and refugees has become increasingly blurred. Also, the distinction between regular and irregular (or undocumented) immigrants, although it allows us to understand the legal circumstances of migrants' entry into a territory, is not always relevant because there is considerable porosity between the categories.[29]

POLICY RESPONSES TO IRREGULAR MIGRATION

Migration policies in most receiving states have converged around the combination of a number of varying instruments which include pre-frontier, border, post-entry, and return.[30] Pre-frontier measures aim to affect the geography and direction of irregular migration. These include bureaucratic controls such as visa requirements, information campaigns, punitive sanctions for human smugglers, the implementation of laws such as the Dublin Law, the reversal of the Schengen law, and the EU funding of the Libyan Coast Guard who were incidentally accused of executing the forced return of migrants to inhumane conditions in Libya. The objective of these measures was the prevention of migrants from leaving their territorial waters, and the prohibition of NGO rescue boats from acting as a pull factor and encouraging migrants to risk their lives at sea in the hope of being rescued and taken safely to land.[31]

It has also been suggested that the embassies of third countries and EU institutions be used as sites from which to claim asylum, with the aim of reducing the numbers of migrants illegally landing on EU shores; this acts as an externalization strategy and a bureaucratic fence affecting the geography and presence of potential immigrants.[32]

Border management measures seek to control the scale of irregular immigration by enforcing fencing and gatekeeping practices by strengthening physical borders through the use of structural fences and walls, electronic surveillance, documentation with enhanced security features, employment and training of personnel, and the use of biometric data. Examples are the Melilla border fence which forms part of the Morocco–Spain border, the U.S.–Mexico border, and the Bulgaria–Turkey border fence. Post-entry measures seek to make the destination a less attractive option for prospective migrants, therefore, these measures can include detention, workplace inspections, employer sanction, and restrictions on the right to work, access to social welfare services, and education.[33]

Deportation is another measure which has been used to reduce stocks of irregular migrants. This measure may result in serving as an incentive for migrants to leave the country again if returned to a precarious situation, or may encourage others to employ an alternative smuggler, or head for an alternative destination. However, deportation is a difficult measure to enforce if there is a lack of will to leave; if the immigrant is not in possession of travel or identity documents; if the immigrant is unwell; when the country of origin is unwilling to cooperate; when friends, family, or lawyers fight the deportation process; or the migrant claims asylum, which stalls the process.[34]

Another layer of complexity is added with secondary movement, where the immigrants' country of origin is not the country of their nationality. This is problematic given that states do not return immigrants to third countries. Moreover, it is uncertain to what extent return is an effective mechanism to reduce irregular migration, given that irregular migrants repeatedly demonstrate that risk-taking is a part of their survival strategy so that there is little which can deter them. Even after the difficult journey to get to the country of destination, detention by authorities, and/or harassment by locals; the need to survive and provide for their families is stronger than the fear of reprisal. These policies have been unsuccessful in preventing or limiting irregular immigration because control policies do not address the root causes of irregular migration.[35] On the contrary, control policies may fuel the growth and sophistication of immigrant smuggling and often push migrants to more dangerous and complicated ways of crossing and remaining behind borders;[36] they only make entry into the receiving country difficult and dangerous. This has serious implications given that immigrants constantly seek out new and alternative routes of "least resistance."[37]

Irregular migration tends to polarize opinions, which vary from concern about border control to concern for the human rights of migrants, and reveal the many interests involved, depending on the agreements being negotiated.[38] As a result, cooperation with other countries is difficult when states are con-flicted about their own interests with regard to migration and what they want to achieve through their migration policies.[39] Statistical data can be used to justify a particular policy response to irregular immigration which would be geared toward restricting movement. It can also be used to aid the state in the allocation of resources to address the economic and social impact of irregular migration, and to assist international and non-governmental organizations involved in the management of irregular migration flows to assist irregular migrants, allocate resources, procure assistance, establish logistical systems, raise money, and account for the organization's expenditure.[40] However, as states seek to comply with international obligations and simultaneously limit access to their territory, this presents a key dilemma for policy-making given that at times the principles of sovereignty are difficult to reconcile with the principles of human rights. Consequently, while there may be a willingness to consider new policy alternatives, it is unlikely that any measure introduced by the state will dismantle the existing policies to the extent of opening regular migration channels to a scale that would sufficiently satisfy demand. [41]

THE EMERGING ROLE OF ISLANDS
IN MIGRATION STUDIES

Most destination countries tend to be global or regional hegemons in rela-tion to the countries of origin from which people migrate, and are generally wealthier and strategically and militarily dominant.[42] While island states are generally discussed in the literature in terms of their limited economic and military power, and limited personnel, resources, and space to host and man-age irregular migrants, some small states and island states such as Malta and Cyprus have successfully devised strategies to increase their influence based on nonmaterial power, to the extent that they have been able to increase their influence in regional migration policy through the formation of alliances, the deployment of moral authority, and symbolic capital within their discourses, in spite of their material limitations. [43]

Islands have become relevant to migration studies as a result of the open access and cover they provide to immigrants, and the strict; yet weak migration controls that exist. Maritime borders make islands attractive for irregular migration. They present a challenge for states, as managing these borders is starkly different from controlling land borders which entail checkpoints at road crossings and at airports, and the erection of fences and walls. Maritime control requires surveillance of a broader area, which becomes more vulnerable under the cover of night, as well as checkpoints at various ports and airports.[44]

In the case of the EU, islands have been transformed into emergency locations, and the indispensable enforcers of EU controls as part of a migration management system which reconceptualizes islands as external borders. They function as "hotspots-like spaces" of mobility disruption, and have become channels to institutionally force mobility or immobility, thereby engaging in a practice of blocking migrants from going further into Europe, or pushing them and diverting them in certain directions, essentially determining the migrant's final destination.[45] This is evident in migration controls implemented at the Strait of Gibraltar which provoked a reorientation of flows on the eastern Moroccan coast, Algeria, and Libya toward Italy and Malta; this has incidentally fuelled massive detention, people-smuggling, kidnapping, and slavery for the purpose of sex work. Subsequently, Italy's Mare Nostrum rescue operations were terminated after the country raised concerns about becoming the refugee camp of Europe, its role as a migrant pull factor,[46] and abandonment by the rest of the EU which failed to share the burden brought on by irregular immigration.[47] This led to the reduction of NGO search and rescue operations, the implementation of Frontex,[48] and the defunding of the Libyan Coast Guard[49] in efforts to curtail irregular immigration. These measures have had the effect of reorienting irregular migration to the Turkey–Bulgarian land border and longer routes through the Balkans.

OVERCOMING STRICT IMMIGRATION POLICIES

In response to these increasingly restrictive regulations, migratory trajectories are being reshaped and migrants are evolving toward new schemes by adopting various "bypass strategies."[50] These strategies can be understood under the construct of self-agency, which is a crucial element in attempting to understand immigration patterns and processes from the point of view and experiences of the people making the decision to move, however limited their room for maneuver.[51] Self-agency is also linked to a broader framework in migration studies which distinguishes between forced and voluntary migration, where the former refers to the migrant who has no agency at all, while the other enjoys total freedom.[52] However, migrants' self-agency highlights the voluntary decision-making process of moving in an irregular manner and of the potential risks involved, and this is an important factor to which reference is limited in irregular migration literature.[53]

While some migrants find themselves forced into an irregular migration situation as a result of being moved by human traffickers, some make a deliberate choice to become irregular migrants by seeking the services of migrant smugglers; whose principal function is to assist the migrant to overcome obstacles that have resulted directly from restrictive immigration policies, especially in the form of visa restrictions and border controls. Some irregular migrants, therefore, negotiate payments and acceptable costs, select between competing services, and choose the best route and final destination.[54] However, any evidence of agency undermines their chances of seeking asylum, as it brings their "victimhood" into question and may instead be portrayed as villains who then become securitized and labeled a threat to national security.[55]

In the EU, only Eritreans, Syrians, and Iraqis were able to commence the asylum process because of their eligibility for the EU's Relocation Programme. All other nationalities, including large numbers of people coming from West African countries, were instead illegalized and classified as undocumented economic migrants, excluding them from protection mechanisms. Illegalized persons were then officially required to leave the country within seven days through an expulsion order called "7 days decree," which entailed funding their own removal. Many live in destitution throughout Europe as irregular and undocumented migrants, and this management system has emerged as a mechanism to prevent most persons from accessing the asylum procedure.[56] The Afghan immigrant's response to overcome this legislative barrier has been the adoption of a new strategy of claiming Syrian or Iraqi nationality in order to qualify for relocation and prevent deportation.[57] This process is facilitated by the fact they are often undocumented, and this makes it difficult to verify their nationalities.[58]

Economic migration is considered to be a rational strategy for maximizing lifetime income-earning opportunities,[59] and islands have emerged as strategic migration destinations, having transformed from source countries to host territories. In the past, islanders left for other, more prosperous lands; today islands are points of convergence for return migrants and economic migrants drawn by new employment opportunities.[60] This may have been the rationale for migration flows from Trinidad and Tobago to Venezuela during the 1970s, as a result of the general sense of social restlessness produced by the political and social climate, which was characterized by economic inequality, foreign domination of the economy, ethnically biased employment practices which led to a progression from peaceful revolution to violent guerrilla warfare. This was represented by the Joint National Action Committee in 1969 which later become known as the NJAC, and the National Union of Freedom Fighters (NUFF) during a period which became known as the Black Power Movement and the February Revolution in which months of massive demonstrations and citizen's revolt against the status quo, represented action-oriented demand for social change and significant changes in governance.[61]

Trinidad and Tobago is one of the wealthiest countries in the Americas on a per capita basis and is classified by the World Bank as a high-income state which has been able to develop a robust welfare system as a result of its well-developed oil and gas sector.[62] The state has witnessed intraregional migratory flows into the islands as a result of its geographical proximity, the relative low cost of transport between territories, mutual interests in the energy sector, increasingly porous borders, unmanned coastline, and minimal restrictions at points of entry, and the shared cultural affinities allow immigrants to "blend in" easily with nationals of Trinidad and Tobago.[63] In some countries immigration policy is driven by the perception that the territory is overwhelmed by large numbers of irregular migrants who pose a threat to the state and the society and this is critical for governments, particularly given the view that irregular migration undermines public confidence in the integrity and effectiveness of a state's immigration and asylum policies.[64]

The current state of affairs in the Bolivarian Republic of Venezuela has had significant implications for neighboring countries such as Colombia, Brazil, Peru, and Trinidad and Tobago. Venezuelans are considered one of the most prevalent migrant groupings in Trinidad and Tobago who subsequently seek asylum, although it has been difficult to collect verifiable statistics on irregular migration given that data often underestimates its degree and volume and is unable to capture the number of immigrants who enter in a clandestine manner. However, "as the number of refugees increases, so does xenophobia and exploitation" in a climate migrants describe as hostile.[65]

Xenophobia against the Venezuelans is such a big issue here. We need an anti-xenophobia campaign. The perception so many Trinidadians have is that Venezuelans are just coming here to take our jobs and our husbands. We need Trinidadian organisations to run such campaigns—otherwise no one will listen.[66]

Interestingly, Venezuela was once the most important destination point of international migrations to Latin America as a result of the privileged economic status it enjoyed during the post–Second World War period. Undocumented migrants to Venezuela comprised a significant proportion of immigrants, whose numbers grew with the increased demand for manpower in the rural sector as a result of increased economic activity; Trinidad and Tobago immigrants comprised 2 percent of the total registered undocumented migrant population and represented the second largest group of Caribbean immigrants. In 1980 Venezuela regularized the undocumented migrant population, via Presidential Decree 616 titled "Regulations on the Admission and Permanence of Foreigners in the Country," based on sections from an instrument which underscored a commitment to labor mobility; the "Instrumento Andino de Migraciones Laborales," Article 1 of the decree called for the registration of all irregular or undocumented migrants who had entered legally but had stayed beyond the expiration date of their visas, those who had entered illegally, and those employed in illicit activities but lacked the documentation permitting their legal residence; this also included their spouses and children.[67]

In Trinidad and Tobago irregular migrants are unable to find legal employment and face detention and deportation; in 2018 a Refugees International (RI) team traveled to Trinidad and Tobago to assess the situation of Venezuelan refugees and migrants in that country.[68] The strict immigration controls in Trinidad and Tobago have led immigrants to seek asylum in an attempt to increase their opportunities to stay in the country for an unlimited period, or perhaps to minimize the chances of—or at least delay—deportation. The absence of a national refugee policy, the implementation of an Immigration Act which criminalizes irregular migration as illegal immigration, and a population that views the arrival of immigrants as a threat to their sovereignty and human security, all present a challenge for the governance of immigration and the asylum system in Trinidad and Tobago. Why then, are immigrants seeking asylum in a country which does not recognize refugees?

Immigrant motivation to seek asylum and refugee status is motivated by the number of rights[69] which are stipulated under the 1951 UN Convention, including the right of non-refoulement, in which asylum-seekers and refugees are protected from forcible return to a country in which their lives or freedom may be in danger. Even in cases where they enter the country without a visa or entry permit, they may not be deported while their asylum claim is being processed to determine their status. The principle of non-refoulement has attained the status of customary international law.

Asylum-seekers are not supposed to be penalized for illegal entry or illegal presence as in many instances they flee their countries without documentation. The right to family unity recognizes the nuclear family and other dependent relatives up to the second degree of blood or family relationship, so although applicants are often forced to flee alone because they do not have the financial means to travel as a family, refugees who have been recognized by the UNHCR can bring their immediate family members to Trinidad and Tobago, including, their spouses, children under 18 years of age, or parents if the refugee is an unaccompanied or separated child. The request for reunification is made to the Living Waters Community (LWC),[70] who will guide the applicant through the procedure. Moreover, the right of non-discrimination states that asylum-seekers have the right to live in an environment free from discrimination, regardless of ethnicity, color, sex, language, religion, political opinion, nationality, economic position, birthplace, or any other personal attribute. They also have a right to state-provided primary health care which can be accessed from LWC on a case-by-case basis.

As a result, they depend on basic assistance provided by the UNHCR and LWC. In light of this, many find themselves working in the informal sector, vulnerable to exploitation. Moreover, they do not currently have rights to the public and private banking services of Trinidad and Tobago, and they are unable to access money transfer services given that passports are required for transactions to be conducted, and asylum seekers' passports are held by immigration officials. As a result, asylum-seekers are unable to receive financial assistance from friends and/or family members abroad. This has led many asylum-seekers to engage the assistance of local citizens, and they are often required to remunerate these individuals for conducting monetary transactions in their names.

The surrendering of passports also renders them immobile: they are unable to legally move to another destination. In instances where refugee status has been obtained, refugees have stated that their situation has worsened given that there are no laws which allow refugees to seek employment and other services and there is little to no opportunity for resettlement in other countries: they are unable to return to their country of origin, and they are unable to legally leave the state. Moreover, Venezuelan immigrants often incur debts in order to fund their trips. This places them in a precarious position given the need to repay this debt, and may provide incentive to remain in the inland at all cost in order to obtain employment.

Consequently, Venezuelan immigrants often leverage the bureaucratic deficiencies of the current asylum/refugee process caused by the delay involved in processing applications. This allows applicants to seek employment as long as they can avoid detection by the authorities, which could lead to detention at the Immigration Detention Centre (IDC), the imposition of fines, and incarceration followed by deportation. Before August 2017 the government issued an order of supervision as an alternative to detention, and this provided a certain degree of protection from detention and deportation. Under this system, asylum-seekers were required to hand over their passports and report regularly to the authorities, but this practice has been suspended by the high court. The order of supervision can now be obtained only after detention and the payment of a security bond which is reimbursed with a successful asylum application.[71]

The geographic proximity between Trinidad and Tobago and Venezuela and the former's porous borders allow asylum-seekers to periodically travel undetected between the countries to carry food and medicine to their families. This categorizes these immigrants as transnational migrants as they engage in regular activities linking them back to their homeland which include sending remittances, making return visits, supporting hometown associations, trading goods, and maintaining close communication with kin back home.[72] As a result, scholars argue that when migration programs are properly managed, they can benefit both the host country and the country of origin through increased remittances which can contribute to national economies and economic growth in the host country through increased professional and skilled labor.[73] The challenge lies in developing an immigration policy which would incentivize legal entry into the state by advancing the protection and respect of immigrants, asylum-seekers, and refugee rights while discouraging persons from pursuing dangerous, illegal pathways to entry or taking advantage of the asylum system in order to overcome the legislative barriers that currently exist.

CONCLUSION

While the government of Trinidad and Tobago has made progress to integrate refugees and asylum-seekers in Trinidad and Tobago through its Refugee Policy adopted in 2014, after five years it has managed to achieve only the first phase, which is an indication of the lengthy and complex nature of the policy. As long as the provisions of this policy remain unincorporated into domestic law, any refugee or asylum seeker who claims protection in Trinidad and Tobago will be bound by the Immigration Act and its regulations.

If migration experiences in the Mediterranean Sea serve as any example of the dangers involved in the poor management of immigration and asylum policies, greater efforts must be geared toward managing irregular migration. This includes the provision of legal channels of entry and access to work permits, which would allow immigrants to actively participate in the society of the host country. Moreover, in Trinidad and Tobago, the vulnerability of immigrants leaves them with little option but to become involved in illegal activities as a means of survival. Failure to manage irregular migration in a way that benefits both the state and the country of origin will continue to engender xenophobic sentiments in a society which has traditionally been characterized as tolerant, but now sees immigrants as a threat to their human security.

NOTES

1. Russell King, "Geography, Islands and Migration in an Era of Global Mobility," *Island Studies Journal* (2009): 66.

2. Godfrey Baldacchino, "Islands, Island Studies, Island Studies Journal," *Island Studies Journal* (2006): 3–18.

3. King, "Geography, Islands and Migration in an Era of Global Mobility," 76.

4. Government of the Republic of Trinidad and Tobago, A Phased Approach towards the Establishment of a National Policy to Address Refugee and Asylum Matters in the Republic of Trinidad and Tobago, 4.

5. Rhoda Margesson and Clare Ribando Seelke, "The Venezuela Regional Migration Crisis," 2019.

6. Khalid Koser, "Dimensions and Dynamics of Irregular Migration," 2010, 182.

7. Cetta Mainwaring, "Migrant Agency: Negotiating Borders and Migration Controls," *Migration Studies* (2016), 292.

8. Lucy Mayblin, "Imagining Asylum, Governing Asylum Seekers: Complexity Reduction and Policy Making in the UK Home Office," 1.

9. Koser, "Dimensions and Dynamics of Irregular Migration," 2010, 183.

10. John Campbell, "Asylum vs. Sovereignty in the 21st Century: How Nation-State Breach International Law to Block Access to Asylum," 2015. Available at http://eprints.soas.ac.uk/21493/2/Asylum%20v%20sovereignty%20in%20the%2021st%20Century.pdf (Accessed May 10, 2019).

11. Rochelle Nakhid, personal communication, 2018.

12. Government of Trinidad and Tobago, "A Phased Approach towards the Establishment of a National Policy to Address Refugee and Asylum Matters in the Republic of Trinidad and Tobago," 1.

13. Melanie Teff, "Forced into Illegality: Venezuelan Refugees and Migrants in Trinidad and Tobago," Field Report. *Refugees International* (2019), 7.

14. Government of the Republic of Trinidad and Tobago, "A Phased Approach towards the Establishment of a National Policy," 2.

15. Rochelle Nakhid and Andrew Welch, "Protection in the absence of Legislation in Trinidad and Tobago," 2017, 42.

16. Mayblin, "Imagining Asylum, Governing Asylum Seekers: Complexity Reduction and Policy Making in the UK Home Office," 1.

17. UNHCR, "Global Report 2004: North America and the Caribbean," 2005, 460.

18. Mayblin, "Imagining Asylum, Governing Asylum Seekers: Complexity Reduction and Policy Making in the UK Home Office," 1.

19. Nathalie Bernardie-Tahir, and Camille Schmoll, "Islands and Undesirables: Introduction to the Special Issue on Irregular Migration in Southern European Islands," 2014, 88.

20. Koser, "Dimensions and Dynamics of Irregular Migration," 2010.

21. King, "Geography, Islands and Migration in an Era of Global Mobility," 59.

22. Koser "Dimensions and Dynamics of Irregular Migration," 183.

23. Global Commission on International Migration (GCIM), Migration in an Interconnected World: New Directions for Actions, 2005, 7.

24. Koser, "Irregular Migration, State Security and Human Security," 2005, 5

25. Koser, "Irregular Migration, State Security and Human Security," 5.

26. Stewart, Pitts and Osborne, 2011, 183.

27. Bernardie-Tahir and Schmoll, "Islands and Undesirables," 35.

28. Lia Figgou, "Constructions of 'Illegal' Immigration and Entitlement to Citisenship: Debating an Immigration Law in Greece," 2016, 151.

29. Bernardie-Tahir and Schmoll, "Islands and Undesirables," 88.

30. Koser, "Irregular Migration, State Security and Human Security," 14.

31. Bernardie-Tahir and Schmoll, "Islands and Undesirables," 89.

32. Anna Triandafyllidou, "Multi-levelling and Externalising Migration and Asylum: Lessons from the Southern European Islands," 2014, 8.

33. Koser, "Irregular Migration, State Security and Human Security," 14.

34. Liza Schuster and John Solomos, "Race, Immigration and Asylum: New Labour's Agenda and its Consequences," *Ethnicities* 4, no. 2 (2004): 275–280.

35. Roger Zetter, David Griffiths, Silva Ferretti and Martyn Pearl, "An Assessment of the Impact of Asylum Policies in Europe 1990-2000," 2003, 134.

36. UNHCR, "Desperate Journeys: Refugees and Migrants Arriving in Europe and at Europe's Borders," 2018, 12–14.

37. King, "Geography, Islands and Migration in an Era of Global Mobility," 66.

38. Koser, "Dimensions and Dynamics of Irregular Migration," 191.

39. IOM, "World Migration Report," 127.

40. Koser, "Dimensions and Dynamics of Irregular Migration," 182.

41. Koser, "Irregular Migration, State Security and Human Security," 2–4.

42. IOM, "World Migration Report," 128.

43. Mainwaring, "Small States and Nonmaterial Power: Creating Crises and Shaping Migration Policies in Malta, Cyprus, and the European Union," 103–122.

44. King, "Geography, Islands and Migration in an Era of Global Mobility," 66.

45. Tazzioli and Garelli, "Containment beyond Detention," 4.

46. Ella Ide, "Italy Ignores Pleas, Ends Boat Migrant Rescue Operations," (AFP, 31 October 2014). Available at https://news.yahoo.com/italy-confirms-end-boat-migrant-rescue-op-mare-142437512.html (accessed May 19, 2019).

47. Bernardie-Tahir and Schmoll, "Islands and Undesirables," 88.

48. Frontex is a European Union institution aimed at coordinating the monitoring and control of the sea, land and air external borders of EU member States, as well as implementing re-admission agreements with neighboring countries concerning non-EU migrants rejected at the borders (see Ministero della Difesa for additional information, available at http://www.marina.difesa.it/EN/operations/Pagine/MareNostrum.aspx (Accessed May 19, 2019).

49. VOA News "Migrants Sue Italy over Collaboration with Libyan Coast Guard." Available at https://youtu.be/c2qGl9Sh40U (Published 9 May, 2018).

50. Bernardie-Tahir and Schmoll, "Islands and Undesirables," 90.

51. International Organisation for Migration (IOM) "World Migration Report," 2017, 172.

52. Mainwaring, "Migrant Agency: Negotiating Borders and Migration Controls," 1.

53. Stephen Castles' "The International Migration Review" for his discussion of why certain policy approaches have failed and the importance of migrant agency, 871.

54. Koser, "Irregular Migration, State Security and Human Security,"188.

55. Cetta Mainwaring, "Migrant Agency: Negotiating Borders and Migration Controls," 290.

56. Tazzioli and Garelli, "Containment beyond Detention," 7.

57. Al Jazeera English "EU – Afghanistan sign deal to deport unlimited number of Afghanistan refugees." Available at https://youtu.be/aH8f4OLGWzI.

58. Admir Skodo, "How Afghans became Second-Class Asylum Seekers," Available at http://theconversation.com/how-afghans-became-second-class-asylum-seekers-72437 (Accessed May 20, 2018; Published: 20 February, 2017).

59. Marlon Anatol, Mark Kirton, and Nia Nanan, "Becoming an Immigration Magnet," 2013, 15.

60. Bernardie-Tahir and Schmoll, "Islands and Undesirables," 87–88.

61. Brinsley Samaroo, "The February Revolution (1970) as a catalyst for change in Trinidad and Tobago in Black Power and the Caribbean," (Ed) by Quinn K. 2014, 118.

62. John McCoy, and W. Andy Knight, "Homegrown Violent Extremism in Trinidad and Tobago: Local Patterns, Global Trends," *Studies in Conflict and Terrorism* (2017): 271.

63. Marlon Anatol' et al., "Becoming an Immigration Magnet," 71.

64. Koser, "Irregular Migration, State Security and Human Security," 2005.

65. The Guardian, "Venezuelan migrants live in Shadows on Caribbean's Sunshine Islands," (13 November 2018). Available at https://www.theguardian.com/world/2018/nov/13/venezuelan-migrants-caribbean-islands. (Accessed May 20, 2019).

66. Teff, "Forced into Illegality: Venezuelan Refugees and Migrants in Trinidad and Tobago," 19.

67. Ralf Van Roy, "Undocumented Migration to Venezuela," *The International Migration Review* (1984): 541–554.

68. Teff, "Forced into Illegality: Venezuelan Refugees and Migrants in Trinidad and Tobago," 4.

69. See UNHCR Trinidad and Tobago, Asylum Seeker Duties, Available at https://help.unhcr.org/trinidadandtobago/rights-and-duties/refugee-duties/ (Accessed November 19, 2018).

70. The Living Water Community (LWC) is the implementing partner of the United Nations High Commission for Refugees (UNHCR) in Trinidad and Tobago. It is a Catholic Ecclesial Community which began in Port of Spain, Trinidad in 1975. It was founded by Rhonda Maingot and Rose Jackman. The organisation has been assisting asylum seekers and refugees for over 30 years.

71. Teff, "Forced into Illegality: Venezuelan Refugees and Migrants in Trinidad and Tobago," 12.

72. King, "Geography, Islands and Migration in an Era of Global Mobility," 62.

73. Anatol et al., "Becoming an Immigration Magnet," 77.

REFERENCES

Anatol, Marlon, Mark Kirton, Nia Nanan. "Becoming an Immigration Magnet: Migrants' profiles and the impact of migration on human development in Trinidad and Tobago." *African, Caribbean and Pacific Observatory on Migration* (2013).

Baldacchino, Godfrey. "Islands, Island Studies, Island Studies Journal." *Island Studies Journal* 1, no. 1 (2006): 3–18, https://files.eric.ed.gov/fulltext/EJ1000212.pdf.

Bernardie-Tahir, Nathalie and Camille Schmoll. "Islands and Undesirables: Introduction to the Special Issue on Irregular Migration in Southern European Islands." *Journal of Immigrant & Refugee Studies* 12 (2014): 87–102. https://doi.org/10.1080/15562948.2014.899657.

Campbell, John. "Asylum vs. Sovereignty in the 21st Century: How Nation-State Breach International Law to Block Access to Asylum" (2015). http://eprints.soas.ac.uk/21493/2/Asylum%20v%20sovereignty%20in%20the%2021st%20Century.pdf.

Castles, Stephen. "The International Migration Review, Conceptual and Methodological Developments in the Study of International Migration." *Sage Publications: New York* 38, no. 3 (2004): 852–884.

Cusumano, Eugenio, and Kristof Gombeer. "In Deep Waters: The Legal Humanitarian and Political Implications of Closing Italian Ports to Migrant Rescuers." *Journal Mediterranean Politics*. doi: 10.1080/13629395.2018.1532145.

Figgou, Lia. "Constructions of 'Illegal' Immigration and Entitlement to Citizenship: Debating an Immigration Law in Greece." *Journal of Community & Applied Social Psychology* 26, no. 2 (2016): 150–163. https://doi.org/10.1002/casp.2242.

Global Commission on International Migration (GCIM). "Migration in an Interconnected World: New Directions for Action: Report of the Global Commission on International Migration." 2005. https://www.iom.int/jahia/webdav/site/myjahiasite/shared/shared/mainsite/policy_and_research/gcim/GCIM_Report_Complete.pdf.

Government of the Republic of Trinidad and Tobago. "A Phased Approach towards the Establishment of a National Policy to Address Refugee and Asylum Matters in the Republic of Trinidad and Tobago." *Draft Working Document*. https://www.acnur.org/fileadmin/Documentos/BDL/2016/10346.pdf?file=fileadmin/Documentos/BDL/2016/10346.

King, Russell. "Geography, Islands and Migration in an Era of Global Mobility." *Island Studies Journal* 4, no.1 (2009): 53–84. https://www.researchgate.net/publication/26624929_Geography_Islands_and_Migration_in_an_Era_of_Global_Mobility.

Koser, Khalid. "Irregular Migration, State Security and Human Security." Global Commission on International Migration (2005). https://www.iom.int/jahia/webdav/site/myjahiasite/shared/shared/mainsite/policy_and_research/gcim/tp/TP5.pdf.

———. "Dimensions and Dynamics of Irregular Migration." *Population, Space and Place* 16, no. 3 (2010): 181–193. https://doi.org/10.1002/psp.587.

Mainwaring, Cetta. "Migrant Agency: Negotiating Borders and Migration Controls." *Migration Studies* 4, no. 3 (2016): 289–308. https://ccis.ucsd.edu/_files/journals /13mnw013.pdf.

———. "Small States and Nonmaterial Power: Creating Crises and Shaping Migration Policies in Malta, Cyprus, and the European Union." *Journal of Immigrant and Refugee Studies* 12, no. 2 (2014): 103–122. doi: 10.1080/15562948.2014.909076.

Margesson, Rhoda, and Clare Ribando Seelke. "The Venezuela Regional Migration Crisis." Congressional Research Service. In Focus. (2019). https://fas.org/sgp/crs/ row/IF11029.pdf.

Mayblin, Lucy. "Imagining Asylum, Governing Asylum-seekers: Complexity Reduction and Policy Making in the UK Home Office." *Migration Studies* 7, no. 1 (2019): 1–20. https://doi.org/10.1093/migration/mnx060.

McCoy, John and W. Andy Knight. "Homegrown Violent Extremism in Trinidad and Tobago: Local Patterns, Global Trends." *Studies in Conflict and Terrorism* 40, no. 4 (2017): 267–299. https://doi.org/10.1080/1057610X.2016.1206734.

Nakhid, Rochelle and Andrew Welch. "Protection in the Absence of Legislation in Trinidad and Tobago." *Forced Migration Review* 56 (2017). https://www. fmreview.org/latinamerica-caribbean/nakhid-welch.

Samaroo, Brinsley. "The February Revolution (1970) as a Catalyst for Change in Trinidad and Tobago in Black Power and the Caribbean." In *Black Power in the Caribbean*, edited by K. Quinn, 97–116. University Press of Florida, 2014.

Schuster, L and John Solomos. "Race, Immigration and Asylum: New Labour's Agenda and its Consequences." *Ethnicities* 4, no. 2 (2004): 267–300. doi: 1177/1468796804042606.

Skodo, Admir. "How Afghans became Second-Class Asylum Seekers." Available at http://theconversation.com/how-afghans-became-second-class-asylum-seekers -72437 (Accessed May 20, 2018; Published: 20 February, 2017).

Stewart, Craig O., Margaret J. Pitts, and Helena Osborne. "Mediated Intergroup Conflict: The Discursive Construction of "Illegal Immigrants, in a Regional US Newspaper." *Journal of Language and Social Psychology* 30, no. 1 (2011): 8–27. https://doi.org/10.1177/0261927X10387099.

Tazzioli, Martina and Glenda Garelli. "Containment Beyond Detention: The Hotspot System and Disrupted Migration Movements Across Europe." *Environment and Planning D: Society and Space* (2018). https://doi.org/10.1177/0263775818759335.

Teff, Melanie. "Forced into Illegality: Venezuelan Refugees and Migrants in Trinidad and Tobago." *Refugees International.* https://www.refugeesinternational.org/ reports/2019/1/27/forced-into-illegality-venezuelan-refugees-and-migrants-in-trinidad-and-tobago.

Triandafyllidou, Anna. "Multi-levelling and Externalising Migration and Asylum: Lessons from the southern European islands." *Island Studies Journal* 9, no. 1 (2014): 7–22. https://www.researchgate.net/publication/289319121_Multi-levelling_and_externalising_migration_and_asylum_Lessons_from_the_southern _European_islands.

UNHCR. 2018a. "Desperate Journeys: Refugees and Migrants Arriving in Europe and at Europe's Borders," 2018. https://www.unhcr.org/desperatejourneys/.

————. 2004. "Global Report 2004: North America and the Caribbean," 2005. https://www.unhcr.org/publications/fundraising/4a0c13d76/global-report-2004.html.

————. 2018b. Asylum Seeker Duties. https://help.unhcr.org/trinidadandtobago/rights-and-duties/refugee-duties/ (Accessed 19 November 2018).

Van Roy, Ralph. "Undocumented Migration to Venezuela." *The International Migration Review* 8, no. 3 (1984): 541–557. doi: 10.2307/2545885.

VOA News. "Migrants Sue Italy over Collaboration with Libyan Coast Guard." https://youtu.be/c2qGl9Sh40U (Published 9 May, 2018).

Zetter, Roger, David Griffiths, Silva Ferretti and Martyn Pearl. "An Assessment of the Impact of Asylum Policies in Europe 1990-2000." *Home Office Research Study* 259 (2003). Retrieved from http://www.temaasyl.se/Documents/Artiklar/hors259.pdf.

Chapter 4

To Expand or Not to Expand?

Utilizing Geopolitical Analysis to Examine CARICOM's Potential Enlargement in the Twenty-First Century

Kai-Ann D. Skeete

THE CARIBBEAN: AN OVERVIEW

The late Caribbean scholar Girvan[1] writes that former historian Gaztambide-Geigel argues that the Caribbean region was an invention of the United States merely for its hemispheric military and economic expansion. Exactly what is or what is not the Caribbean is entirely open for interpretation according to authors Knight and Palmer.[2] More often than not, the Caribbean is defined by a myriad of its characteristics ranging from geographic, historical, cultural, or geopolitical purposes.

This chapter defines the Caribbean as the fifteen full member states of the Caribbean Community and Common Market (CARICOM). These are as follows: Antigua and Barbuda, the Commonwealth of the Bahamas, Barbados, Belize, the Commonwealth of Dominica, Grenada, the Republic of Guyana, the Republic of Haiti, Jamaica, Montserrat, the Federation of St. Kitts and Nevis, St. Lucia, St. Vincent and the Grenadines, the Republic of Suriname, and the Republic of Trinidad and Tobago.

As citizens of the Caribbean, we must be cognizant of our strategic positioning: our size is not as important as our location, especially in the face of different powers across Latin America, the United States, Europe, and Africa. During the Cold War era, the Caribbean was in a very enviable geopolitical location: for the United States, because much of their oil requirements had to transit Caribbean waters, and for the Soviet Union, the Caribbean was an important passageway for U.S. military supplies to Western Europe.[3] It is time that the Caribbean creates its own geopolitical agenda. Caribbean academic William Demas once advocated the "widening and deepening" of the Caribbean integration movement, which some scholars have taken as the substantial argument for integration with the Latin American and Dutch countries of our hemisphere. To this effect, the regional organization of the CARICOM has fostered intimate Latin American Relations, through the creation of a variety of bilateral agreements, free trade areas, and regional arrangements with many hemispheric states.

Contemporary Caribbean International Relations have been characterized by an increasing complexity. In an effort to assess this complexity, Csurgai's geopolitical analysis is a useful tool on the basis of its strategic, geographic, historic, cultural, and socio-economic lens to ascertain the potential impact of any crisis. The methodology of this Caribbean geopolitical analysis follows the classical geopolitical scientist approach advanced by Criekemans[4] which recommends developing overview tables in which individual countries or spaces are compared using five out of eight indicators.

Geopolitical Analysis (GPA)

According to Csurgai,[5] geopolitics is simply the points of intersection between political and geographic spaces. The first and most popular indicator deals with the geographic characteristics and takes into consideration the state's physical characteristics. The second indicator relates to natural resources, and entails an analysis of stocks of water, oil, natural gas, uranium, gold, and different metals as well as of arable land. This indicator is very important in light of water scarcity and land/lease–grabbing within the Caribbean. The third indicator is an analysis of the external and internal boundaries of the space, noting especially the growing importance of maritime boundaries due to the increasing recognition of the potential of the Caribbean country's blue economy. Fourth on the list are geopolitical representations relating to the cognitive dimension of the space, that is, the perception of the country, region, or space by citizens and others, as well as the identification of symbolic places.

The fifth indicator follows on as it relates to the geography of populations dealing with identity factors: ethnic composition, demography, and geographic distribution of populations. The sixth factor examines the historical factors of the space while the seventh factor covers the economic factors and how these influence the internal and external geopolitics of a space—these range from the related Gross Domestic Product (GDP), Gross National Product (GNP), and employment indicators, to self-sufficiency in food production and human development index indicators. The eighth and final indicator relates to the strategy of actors specifically their available resources and outputs.

Today's world continues to observe many shifts in power relations between larger developed countries, thus, geopolitics is very relevant.[6] As regional analysts, our policy toolbox must evolve as countries are simultaneously affected by environmentalism, economic measures, and political events. The small vulnerable economies within the Caribbean region should apply a geopolitical lens to provide significant evidence with which to inform their decisions and policies. This lens allows the practitioner to look beyond the descriptive and chronological presentation of political events as presented by mainstream media to a more in-depth scrutiny. Gagne[7] highlights the indispensability of geopolitics for policy analysts and leaders.

FINDINGS OF A CARIBBEAN GEOPOLITICAL ANALYSIS

The areas of Caribbean states vary greatly. The single islands range in size from 102 km^2 in Montserrat to 10,991 km^2 in Jamaica. Of the dual islands/states, St. Kitts and Nevis measure 261 km^2 and Haiti measures 27,750 km^2. In Central America, Belize is 22,966 km^2 and Guyana comprises 214,969 km^2 of South America. The predominant natural disasters affecting the Caribbean are hurricanes, followed by earthquakes.

CARIBBEAN NATURAL RESOURCES

The Caribbean is generally a water-scarce region apart from members on the South American continent. Although most countries started with mono-crop economies, the stock of arable land as a percentage of agricultural land within the Caribbean ranges from 0.8 percent in the Bahamas to 38.5 percent in Haiti.[8] Concerning different metal stock, Guyana in South America has gold and bauxite, Jamaica in the Northern Caribbean has bauxite, gypsum, and limestone while Trinidad in the Southern Caribbean has deposits of iron, steel, natural gas, and asphalt[9]. Incidentally, Barbados, Belize, Guyana, Suriname, and Trinidad and Tobago have found oil in offshore explorations.

CARIBBEAN BOUNDARIES

Much of the Caribbean—seven islands—is comprised predominantly of islands with one or more neighboring islands such as the Bahamas, Antigua, and Barbuda, and Grenada to mention a few. There are also five singular islands including Barbados, Jamaica, and St. Lucia. In addition, there is

Belize on the Central American continent bordering Guatemala and Mexico. In South America, there is Guyana between Brazil, Suriname, and Venezuela, and Suriname is bordered by Guyana and French Guiana.

Generally, the Caribbean states adhere to the 12 nautical miles of territorial sea, 200 nautical miles of Exclusive Economic Zone (EEZ) and a 24 nautical mile contiguous zone. However, there are several ongoing border conflicts between Caribbean states, such as that between Barbados and Trinidad and Tobago regarding their shared maritime boundary. There are also conflicts between Caribbean states and Third States over territorial ownership: between Guatemala and Belize; Guyana and Suriname; Guyana and Venezuela; Haiti and the United States; Dominica, St. Kitts and Nevis, and St. Lucia with Venezuela.

CARIBBEAN GEOGRAPHY OF POPULATIONS

Within the Caribbean, the population is heavily concentrated in clusters surrounding the capitals and coastal cities. In countries with multiple islands, the population is more densely located in one island as is the case with Antigua and New Providence Island. The ethnic composition of the Caribbean is comprised of predominantly African descendants in eleven out of the fifteen member states, predominantly East Indian descendants in three out of the fifteen member states, and in Belize, the population is a mixed composition of Mestizo, Creole, Mayan, and Garifuna descendants.

CARIBBEAN GEOPOLITICAL REPRESENTATIONS

Geopolitically, the entire Caribbean is considered to be a component of the Global South, the Periphery and the Developing world. However, the continental member states are often classified by the fact that they are the only English speakers in Central America and South America. This indicator also refers to symbolic places linked to collective identities in the member state. In the majority of Caribbean countries, symbolic places are located in or around the country's capital. In several instances, symbolic places are environmental landmarks such as Harrison's Cave in Barbados, the Barrier Reef in Belize, Kaieteur Falls in Guyana, the Blue Mountains in Jamaica, the Pitons in St. Lucia, the Petroglyphs in St. Vincent and the Grenadines, and the Savannah in Trinidad and Tobago. In some instances, national landmarks range from the Atlantis Paradise Hotel in the Bahamas, Fort George in Grenada, St. George's Cathedral in Guyana, the National Presidential Palace in Haiti, Brimstone Hill Fortress in St. Kitts and Nevis, and the Red House in Trinidad and Tobago.

OVERVIEW OF CARIBBEAN INTEGRATION

The Caribbean has continuously developed regional integration schemes to achieve greater independence and development of its states, together, these have resulted in several multipronged approaches to integration. Early approaches in the nineteenth century saw separate federations among the Windward Islands and the Leeward Islands, created to assist Britain in the administrative management of its colonies. Toward the mid-twentieth century, the most notable experiment at regionalism was the British West Indies Federation (BWIF) of ten colonies. However, the BWIF was short-lived due to a plethora of problems affecting its general purpose: these ranged from territorial disagreements, to limited political will, and asymmetrical territorial development. Following the demise of the BWIF, the smaller territories constructed the West Indies Associated States (WIAS) in 1966 in an effort to become more viable. Upon gaining independence, these smaller countries decided to re-join the larger territories of the region to form a Caribbean Free Trade Area (CARIFTA) to combat the challenges posed by their small size, undiversified economies, and limited financial and human resources.

CARIFTA came into effect on May 1, 1968, to assist countries in their efforts to expand and diversify trade, to ensure fair competitive practices, and to advance the harmonious development of Caribbean trade and its liberalization attempts. However, during CARIFTA's existence, trade was skewed in favor of the larger territories within the region—namely Trinidad and Tobago and Jamaica, with their stronger manufacturing and industrial centers—creating additional problems for smaller territories. In the early 1970s, with Britain's accession to the European Community, Caribbean territories decided to transform their regional integration efforts into a Caribbean Community and Common Market (CARICOM). CARICOM was considered to be the next stage of integration, as CARIFTA was only a free trade area and was severely limited since it did not address any movement of factors of production or the regional coordination of policies. The switch to CARICOM was expected to generate greater benefits to its members' national economic development.

Twenty-seven years after the start the of the Regional Independence movement, CARICOM Heads of Government at the 10th Meeting of the Conference at Grand Anse, Grenada in 1989, agreed to deepen the integration process by conceptualizing a regional single market and economy. Thus, former Prime Minister of Barbados aptly described the CSME as the "unique and strategic tool for CARICOM whilst we attempt to reposition our economies to compete effectively in a globalising world."[10] Hence, it was envisaged that the CSME would assist CARICOM in achieving its goals ranging from improving national standards of living, increasing levels of employment, increasing regional trade, and achieving comprehensive development.

In essence, the CSME can be simply deconstructed into the CARICOM Single Market and Economy. The former's main feature is the enabling of the free movement of labor, services and capital throughout CARICOM member states in order to create a single, large, economic space. Whereas, the Single Economy will comprise of integrated capital markets, harmonized fiscal incentives, fiscal policy harmonization as well as coordinated interest and foreign exchange rates policies throughout CARICOM.

To regional economists, the movement of labor is a critical tool to increase regional efficiency and actualize economic integration according to Worrell.[11] Since within a single market, the factors of production are allowed to transfer and inhabit spaces where there is scarcity.[12] This may be achieved by the creation of a larger skills pool suitable to the firms' demands and available technology and lowered currency risks.

One of the key pillars of CARICOM is economic integration. However, the recent IMF report emphasizes the point that Caribbean economic integration has taken place on a number of levels but significantly lags behind other "well-integrated regions." Todaro makes the point that conditions must be met for economic integration to be successful. These conditions include a grouping of countries within the same geographic region, of relatively equal size and at equal stages of development. The IMF 2020 Working Paper laments that the Caribbean needs to address resource and capacity constraints which could be ameliorated by leveraging existing regional institutions. However, general progress with institutional integration within CARICOM has been slow and the stages are incomplete. Based on the CARICOM Secretariat CSME Status Reports, only 56.5 percent of the actions required to establish the CSME had been completed as of 2017, suggesting some limited progress since the last assessment in the early 2000s.

GOVERNANCE OF THE CARICOM ARRANGEMENT

CARICOM is a unique arrangement. Payne, writing in the second decade of its existence, stated that CARICOM's survival was secured on the basis that it would steer clear of Caribbean political integration and all its facets, namely supranationalism, which threatens national independence and sovereignty.[13] With respect to its governance mechanisms, Payne describes the CARICOM system as being managed by a chain of organs comprised of member states' politicians and as merely "serviced by its secretariat." Paradoxically, decision-making within the Community has to be by unanimous agreement but, the implementation of all decisions is up to the individual member state and "its own constitutional procedures."[14]

According to Anderson et al., as the result of its "implementation of decisions," by the late 1980s CARICOM had failed to meet its objectives.'[15] This conclusion was supported by Demas who argued that CARICOM was not meeting its potential.[16] Demas' position was based on the Treaty's disregard of supranationality with respect to decision-making, stating instead, that regionally agreed decisions were to be implemented independently in each member state.

CARICOM has struggled over the years to remain relevant. Sadly, it has been demoted to become an outdated piece of Caribbean economic and political equipment that has not garnered significant intra-regional support. Perhaps CARICOM's demotion is due to a longstanding history of ill-defined regionalization grounded in competing tensions between national interests and regional intentions. Over the years and over the course of the different regional configurations, the Caribbean has tried every conceivable strategy to boost its economies. This author proposes strategically enlarging the community with countries that could help the Caribbean overcome its inherent challenges and increase its trade and by extension its economic and social development.

CARICOM ENLARGEMENT?

According to the prime minster of St. Vincent and the Grenadines, Dr. Ralph Gonsalves, in Hall and Benn,[17] the small states of the Caribbean operate within "a condition of learned helplessness." Size and geographical features isolate them from markets, heighten their susceptibility to natural disasters and general ecological vulnerability, and affect their democracies. However, despite our small size and our economic limitations, Fauriol and Hughes[18] argue that the Caribbean has the potential to be more active and vocal within the multilateral fora while addressing regional and global problems.

One way in which the Caribbean can decrease its marginalization is through "economic coalition-building," according to Erisman in Hillman and D'Agostino.[19] Or—as Caribbean academic, William Demas, once advocated for—the "widening and deepening" of the Caribbean integration movement, which some scholars have taken as the substantial argument for integration with the linguistically Spanish, French, or Dutch countries of our hemisphere.

In 1990, seventeen years after the formation of CARICOM, the chief decision-making body recalled the Founders' vision of expanding the regional movement to include all Caribbean people. According to the CARICOM Secretariat[20] the regional leadership agreed to the dynamic widening of the Community. Hence applications for associate and full membership as well as for observation were considered. When the dust settled, CARICOM's Associate States included the British Virgin Islands and Turks and Caicos Islands: the new Observers on the Conference of Ministers of Health, Committees on Agriculture, Education, Science and Technology were Mexico, Venezuela, and Puerto Rico. Concerning new full membership, the CHOG requested that the Dominican Republic's application be considered within the West Indian Commission.

In 2012, the CHOG initiated the process for the Dutch territories of Curacao's and Aruba's applications for Associate Membership of the Community. CARICOM chief administrative officer, the secretary general, was instructed to engage the Dutch territories and initiate negotiations for associate membership while ascertaining the intentions of all parties and how these could benefit the wider Community. Furthermore, the region would consider the applications of the French Overseas territories in the Caribbean.

Six years later, in 2018, the principle of "acquis communtaire" was adopted by the CHOG as a requirement for membership into CARICOM. According to the CARICOM 2018 Press Release, this principle outlines the mandatory membership terms and conditions for new member states. This was necessary as the region was considering several applications for Associate Membership from French Guiana, Guadeloupe, Martinique, Curacao, and St. Maarten. The President of the Regional Council of Martinique in 2018 expressed the desire to assist in expanding the Community. To date, the CARICOM Secretariat has conducted fact-finding missions to the Dutch territories in an attempt to build relations with these countries.

This author argues that although "fact-finding missions" may yield considerable benefits for gauging the suitability of accepting the membership of the Dutch territories, the utility of conducting a geopolitical analysis must be emphasized. Geopolitics provides regional leadership with a holistic lens to carefully collect data and analyze the feasibility of pursuing strategic actions. At a time when the regional leadership is forced to strategically innovate while juggling the demands of precarious national economic variations, global crises, and climate change adaptation/mitigation efforts, a geopolitical analysis must be a prerequisite. A geopolitical analysis assists in establishing a baseline for CARICOM decision makers to determine the feasibility of expanding to include new member states.

As it relates to the Dominican Republic (DR), CARICOM already has strong affiliation with the DR due its membership in the Caribbean Forum (CARIFORUM) created to service dialogue with the European Union while in negotiating theaters. CARIFORUM originated during the ACP negotiations within the Lome Convention and then endured until the arrangement became formalized within the Economic Partnership Agreement with the EU.

Table 4.1 Dutch Caribbean Territories Applications to CARICOM

DUTCH CARIBBEAN TERRITORIES APPLICATION
• 2011—Prime Minister of St. Maarten engaged in **preliminary discussions** on formal membership.
• —*Aruba granted Observer Status to a number of CARICOM Institutions.*
• 2013—Prime minister of St. Maarten discussed with the heads **submitting a formal request to become an associate member.**
• 2014—Heads agreed to **further deliberate on the applications** for associate membership of French Guiana, Guadeloupe, Martinique, Curacao, and St. Maarten.
• 2018—Heads agreed to **proceed with the applications of the Dutch Caribbean** after **determining their expectations** of associate membership and what **benefits** this relationship could yield for the Community.

CARICOM ADMITTANCE OF THE DUTCH CARIBBEAN TERRITORIES

In light of the above, the GPA of the Caribbean illustrates that within our space there is the peaceful presence of asymmetries, contradictions, and heterogeneity. As much as there are microstates, there are states with large populations and land masses: as much as some states are insular islands, others are large continental swathes of land surrounded by states who lay claim to their territory. Thus, Caribbean integration as a process has always been complex and sometimes awkward. However, the present Caribbean family has remained committed to their goals, and this has resulted in success stories in the areas of security coordination and functional cooperation, albeit with deficiencies in the realms of economic integration and foreign policy coordination.

Aruba and Curacao are located in the Caribbean Sea, north of Venezuela while St. Maarten is located within the Leeward Islands. They are constituent countries of the Kingdom of Netherlands, thus, the Dutch Government is responsible for their defense and foreign affairs. Similarly, to most CARICOM States, these countries have small populations that are heavily dependent on imports and tourism receipts. Geographically, Aruba and Curacao are located outside of the Hurricane Belt but St. Maarten continues to battle with the vagaries of the climate following Hurricane Maria's passage in 2017.

Geopolitical analyses illustrate that the Dutch Caribbean territories are the "right fit" for CARICOM. However, CARICOM must cautiously proceed with these membership negotiations to determine the expectations and anticipated benefits of the joining countries. The Functional Cooperation and Security Coordination pillars are often seen as the successes of CARICOM but as the economic integration pillar is revitalized by regional leadership, CARICOM must ensure its agenda remains focused, relevant, effective, and complements the activities of all of its members.

CARICOM leadership must not allow newly admitted member states to carefully select aspects of the Caribbean Community to engage or participate in. They must remain firm, that admittance into CARICOM requires complete acceptance and participation in all CARICOM regimes and institutions.

CARICOM ADMITTANCE OF DOMINICAN REPUBLIC

Reflecting on the CARICOM Arrangement, CARICOM's core membership was originally Anglophone but previous expansion served to admit the Francophone state of Haiti, then the Dutch-speaking Suriname. Together these have offered significant trading bridges for CARICOM citizens, businesses and governments to take advantage. Continuing along this trajectory, the DR could continue to provide an opportunity to build a bridge within the Hispanic countries.

The CARICOM Regional Trade and External Economic Strategy developed in 1995 identified the DR as one of the hemispheric countries with which to engage in a free trade agreement. The CARICOM-DR FTA was signed in 1998 and provisionally applied since 2001.

It would be remiss of the author not to mention that the DR has previously requested to deepen its relations with CARICOM by joining as a full member in CARICOM in the early 1990s but there been no action by the regional arrangement following the original granting of DR as an Observer in 1982. Unfortunately, the regional response has been relatively limited and CARICOM has not been positive toward the DR application for a myriad of reasons. The DR has continued to build on expressing its interest in CARICOM and has engaged in the joint commissions and councils to increase trade.

Although bound to cooperate in the areas of trade negotiations, the DR has not been the friendliest CARICOM Observer state as the region could point to a number of community infractions committed by the DR, the most recent being the rendering of Haitian nationals and descendants in DR as stateless, all while Haiti is a full, active, and participating member state of CARICOM. Looking toward the future economic growth and development of the CARICOM region, the region must acknowledge a place for the larger, more competitive market of the DR to assist the regional private sector in building their capacity to trade, enter global value chains, and increase their competitiveness.

THE WAY FORWARD

Strategically, CARICOM must build its capacity to strengthen its regional policy efforts. This author opines that it is with the increase in membership, the expansion, and the augmenting of the CARICOM voice, will CARICOM be able to address several regional injustices within the hemisphere such as Venezuela's continued claimed to large swathes of CARICOM Member States space to even the United States' claim to the Navassa Island which is squarely located with the EEZ of Haiti. It is hoped with a hemispheric power-house like the DR, CARICOM foreign policy position could be ameliorated.

Proceeding in the future, the CARICOM region could benefit from the creation and application of an Admission Criteria or an Enlargement Policy, which clearly outlines the requirements for the incoming member and the expectations of the CARICOM community. Such a criteria or policy should be grounded in principles such as respect for CARICOM's Democratic values, enhancing fair and transformative trade, respect for CARICOM's Charter of Civil Society, and the adoption and implementation of the Revised Treaty of Chaguaramas.

Therefore, the region should carefully consider admittance to like-minded states interested in joining the entire CARICOM system in all four realms—economic integration, collective security, functional cooperation, and foreign policy coordination—which can strengthen the region's ability to correct its deficiencies.

NOTES

1. Norman Girvan (2002 June). *El Gran Caribe.* Web Published.

2. Franklin Knight and Colin Palmer (1989). "The Caribbean: A Regional Overview," in *The Modern Caribbean.* Chapel Hill: UNC Press.

3. Ronald Sanders (1997) "The Growing Vulnerability of Small States: The Caribbean Revisited," *Round Table*, Issue 343.

4. David Criekemans (2017) *Introduction to Geopolitics and Geopolitical Schools of Thought*, 2nd Latin American and Caribbean Institute for Geopolitics Winter Course.

5. Gyula Csurgai (2017) *Enduring and Variable Factors of Geopolitical Analysis,* 2nd Latin American and Caribbean Institute for Geopolitics Winter Course.

6. David Criekemans, (2009). *Geopolitical Schools of Thought: A Concise Overview from 1890 till 2015, and beyond* Antwerp: University of Antwerp & Flemish Centre for International Policy.

7. Jean-Francois Gagne (2007). *Geopolitics in a Post-War Context: From Geo-Strategic to Geo-Economic Considerations.* Montreal: Raoul Dandurand Chair of Strategic and Diplomatic Studies.

8. CIA Factbook (2020). "Bahamas" & "Haiti."

9. CIA Factbook (2020). "Bahamas" & "Haiti."

10. Owen Arthur (2004). "Lecture to the 15th Triennial Delegates of the Caribbean Congress of Labour."

11. Delisle Worrell (2001). "Economic Integration With Unequal Partners: The Caribbean and North America." In *The Caribbean Community: Beyond Survival*. Kingston: Ian Randle Publishers.

12. John Springford (2013). *The UK and The Single Market*. Centre for European Reform.

13. Anthony Payne (1994). "The Politics of Regional Cooperation in the Caribbean: The Case of CARICOM," in *The Political Economy of Regional Cooperation: Comparative Case Studies* (London: Pinter Publishers, 1994).

14. Ibid.

15. Alison, Anderson, Marie Freckleton, and Claremont Kirton (2002). "New Regionalism in CARICOM: Prospects and Challenges," in *Caribbean Economies and Global Restructuring*. Kingston: Ian Randle Publishers.

16. Peter Wickham et al. (2004). *Freedom of Movement: The Cornerstone of the Caribbean Single Market and Economy*. Bridgetown: CADRES.

17. Kenneth Hall and Denis Benn (2003). *Contending with Destiny: The Caribbean in the 21st Century*. Kingston: Ian Randle Publishers.

18. Georges, Fauriol and G. Philip Hughes (1995). *US–Caribbean Relations into the 21st Century*. Washington, DC: Center for Strategic and International Studies.

19. Richard, Hillman and Thomas D'Agostino (2003). *Understanding the Contemporary Caribbean*. Kingston: Ian Randle Publishers.

20. CARICOM Secretariat. 11th Heads of Government Conference in Kingston, Jamaica, August 2, 1990 http://www.caricom.org/jsp/communications/communiques /11hgc_1990_communique.jsp.

REFERENCES

Anderson, Alison, Marie Freckleton, and Claremont Kirton. 2002. "New Regionalism in CARICOM: Prospects and Challenges." In *Caribbean Economies and Global Restructuring*, edited by Marie-Claude Derne and Keith Nurse, 115–158. Kingston, Jamaica: Ian Randle Publishers.

Arthur, Owen. 2004. "Lecture to the 15th Triennial Delegates of the Caribbean Congress of Labour." Speech presented at the Caribbean Congress of Labour 15th Triennial Congress of Labour, Paramaribo, Suriname, October 19, 2004.

Caribbean Community Secretariat. 2018. *Inter-Sessional Meeting of the Conference of Heads of Government of the Caribbean Community*. Port-au-Prince: CARICOM Secretariat.

———. 2012. *Communique: 33rd Regular Meeting of the Conference of Heads of Government of the Caribbean Community*. Castries: CARICOM Secretariat.

———. 1990. *Communique: 11th Regular Meeting of the Conference of Heads of Government of the Caribbean Community*. Kingston: CARICOM Secretariat.

———. 2005. *CARICOM, Our Caribbean Community*. Kingston: Ian Randle Publishers.

CIA Factbook. 2019. "The Bahamas." Accessed October 1, 2019. https://www.cia .gov/library/publications/the-world-factbook/geos/bf.html.

————. 2019. "Haiti." Accessed October 1, 2019. https://www.cia.gov/library/publications/the-world-factbook/geos/ha.html.

————. 2019. "Jamaica." Accessed October 1, 2019. https://www.cia.gov/library/publications/the-world-factbook/geos/jm.html.

————. 2019. "Trinidad and Tobago." Accessed October 1, 2019. https://www.cia.gov/library/publications/the-world-factbook/geos/td.html.

Criekemans, David. 2009. *Geopolitical Schools of Thought: A Concise Overview from 1890 till 2015, and beyond.* Antwerp: University of Antwerp & Flemish Centre for International Policy.

————. 2017. *Introduction to Geopolitics and Geopolitical Schools of Thought,* 2nd Latin American and Caribbean Institute for Geopolitics Winter Course, 6–10 November 2017.

Csurgai, Gyula. 2017. *Enduring and Variable Factors of Geopolitical Analysis,* 2nd Latin American and Caribbean Institute for Geopolitics Winter course, 6–10 November 2017.

Fauriol, Georges and G. Philip Hughes. 1995. *US–Caribbean Relations into the 21st Century.* Washington, DC: Center for Strategic and International Studies.

Gagne, Jean-Francois. 2007. *Geopolitics in a Post-War Context: From Geo-Strategic to Geo-Economic Considerations.* Montreal: Raoul Dandurand Chair of Strategic and Diplomatic Studies.

Girvan, Norman. 1999. "Reinterpreting the Caribbean." In *New Caribbean Thought,* edited by Folke Lindhal and Brian Meeks, 3–22. Kingston: Mona Publishing.

————. 2002. "El Gran Caribe." Accessed October 1 2007. www.normangirvan.info/el-gran-caribe/.

Hall, Kenneth, and Denis Benn. 2003. *Contending with Destiny: The Caribbean in the 21st Century.* Kingston: Ian Randle Publishers.

Hillman, Richard, and Thomas D'Agostino. 2003. *Understanding the Contemporary Caribbean.* Kingston: Ian Randle Publishers.

Knight, Franklin, and Colin Palmer. 1989. "The Caribbean: A Regional Overview." In *The Modern Caribbean,* edited by Franklin Knight and Colin Palmer, 1–20. Chapel Hill: University of North Carolina Press.

Payne, Anthony.1994. "The Politics of Regional Cooperation in the Caribbean: The Case of CARICOM." In *The Political Economy of Regional Cooperation: Comparative Case Studies,* edited by W. Andrew Axline, 72–104. London: Pinter Publishers.

Payne, Anthony, and Paul Sutton. 2001. *Charting Caribbean Development.* London: MacMillan Education Ltd, 2001.

Sanders, Ronald. 1997. "The Growing Vulnerability of Small States: The Caribbean Revisited." *Round Table,* Issue 343.

Springford, John. 2013. *The UK and The Single Market.* Centre for European Reform.

Wickham, Peter et al. 2004. *Freedom of Movement: The Cornerstone of the CSME.* Report, Bridgetown: Caribbean Policy Development Centre.

Worrell, Delisle. 2001. "Economic Integration With Unequal Partners: The Caribbean and North America." In *The Caribbean Community: Beyond Survival,* edited by Kenneth Hall, 427–474. Kingston: Ian Randle Publishers.

Chapter 5

The Foreign Policy of the Cuban Revolution

Half a Century of Cuba–Caribbean Relations

Jacqueline Laguardia Martinez and
Milagros Martinez Reinosa

INTRODUCTION

In 2019, the Cuban Revolution celebrated its sixtieth anniversary. As part of the many and multiple reflections produced about the Revolution's achievements, let-downs, and historic significance, this chapter proposes an examination of sixty years of Cuba's foreign policy with emphasis on Cuba–Caribbean relations. First, we offer a characterization on the key foreign policy principles during the Revolution, since it serves as a basis from which to understand the Cuba–Caribbean relationship. This is followed by a brief historical review of the evolution of Cuba–Caribbean relations, highlighting key moments in the uneven progression of these relations. Finally, we evaluate the current situation of the links and the potential obstacles that might hinder its positive development.

For this purpose, we understand the Caribbean as the group of Caribbean countries recognized as part of the Small Island Developing States (SIDS) as defined by the United Nations. With the exception of the Dominican Republic and Cuba, the other countries are member states of the Caribbean Community (CARICOM). Caribbean SIDS share common development challenges that bring them together and influence their foreign relations strategy and multilateral activity, the election of international allies, and their commitments to regional integration mechanisms. Non-independent territories located in the Caribbean are not to be considered in this analysis since unlike the foreign policy agents, they do not have the capacity to determine rules of engagement with Cuba as sovereign states.

THE FOREIGN POLICY OF THE CUBAN REVOLUTION

The triumph of the Revolution in 1959 followed by Cuba's decision to declare itself a Socialist state in 1961 have led exogenous actors to believe that Cuba's foreign policy was absolutely determined by its alliance with the USSR and subsequent antagonism to the United States as a result of Cold War polarities. Of course, Cold War dynamics heavily influenced international relations for all developing countries, especially in Latin America and the Caribbean—the "backyard" of the United States—and mostly for Cuba. However, Cuba's foreign relations have been historically subordinated to the island asymmetric relation with the United States, located merely 90 miles away from the Cuban shores. Before the Revolution, Cuba's international relations were almost monopolized by the United States[1] and since 1959 Havana's foreign policy has been conditioned by its conflictive relationship with the United States.[2]

Despite declaring itself a Socialist state in the vicinity of the United States in the years of the Cold War, after the Revolution Cuba was able to practice a foreign policy with a noteworthy degree of autonomy, while maintaining a unique and complex arrangement with the USSR that lasted until the end of the Cold War.[3] Since 1959, Cuba's foreign policy has been based on the respect for national sovereignty and discouraged any form of intervention in the internal affairs of sovereign states—Third World, Global South, among other denominations. Latin American nationalism, together with internationalism, anti-Pan-Americanism, anti-imperialism, and anti-colonialism became key concepts of Cuba's foreign policy after the triumph of the Revolution. However, all of these concepts existed in the island's revolutionary ideology since the times of José Martí.[4]

According to Alzugaray (2015), the basic concept to understand Cuba's foreign policy is its anti-hegemonic character, linked (but not limited) to the purpose of maintaining national independence, sovereignty, and self-determination. "Anti-hegemony means not only emphasizing the independence of a state, in this case Cuba's, but also the decision to challenge the existing world order and propose alternative solutions to global problems such as underdevelopment, trade, finance, production, disarmament, and so forth."[5]

According to Article 16 of the Constitution of the Republic of Cuba, the principles that guide the country's international relations are anti-imperialism and internationalism. Cuba defends multilateralism and multipolarity (Article 16.o); and solidarity with peoples who fight for their national liberation and right to self-determination (Article 16.j). The island affirms its will to integrate and collaborate with Latin American and Caribbean countries (Article 16.d).[6] These principles have been consistent and have endowed Cuba's foreign policy with a globalist vocation based on three main axes:

belonging to the community of Socialist states until 1989, active participation in the Non-Aligned Movement (NAM)—whose presidency Cuba assumed twice (1979–1983 and 2006–2009), and a determined Latin American and Caribbean vocation.[7]

Cuba maintains a strong ideological affinity with developing nations which is reinforced by common indigenous and African ancestries, colonial legacies, and exploitation by outside powers.[8] This international position paved the way for Cuba to assume leadership positions among the developing world, and to accumulate political capital in Asia, Africa, Latin America, and the Caribbean. Havana's foreign policy has been able to show an unusually broad range of influence in relation to Cuba's landmass, population, and economic power.

It is important to note that, for Cuba, foreign policy constitutes a central element of the country's international relations. Within the rationale of Cuba's Socialist order, the state is the dominant actor in the formulation and implementation of the country's foreign policy, a policy that encompasses many dimensions such as trade, investment, and large cooperation initiatives on education and health. Foreign policy responds to a highly centralized political system that enables the government to act as a unified rational actor in its formulation and implementation without being forced to build domestic consensus.[9]

According to Luis Suárez, Cuba's foreign policy lies fundamentally in the activity of the Ministry of External Relations (MINREX) together with the Cuban Communist Party's International Relations and America's Departments with a lesser participation of other NGOs .[10]

The Cuban government has maintained the principles and key objectives of its foreign policy since 1959. Coherence and continuity have been possible since there have been no fundamental changes in the country's ideological principles, institutions and, until 2016, its key strategist: President Fidel Castro.[11] However, approaches on how to exercise foreign policy have changed. Cuba has been very successful in implementing a flexible foreign policy that wears different "hats" on the global scene: member of the Socialist bloc, a Non-Alignment country, and a developing nation inserted into the North–South dynamic.[12] Since 1992, with the celebration of the United Nations Conference on Environment and Development, also known as the Rio Summit or the Earth Summit, Cuba has added a new "hat" related to environmental action and climate change's adverse impacts.

Looking closely at Cuba's foreign policy and the island's motivations to cultivate international relations, it is possible to identify a balanced combination between idealism and realism driven from the urgency to survive as a sovereign, independent, and Socialist state. The basis of Havana's foreign policy has two pillars: the first is a realistic one based on promoting solid

economic partnerships through the diversification of foreign trade and investment on one hand, and aiming for a pacific coexistence with the United States
on the other; the second is an idealistic pillar based on solidarity with progressive governments and emancipatory movements in developing countries.
This idealistic dimension nurtures Cuba's reputation as a revolutionary force
in Latin America, the Caribbean, and the rest of the world.[13]

Pragmatism was fundamental for Cuba to prevail through the chaos that
followed the disbanding of the Eastern Bloc. After the disappearance of the
USSR and the Eastern Bloc, it was imperative for Cuba to stimulate international relations with countries that could play a positive role in the recovery
of its economy while accepting its political system and refraining from interference in domestic affairs. Since the last decade of the twentieth century, the
objectives of Cuba's foreign policy have been directed toward promoting the
incorporation of the island into the new multipolar world configuration by
building the necessary alliances both to face U.S. hostile actions, and achieving more effective participation in the global and regional economy.[14] Cuba
has been able to build profitable relationships with Western Europe—mostly
Spain—Canada, Japan, Latin America, and the Caribbean. The country began
to exploit its cumulated political capital to boost its depressed economy and
attract foreign investment and trade partners. The quest was to find a balanced
blend of national interests and moral values in the right proportions.[15]

This synthesis of pragmatism and ideology is not strange to Latin American
foreign policy. According to Gardini and Lambert (2011), these two elements
are integral components of political behavior in the continent and, like in the
case of Cuba, both concepts help to explain what might look as divergent
agendas and policies in Latin American international affairs since the end
of the twentieth century.[16] Cuba's foreign policy could be understood as
well under the rationale of "pragmatic idealism," an International Relations
theoretical approach that describes a foreign policy built upon a pragmatic
compromise between realism and idealism. The result is a foreign policy that
pursues national interests—usually regarded as "selfish'—while advocating
for the use of the state's influence to promote higher liberal ideals such as
peace and cooperation.

> Pragmatic idealism, according to the original formulation, constitutes both an
> empirical description of actual foreign policies of states as well as a normative
> stance in international relations theorizing. Pragmatic idealism rejects the two
> extremes of international relations theorizing, that is, realism and idealism (. . .)
> It tries, however, to retain what is valid in both. Thus, like realism, it accepts
> as self-evident the need of any state to safeguard security but emphasizes deter-
> rence as far more reasonable and rational. It also adopts the idea of increasing
> power but is careful to oppose it as an end in itself. Instead, it embraces it as

a means to raise the quality of life of society. Similarly, pragmatic idealism endorses the fundamental notions of political idealism, to include social justice, human rights, caring, sharing, and ecological sensitivity, but resists their utopian open-endedness.[17]

Pragmatic idealism has an explicit moral dimension due to the strong endorsement of international ethics and international law. It is character-ized by "an authentic commitment to international law, multilateralism, the principles and values of the United Nations Charter, moderation, solidarity with countries in need, and an emphasis on diplomatic solutions to interna-tional problems."[18] By examining the country's multilateral engagements and international relations, it can be concluded that beyond the narrow realpolitik conception of national interests, Havana's foreign policy also derives from "a rich nexus of friendly attitudes and bonds, resulting in support for legal norms, ethical values, and political choices that are essentially idealist."[19]

Even if this is an interesting theoretical proposal to frame the pecu-liarities of Cuba's foreign policy, it is debatable whether the pragmatic idealist hypothesis is an approach distinct from constructivism. According to Vamvakas, pragmatic idealism is similar to Alexander Wendt's constructivist argument that recognizes the existence of elements beyond geopolitical and national interests that guide foreign policy and international relations.[20]

Finally, when characterizing Cuba's foreign policy, it is important to consider the weight of Cuba's SIDS condition and its geopolitical location. Cuba's insular position, limited size, colonial past, and dependent economy have determined the country's international relations together with the men-ace from a variety of powers, particularly the United States, to control the island considering its geographical location. These "material" elements[21] have been key in the design and implementation of Cuba's foreign policy. Another important factor to consider is the multi-ethnic origin the Cuban society which has facilitated the establishment of close cooperative relations with African and Caribbean states.

Examining the changing dynamics of the world during the twenty-first cen-tury, it is evident that Cuba's foreign policy must creatively adapt to changes in the international order. However, the country's responses to fluctuating domestic events have become just as important. Nowadays, the central threat to the stability of the Cuban political system comes mostly from endogenous economic dares. Cuba is immersed in an ambitious transformation plan, known as the implementation of Guidelines on the Economic and Social Policy of the Party and the Revolution, approved by the Communist Party of Cuba (PCC) during its 6th Congress in 2011. At the 7th Congress of the PCC held in 2016, a revised version of the Guidelines was approved, and its imple-mentation is scheduled until 2021. The 8th Congress of the PCC, scheduled for April 16–19, 2021, will focus on examining the economic performance of the last five-year period. The Cuban economy—heavily impacted by new sanctions under the Trump Administration and the Venezuelan crisis—registered a very modest growth at a rate of one percent as an annual average of the GDP. For 2020, a contraction of around 11 percent is estimated due to the added impact of the COVID-19 pandemic.[22]

CUBA AND THE REST OF THE CARIBBEAN: A HISTORIC REVIEW OF A CEMENTED RELATIONSHIP

Since the triumph of the Revolution in 1959, Cuba's foreign relations with the rest of the Caribbean—especially with English-speaking Caribbean islands—have transited different stages. Following the periodization proposed by González Núñez, we recognize four initial stages until the Cold War.[23] From the 90s until 2019, we propose two new stages, for a total of six (table 5.1).

Restricted Cuba-Caribbean Relations (1959–1970)

During the first years of the Revolution, the Cuban government was absorbed in securing its survival in a context of growing animosity from the United States. Foreign policy focused on rebuilding the country's foreign relations since traditional partners distanced themselves from the government following the U.S. mandate to isolate the island. In 1964, after a call from the Organization of American States (OAS) for all member states to discontinue diplomatic or consular relations with Cuba, most Latin American countries ceased diplomatic relations with the island, including the Dominican Republic and Haiti. The only exceptions at the time were Mexico, Bolivia, and Uruguay.[24]

During the 60s, Cuban formal relations with Caribbean territories were limited since there were few independent countries in the region at the time. Exchanges existed though, at the consular level, as a consequence of the growing Caribbean migration to Cuba, especially from Haiti and Jamaica. Caribbean workmen came to labor on the sugar harvest, and many of them stayed in Cuba and formed families there.

Links also existed between political and intellectual classes. In April 1959, for example, on his way to Argentina, Prime Minister Fidel Castro made a technical stopover in Trinidad and Tobago where he was received by Premier Eric Williams.[25] In April 1960, Guyana's Premier Cheddi Jagan met with guerilla leader and then President of the National Bank of Cuba, Ernesto "Che" Guevara. They met several times during the following years and established a firm friendship.[26]

Table 5.1   Stages of Cuba–Caribbean Relations after the Cuban Revolution

Period	Stages
1959–1970	Restricted Cuba–Caribbean relations
1970–1979	Rise of Cuba–Caribbean relations
1979–1983	Decline of Cuba–Caribbean relations
1983–1990	Regression of Cuba–Caribbean relations
1990–2004	Reconstitution of Cuba–Caribbean relations
2004–2019	Regional projection of Cuba–Caribbean relations

Source: Authors' elaboration based on González Núñez (1991).[1]
[1]Gerardo González Núñez, (1991). *El Caribe en la política exterior de Cuba. Balance de 30 años: 1959–1989*. Santo Domingo: Ediciones CIPROS.

Rise of Cuba-Caribbean Relations (1970–1979)

During the 70s there was an upsurge in Cuba–Caribbean relations, contributed to by regional political leaders such as Michael Manley, Eric Williams, and Forbes Burnham who were Prime Ministers of Jamaica, Trinidad and Tobago, and Guyana respectively.

In 1972, at a meeting of the NAM held in Guyana, Caribbean delegates discussed establishing relations with Cuba.[27] Later that year, on December 8, Trinidad and Tobago, Jamaica, Barbados, and Guyana simultaneously announced the establishment of diplomatic relations with Cuba. The first three joined the OAS after the sanctions were imposed.[28] Guyana joined the OAS in 1991.

The decision was a demonstration of a novel Caribbean vision on the exertion of sovereignty and self-determination. These four Caribbean countries reaffirmed their independence and broke the hemispheric isolation that surrounded Cuba. Their decision paved the way for CARICOM foreign policy toward Cuba.[29] This concerted action from four Caribbean governments was a key factor for the approval, in 1975, of the OAS resolution that ended political and economic sanctions against Cuba from 1964. The resolution allowed each OAS member to determine for itself the nature of its bilateral relations with Cuba.[30]

In the second half of the decade there was an expansion of Cuba–Caribbean relations, especially economic and scientific-technical cooperation. Trade exchanges were energized and Cuban embassies were established in Jamaica and Guyana, as well as a trade office in Kingston. In 1974, Cuba established diplomatic relations with the Bahamas, and in 1979, expanded its diplomatic ties in the region by establishing diplomatic relations with St. Lucia and Suriname.

The visits to Cuba of Prime Ministers Forbes Burnham, Eric Williams and Michael Manley in 1975 were landmarks of the period. During their visits, Prime Minister Williams was awarded with an Honorary Doctorate from the University of Havana, and Prime Ministers Burnham and Manley were distinguished with the Order of José Martí, the highest state honor in Cuba. During Burnham's visit it was agreed that Guyana would provide Cuba with timber and rice in exchange for cement, and Guyana and Cuba signed an Air Agreement and a Scientific-Technical Agreement, as well as a Joint Communiqué saluting Suriname's upcoming independence and expressing solidarity to progressive forces around the world.

Prime Minister Williams's visit had a more scholarly and cultural orientation. He visited Casa de las Américas and the University of Havana. Prime Minister Williams met with Cuban writers and intellectuals and was presented with the first Spanish language copy of his book *Capitalism and Slavery*. As a result of the visit, the celebration of the First Meeting of the Caribbean Committee of the Economic Commission for Latin America and the Caribbean (ECLAC) in Havana was proposed. Cuba established its first agreement with an English-speaking Caribbean country in the area of higher education, since both governments decided to initiate cooperation between the University of Havana and the corresponding institutions of Trinidad and Tobago. Both delegations discussed Maritime Law and the need for a special policy for the Caribbean Sea.

A significant outcome of the meeting between Eric Williams and Fidel Castro was the creation, in October 1975, of the ECLAC Caribbean Development and Cooperation Committee (CDCC). The objectives of the CDCC included the promotion and strengthening of cooperation and economic and social integration among Caribbean countries and territories, fostering cooperation between them and other countries, and integration processes between Latin America and Caribbean states.

As a result of Manley's visit, a Joint Communiqué was released demanding the removal of the U.S. economic blockade against Cuba and the establishment of a New International Economic Order. A Cultural Agreement was signed and it included, for the first time, the granting of Cuban scholarships to the Caribbean. An Economic Partnership Agreement establishing the Cuba–Jamaica Joint Commission was also signed: this agreement included actions on fisheries, sugar derivative industries, agriculture, tourism, foreign trade, and aluminum production. The possibility of using the port of Kingston as a transhipment port for goods was discussed, as well as increasing cooperation in the construction sector.

In spite of the establishment of these relationships with Caribbean countries, Cuba did not take full advantage of the possibilities which arose from them. This was due to the fact that Havana's foreign policy toward the region suffered from a lack of knowledge of historic particularities, national idiosyncrasies, political systems, and social beliefs of the West Indies. The Caribbean was still understood as a sub-region of Latin America in Cuba's foreign policy strategy.

Decline of Cuba–Caribbean Relations (1979–1983)

During this period there was a gradual deterioration of Cuba–Caribbean relations. The main causes were the changes in the regional political climate, mostly associated with the electoral defeat of Michael Manley in the 1980 elections in Jamaica and the defeat of the revolution in Grenada. The 80s marked the rise of right-wing governments and economic neoliberalism, with President Ronald Reagan in the United States and Prime Minister Margaret Thatcher in Great Britain at the top. Both countries had—and still have— major influence in Caribbean economies, politics, and societies. However, from 1979, certain events in the Caribbean basin triggered U.S attention to the area. These included the aforementioned Grenadian Revolution, the Nicaraguan Revolution, and Cuban military support to African countries in their fight against colonialism and foreign intervention.

A defining characteristic of right-wing politics is its fierce anti-communism. Tensions in the Caribbean region were exacerbated as a result of the U.S. discourse against the "Cuban danger." The U.S. campaign against Cuba had the clear goal of representing the objectives of Cuban cooperation with the West Indies as the means of exporting communism under Moscow's orders.

This was a challenging period for the Cuban government. Several actions were taken to counteract the U.S.-led push against the island. One of them was to consolidate ties with Caribbean political forces and social organization sympathetic to the Cuban Revolution. Another was to reinforce diplomatic dialogue with the Caribbean and support regional positions in international affairs. One example of this was the Caribbean tour completed by the Cuban Vice-Minister of Foreign Relations, Ricardo Alarcón de Quesada, in November 1981. During the tour, Vice-Minister Alarcón reiterated Cuba's support for Guyana's position regarding the Venezuelan claim to Essequibo by stating that Guyana has the full right to enjoy its entire territory in full freedom. Earlier that year, during the 6th seminar of Latin American journalists, held in Cuba, Minister Alarcón echoed Cuba's position noting that the claim by Venezuela was hindering Guyana's development.[31]

Regression of Cuba–Caribbean Relations (1983–1990)

The invasion of Grenada lead by the United States is considered to be the turning point for a major change in the Cuba–Caribbean relationship. The internal divisions of the New Jewel Movement, which led to the assassination of Maurice Bishop, not only caused the freeze and eventual rupture of bilateral ties but also reinforced the regional turn in favor of conservative forces that mistrusted Socialist Cuba.

On October 13, 1983, a faction led by Deputy Prime Minister Bernard Coard ousted Prime Minister Bishop in an armed coup and placed him under house arrest. Six days later, People's Revolutionary Army (PRA) troops executed Bishop and his closest deputies. On October 24, Jamaica, Barbados, and four members states of the Organization of Eastern Caribbean States (OECS)—Antigua and Barbuda, Dominica, St. Lucia, and St. Vincent and the Grenadines—requested U.S. military action in Grenada. The invasion of Grenada, named Operation Urgent Fury, occurred between October 25 and November 1. According to Bell, estimates of the casualties were "19 Americans killed and 115 wounded; 24 Cubans killed and 57 wounded; 16 Grenad[i]an soldiers and 34 civilians killed and 357 civilians wounded."[32]

President Reagan authorized the invasion citing the threat posed to U.S. nationals in Grenada. However, it has been established that the invasion of Grenada was not a justifiable self-defense action because there was no credible imminent threat to the United States and neither a humanitarian intervention nor rescue was necessary since there was no credible immediate danger to U.S. citizens.[33]

Among the arguments presented by the U.S. government to justify its military intervention was that the planned airport at Point Salines, to be built with the support of Cuban engineers and construction workers, was intended to be a future Soviet–Cuban military base. The Reagan administration portrayed Grenada as a potential Soviet–Cuban military bastion for the export of communism throughout the West Indies. The airport was said to be a threat to the vital interests and the national security of the United States.[34]

The facts were that Cuban aid had increased when Bishop came into power, particularly due to the presence of doctors, nurses, teachers, military advisers, and construction workers. "There were many signs of progress and some improvement in the lives of the people, especially in the areas of health, welfare, education, and employment."[35] On the contrary, there was no evidence of plans to make Grenada a Soviet-—Cuban colony or to use it as a base for exporting Socialism into the Caribbean. The greatest irony was that Cuba was not exporting the revolution as a satellite of the USSR (Fabbri 1993).

> Quite to the contrary, even in the 1980s, most of the Cuban commitments were maintained as a continuation of political relations woven only on the margin, and at times against the grain, of Cuba's Soviet alliance. In general, these were responses to national struggles and political movements that were not endangered by the Cold War or the logic of the East-West conflict.[36]

On November 2, 1983, by a vote of 108 in favor/9 against (Antigua and Barbuda, Barbados, Dominica, El Salvador, Israel, Jamaica, Saint Lucia, Saint Vincent and the Grenadines, and the United States), and 27 abstentions, the United Nations General Assembly adopted a resolution which "deeply deplores the armed intervention in Grenada, which constitutes a flagrant violation of international law and of the independence, sovereignty and territorial integrity of that State."[37] The Reagan administration, on the other hand, claimed a great victory, calling it the first "rollback" of communist influence in the Cold War era.

The Grenada invasion marked the final act in the displacement of the United Kingdom by the United States as the West Indies global power of reference. It also indicated the beginning of the alienation of Cuba from the rest of the Caribbean. Even though Guyana and Trinidad and Tobago maintained bilateral relations with the Socialist island, they remained at a low level until the end of the Cold War.

It is important to note that, in 1983, the United States approved the Caribbean Basin Economic Recovery Act (CBERA), which began to be implemented in 1984. The goal of the program was to provide trade benefits to Central American and Caribbean countries as well as to expand investment in non-traditional sectors. Provisions in the CBERA prohibited extending economic preferences to countries considered to be contrary to U.S. interests.[38]

Reconstitution of Cuba–Caribbean Relations (1990–2004)

The 90s brought fundamental changes to the international scene. The disappearance of the USSR and the Eastern bloc favored a rapprochement between Cuba and the rest of the Caribbean. The post–Cold War era highlighted both the common development challenges faced by Caribbean islands, and the necessity of joining efforts to navigate in a less predictable world. The recognition of similar vulnerabilities anchored in a common colonial past, cultural identity, and insular condition, paved the road to the resumption of relations and boosted economic and cooperation links.

The new context compelled MINREX to establish the basis for the articulation of a coherent strategy toward the Caribbean region. Cuba's government recognized the key role of the Caribbean in Havana's foreign policy goals and understood the importance of close alliance with its neighbors in a multipolar world.

Cuba resumed and established diplomatic relations with all Caribbean countries during the 90s. In 1994, for example, Cuba and Grenada re-established diplomatic relations. In 2017, Grenada unveiled a monument commemorating the Cuban workers who died during the 1983 military invasion.

There was also a joint regional effort to launch Cuba–CARICOM relations. At the 11th CARICOM Summit in 1990, exploring economic cooperation with Cuba was discussed. The CARICOM–Cuba Joint Commission was established in 1993 to "promote co-operative relations between the Caribbean Community and Cuba in economic, social, cultural and technological fields."[39] The establishment of the Joint Commission could be understood as the first step toward Cuban membership of CARICOM.[40]

The CARICOM vote at the United Nations General Assembly on Cuba's annual resolution advocating for the end of the U.S. embargo is also an illustrative example of Cuba–Caribbean rapprochement. In 1992, the first time the resolution was presented, three Caribbean countries voted in favor of Cuba, eight abstained, and four were absent. In favor: Barbados, Haiti, Jamaica. Abstaining: Antigua and Barbuda, Bahamas, Belize, Guyana, St. Lucia, St. Vincent, and the Grenadines, Suriname, Trinidad and Tobago.[41] One year later, CARICOM's voting at the UNGA had changed in Cuba's favor, with ten CARICOM members voting against Washington's position.[42]

The momentum in the relations between Cuba and the Caribbean continued in the twenty-first century. In 2000, during the meeting of the CARICOM–Cuba Joint Commission, the CARICOM–Cuba Trade and Economic Cooperation Agreement (TECA) was signed. The Agreement covers trade, tourism, transportation, business facilitation, and capacity-building among other areas. The goal is to strengthen economic and trade relations.[43] Two Protocols to the TECA were signed later; one to implement the Agreement and a second one containing additional provisions.

The TECA creates a framework for the progressive liberalization of trade while seeking "to lay the foundation for increased economic integration through new levels of partnership and the gradual reduction of tariffs and other obstacles to trade."[44] The TECA makes provisions for duty-free treatment for a group of goods such as clothing, condiments, fruit juices, and agricultural products among others. During the 10th Meeting of the CARICOM–Cuba Joint Commission in 2017, the parties agreed on the expansion of the preferential access provisions by signing a third Protocol.[45] The Protocol was signed on November 2017 in the 45th Meeting of the Council for Trade and Economic Development (COTED) celebrated in Georgetown.[46]

In 2002, the First Cuba–CARICOM Summit was celebrated in Havana. All CARICOM Head of Governments and Head of States attended the meeting. These summits constitute the most important meetings between Cuba and the regional bloc, and are scheduled every three years. The next summit is to be celebrated in Cuba in 2022.[47] At the first Summit it was agreed to commemorate Cuba–CARICOM day on December 8 to remember the date in 1972 when four Caribbean nations simultaneously established diplomatic relations with Cuba.

The dynamism gained in the Cuba–Caribbean relationship in these years can be appreciated when examining high-level visits from Caribbean statespersons to Cuba. Until 2003, all Caribbean Prime Ministers and Presidents, as well as Ministers of Foreign Affairs visited Cuba. However, between 2004 and 2005 the intensity of such visits rose: on average, every two months, a Caribbean Head of Government or Head of State arrived in the country.

The creation of the Association of Caribbean States (ACS) in 1994 also functioned to enhance Cuba–Caribbean cooperation. The ACS has as its key goal to be an organization for consultation, cooperation, and joint action for its member states. It provides a forum for dialogue in order to identify areas of common interest to be addressed at the regional level.[48] The ACS became an optimal space for Cuba to promote its internationalist vocation toward the Caribbean since the regional association does not focus on free trade promotion and, as a bonus, does not include the United States as a member.

The ACS has been an appropriate setting for Cuba to develop triangular cooperation projects involving other Caribbean countries, as well as promoting South–South cooperation. For instance, Cuba participates in the Maps of Maritime Routes of the Greater Caribbean project that is funded by South Korea, Turkey, Cuba, Panama, and the Central American Commission of Maritime Transport. The project goal is to "create an updated map of maritime routes in the Greater Caribbean, to allow exporters, importers, vendors or buyers, both internationally and regionally to know when, how, through which operators and under what conditions they may transport their goods."[49]

In March 2017, the ACS hosted its Inaugural Cooperation Conference in Havana. The meeting provided information on the status of diverse cooperation initiatives and had the additional purpose of mobilizing resources for ongoing and future projects. The Conference attracted over a hundred participants among state delegations and international agencies to discuss collaboration opportunities in regional cooperation, and focused on the areas of climate change and transport.[50]

Regional projection of Cuba–Caribbean Relations (2004–2019)

Since the end of the twentieth century, Cuba has pursued both bilateral and regional aspects of its relations with the Caribbean. Bilateral relations continue to function as an optimal framework for cooperation actions. At the same time, the regional dimension was reinforced with Cuba's institutional engagements with CARICOM. However, the beginning of the new century served as scenario for more ambitious projects and for advancing regional consensus not only in the Caribbean but also in the wider Latin American space.

Relations with Latin America and the Caribbean became even more important for the Cuban government. This is largely because of the rise of the "pink tide" and the emergence of progressive governments in Venezuela, Bolivia, Ecuador, Nicaragua, Brazil, Argentina, and Uruguay. A second factor was the growing autonomy of the governments of the region from the United States. There was a boom of regional integration projects that appeared as alternative to the traditional Pan-American order managed by Washington, with initiatives such as UNASUR, ALBA-TCP, and CELAC.

The Bolivarian Alliance for the Peoples of Our America (ALBA) was launched in December 2004 by Presidents Hugo Chávez and Fidel Castro. The agreement was designed to be a regional platform to promote development for Latin America and the Caribbean. Unlike most of the regional integration schemes in the hemisphere, the ALBA-TCP initiative proposed a new type of regionalism less centered on trade facilitation and economic integration and more focused on building an alliance in defense of independence, self-determination, and the identity of Latin American and Caribbean peoples.[51]

ALBA was born as a reaction to the failed Free Trade Area of the Americas (FTAA). It proposed a commercial alternative to the FTAA, but also incorporated concepts of social, political, economic, environmental, and cultural orientation. The ALBA-TCP put emphasis on the political and social dimensions of regional integration, particularly on fighting poverty and promoting health, education, and cultural cooperation.[52] The initiative is based on the principles of solidarity, cooperation, and complementarity among its members. Its inception distinguished a new moment in Latin American and Caribbean relations. With the exception of Bolivia, all ALBA-TCP countries have a coastline on the Caribbean Sea. From the current ALBA membership, seven members are Caribbean SIDS which represents more than 50 percent of the total.

In 2005, President Chávez launched an energy alliance

> to provide a preferential payment arrangement for petroleum and petroleum products to some Caribbean and Latin American countries (. . .) PetroCaribe also provides cooperation support for efficient use of energy, technological cooperation, training, the development of energy infrastructure, and the promotion and use of alternative energy sources, such as wind, and solar energy, among others.[53]

Cuba, together with other Caribbean SIDS—with the exception of Barbados and Trinidad and Tobago—joined the PetroCaribe Agreement. The main goal of PetroCaribe was to contribute to energy security, socioeconomic development, and regional integration through the sovereign use of energy resources.[54]

Clear signs of growing interaction between Caribbean and Latin American countries were evident not only through the ALBA-TCP and the PetroCaribe Agreement. The goal of advancing regional integration based on cooperation

Table 5.2 ALBA–TCP Member States (up to December 2020)[2]

ALBA–TCP Member States	Year of Ascension
Cuba	2004
Venezuela	2004
Bolivia	2006
Nicaragua	2007
Dominica	2008
Antigua and Barbuda	2009
St. Vincent and the Grenadines	2009
Surinam	2012
St. Lucia	2013
Grenada	2014
St. Kitts and Nevis	2014

Source: Author's own elaboration based on https://albainfo.org/.
[2] Honduras was a member for a short period between 2008 and 2009. Ecuador was member between 2009 and 2018. Bolivia suspended its membership between 2019 and 2020 as result of the coup d'état and during the interim presidency of Jeanine Áñez Chávez. Since 2017, St. Lucia has stopped its active participation in the ALBA-TCP mechanism as result of the island's adherence to the Lima Declaration that criticizes Venezuela's government and President Nicolás Maduro.

and complementarity was embraced by other regional mechanism with major political ambitions, such as the Community of Latin American and Caribbean States (CELAC).

The CELAC was founded on February 2010. The organization pursues the enhancement of regional cooperation and the consolidation of a Latin American and Caribbean identity based on shared values and the unity-within-diversity principle. Cooperation within CELAC was intended to develop economic complementarities and South–South cooperation. This regional cooperation should act as a mechanism for integration and reducing asymmetries between Latin America and the Caribbean.[55]

This alternative conceptualization of regional integration allowed a renewed approach to Cuba's relations with the Caribbean. The strengthening of Cuba–Caribbean relations at the regional level was reinforced with the creation of regional mechanisms encompassing Caribbean SIDS. In this fresh context, the drive for Cuba–Caribbean relations flourished within the wider framework of Latin American–Caribbean relations.

The Caribbean as a sub-region has increased its relevance within larger integration schemes comprising Latin America and Caribbean countries. Caribbean SIDS wield diplomatic leverage by carrying sixteen votes in multilateral fora—a number of votes disproportionate to its size.[56]

In this more regional-orientated model, Havana favored Cuba's role as a mediating power in the area. A clear example is Cuba's role in making Latin American governments more sensitive and aware of Caribbean

SIDS vulnerabilities and development challenges. During Cuba's CELAC Presidency in 2013, modifications to the working procedure of this regional forum were formalized. The Pro-Tempore Presidency changed to a Quartet instead of a Troika so that each semester one CARICOM member state could preside over the regional organization and directly represent Caribbean interests in the maximum direction organ of CELAC.[57]

On the other hand, regional support for Cuba's full integration into the hemispheric diplomatic dialogue was evident on several statements made prior to the 5th Summit of the Americas held in Port of Spain in April 2009— many of them touching on Cuba's absence from the meeting. In his speech, President Obama announced that the United States sought a new beginning with Cuba and that he was ready to have his administration engage the Cuban government on various issues.[58] In 2015, Panama extended an invitation to Cuba to attend the 7th Summit of the Americas. At the occasion, Presidents Raúl Castro and Barack Obama shook hands in a historic moment that commemorated the reestablishment of bilateral relations between Cuba and the United States a few months later in December 2014.

Even after the arrival of Donald Trump to the U.S. presidency in 2017 and the retrogression of Cuba–U.S. relations, Cuba and the Caribbean progressed in their goals to strengthen regional mechanisms and institutions. However, the worsening of the Venezuelan crisis and the turn into the right of some governments in the area have been the key factors that have negatively influenced the most recent regional initiatives and damaged regionalism in Latin America and the Caribbean, and by extension, the regional projection of the Cuba–Caribbean relations. Main impacts are reflected in a weakened CELAC and ALBA-TCP.

In 2019, the Venezuelan crisis aggravated as a result of a divided recognition of the legitimate president of the nation. Following the widely disputed presidential elections of 2018 that resulted in the victory of President Nicolás Maduro, the Venezuelan National Assembly declared Juan Guaidó as the legitimate president of the country. In the Caribbean, Bahamas, Dominican Republic, Haiti, Jamaica, and St. Lucia greeted the decision of the Venezuelan National Assembly, contrary to CARICOM's position. The presidents of these five nations were invited to meet President Trump on March 2019 in Mar-a-Lago.[59] The governments of Guyana, Haiti, and Saint Lucia are members of the Lima Group while Barbados, Grenada, and Jamaica attended its initial meeting. On the other hand, Cuba has declared its uncontested support to President Maduro and the Bolivarian Revolution.

Tensions between Venezuela and Guyana in the region are also associated to Venezuela's claim over the Essequibo region, a position that has been firmly rejected by CARICOM.

CUBA'S COOPERATION IN THE CARIBBEAN:
A MAJOR CORNERSTONE FOR HEMISPHERIC RELATIONS

Havana's relations with the rest of the Caribbean have touched many areas through the years, but the dimension that has the most impact is the cooperation agenda. Cuba's cooperation with developing countries is a trademark of its foreign policy. The island has acted as a donor to Caribbean countries in times of catastrophe and has established cooperation agreements in the areas of health, education, science and technology, and professional training, among others. Cuba has deployed scholarship programs for Caribbean youth to complete tertiary education in Cuba, most of them in the area of medical studies.[60]

Cuba's assistance in the regional medical sector is widely commended. By 2018, from a total of 1,773 Cuban collaborators in the region, 1,454 Cuban health professionals worked in cooperation programs in the Caribbean.[61] The sole CARICOM state that did not have a medical cooperation program with Cuba is Barbados until the arrival of Cuban medical personal to combat COVID-19.[62] As medical cooperation to face the pandemic, Cuba sent over 650 highly trained medical professionals to Caribbean territories to reinforce local resources.[63]

The Latin American School of Medicine (ELAM) is an important institution for training Caribbean youth as doctors. The school was inaugurated in 1999 as part of Cuba's humanitarian response to Hurricane Mitch and Hurricane George. The first students arrived in February 1999, and the school is considered the world's largest of its kind. Its goal is to educate socially committed doctors. Most of them come from low-income families; therefore, the six-year medical program is free for these students. The expectation is for these young doctors to return to their countries of origin and practice medicine in underserved communities.[64]

Caribbean nationals have pursued undergraduate and graduate studies in various fields besides medicine, such as veterinary science, engineering, computer sciences, journalism, cinema and arts, economy, and international relations, among others, and many have benefited from scholarships awarded by Cuba. In 2018, 6,623 Caribbean nationals had graduated from Cuban institutions while 1,094 Caribbean youth were studying in the island.[65]

Cuba is committed to rapid response when extreme climatological events hit Caribbean countries. Medical brigades have been sent after the occurrence of floods as in Haiti in 2004 and Guyana in 2005. In response to the damage caused by Hurricane Ivan and Hurricane Emily, Cuba sent electrical engineers and technicians to Grenada and food supplies to Jamaica. After Hurricane Maria, Cuba sent 300 tons of cargo to Dominica.[66]

When the 2010 earthquake hit Haiti, Cuba sent additional health personnel to reinforce the medical brigades already in the country. Since Cuban medical staff were already working in Haiti and had been in the country since 1998, they could be considered the first foreigners to respond to the earthquake. "After three weeks, the Cuban medical staff had assisted over 50,000 people, performed 3,000 surgeries, delivered 280 babies, vaccinated 20,000 people against tetanus, established nine rehabilitation wards, and begun providing mental health care."[67]

Hurricane seasons in the Caribbean have become more lethal. The region is highly affected by climate change, and has begun to join efforts to adapt and mitigate its effects. The circumstances of SIDS emphasize the environmental vulnerabilities of Caribbean countries and stress the urgency of coming together to combat climate change's negative consequences.

Most of the initiatives on environmental cooperation are oriented toward "designing, organizing and delivering training courses and joint programs for weather modelling and forecasts."[68] Cuban institutions have cooperated with CARICOM counterparts at the Caribbean Community Climate Change,[69] and Cuba has supported St. Kitts and Nevis and Haiti in the preparation of their First National Communication on Climate Change; St. Vincent and the Grenadines in the making of the country's greenhouse gases inventory; and Belize in evaluating coastal vulnerability.[70]

An interesting example of Caribbean initiatives in joining efforts for environmental protection is the agreement signed in 2007 for creating the first biological corridor in the Caribbean. The agreement, signed by Cuba, the Dominican Republic and Haiti, aims to reduce the loss of biological diversity in the region.[71] The initiative is an example of triangular cooperation that has continued for over a decade. In July 2018, the meeting of the Ministerial Committee on the Caribbean Biological Corridor inaugurated a new phase with the support of the United Nations Environment Program (UNEP) and the financial contribution of the European Union.[72]

In the cultural field, there is growing exchange. Besides participating in art festivals and book fairs, Cuba promotes two regional events to bring together Caribbean artists and societies: The Festival of Fire and the Caribbean Traveling Exhibition.[73] In 2005, CARICOM and Cuba signed a Cultural Cooperation Agreement.[74] In 2018, the Ministry of Culture of Cuba and the Organization of Eastern Caribbean States (OECS) signed a Memorandum of Understanding to cooperate in creative industries, mainly the craft arts.[75]

One key element for the success of Cuba's cooperation with the rest of the Caribbean is Cuba's foreign policy conviction of respecting self-determination and embracing the diversity of political systems as a pillar of peaceful coexistence.

In a region such as the Caribbean, with political regimes, leaders, and situations of sovereignty as diverse as Antigua and Barbuda and Panama, Belize and the Dominican Republic, Puerto Rico and Cuba, Trinidad and Tobago and Martinique, pluralism would appear to be a sine qua non for any type of international cooperation arrangement.[76]

CLOUDS ON THE HORIZON

In spite of the positive balance of Cuba–Caribbean relationships almost half a century after the establishment of diplomatic relations between Cuba and four Caribbean countries, there are some factors that challenge the expansion of these relations. They are the deficient regional transportation infrastructure, linguistic barriers, insufficient knowledge regarding the economic logistics on both sides, foreign exchange constraints, and the U.S. economic sanctions against Cuba, among others.[77]

To these obstacles that Cuba and its Caribbean counterparts have been tackling in order to advance their relationships, since the end of the last decade we can add two hemispheric developments that tested the fluid dialogue between Cuba and the Caribbean: The Trump Administration and the Venezuela crisis.

The current regional context is less favorable to Cuba as it was at the beginning of the twenty-first century. The Trump administration openly declared a return to the Monroe Doctrine as a valid approach to orientating U.S. foreign policy,[78] and left little room to expect a constructive hemispheric environment for countries which follow an alternative path to the neoliberal capitalism that governs the White House. As part of the U.S. policy of confrontation with Socialist and progressive forces, the Trump Administration promoted a belligerent discourse against Cuba. The central argument is that the island is part of what former U.S. national security adviser John Bolton's identified as the "Troika of Tyranny in this Hemisphere."[79] The U.S. approach to battle the "axis of evil" was to undertake actions—regardless of whether they constitute open interventionism in other states' affairs—to increase economic and diplomatic sanctions while supporting opposition groups that advocate for a regime change.

In the case of Cuba, Donald Trump was determined to review Obama's policy toward the island arguing that President Obama did a "bad deal." Such a revision resulted in dismantling the improvements in advancing the normalization of bilateral relation between Cuba and the United States made under Obama's Administration. To undermine the bilateral environment even more, in September 2017 President Trump removed all non-essential staff from the U.S. embassy in Havana, accusing Cuba of "sonic attacks" affecting the health and well-being of the diplomatic personnel stationed there. Later in 2018, all U.S. consular services in Havana were suspended under the same allegation.[80] In January 2021, just days before leaving the White House, the Trump's administration announced that the United States has placed Cuba back on a list of state sponsors of terrorism as response to the island's support to Venezuela.[81]

Besides reversing U.S. policy toward Cuba to that of the pre-Obama era, the Trump Administration undertook unique decisions to mark a significant policy shift. In April 2019, the White House announced that the United States will no longer suspend Title III of the Helms–Burton Act. The Act from 1996 pursues the strengthening of the U.S. embargo against Cuba and, to do so, promotes the extraterritorial application of the U.S. embargo under its Title III. Since President Clinton, the Title III has been systematically suspended to avoid conflicts with European and Canadian investors in Cuba. With its application in effect, it is possible for U.S. courts to penalize foreign companies that are allegedly "trafficking" in the now nationalized property formerly owned by U.S. citizens and by Cubans who have become U.S. citizens.[82]

Due to the multiple and close links that Caribbean states maintain with the United States, the renewed tensions between Cuba and the United States influence the Cuba–Caribbean relationship. For instance, Caribbean investors could hesitate to invest in Cuba due to the potential sanctions they may suffer under the embargo regulations. Caribbean tourists may be discouraged to visit Cuba if they fear future problems in getting a U.S. visa. And the list goes on.

The other factor that might challenge the expansion of Cuba–Caribbean relations is the crisis in Venezuela. As we previously mentioned, the Cuban government has undoubtedly supported the Bolivarian Revolution and the Chávez legacy. Therefore, Havana has persistently declared its backing for President Nicolás Maduro, denouncing Washington's attempts to promote a coup d'état and a civil war in Venezuela, both of which would be the perfect excuse for a military intervention.

The Caribbean is politically divided regarding the situation in Venezuela. Breaking the inured CARICOM consensus when it comes to maintaining a common position regarding international and hemispheric affairs, five CARICOM countries: The Bahamas, Jamaica, St. Lucia, Guyana, and Haiti, supported the OAS resolution of January 10, 2019, that declared President Maduro's election illegitimate, three CARICOM states: St. Vincent and the Grenadines, Dominica, and Suriname voted against the resolution, while five others: St. Kitts and Nevis, Trinidad and Tobago, Antigua and Barbuda, Barbados and Belize abstained from voting. The vote clearly divided the OAS' CARICOM member states; a division continued in the following weeks after Juan Guaidó declared himself interim president of Venezuela.[83]

CARICOM holds a neutral position of non-intervention toward Venezuela. The group supports international mediation through a peaceful resolution. The position of rejecting external interference is supported by Mexico and Uruguay: these two countries, together with CARICOM and Bolivia have formed the Montevideo Mechanism that calls for dialogue and a peaceful way out of the political crisis in Venezuela. At the 30th Inter-Sessional Meeting of the Conference of CARICOM Head of Governments and Head of States on February 27, 2019, in Frigate Bay, St. Kitts and Nevis, regional leaders recognized that:

> The people of Venezuela must be allowed to decide their own future in accordance with the principles of the United Nations Charter—non-intervention, non-interference, prohibition of the threat or use of force, respect for the rule of law, human rights and democracy. As CARICOM has ceaselessly advocated, for this objective to be attained, there has to be a meaningful and internal dialogue between the contending parties.[84]

Along with these two critical issues that hinder the progress of Cuba–CARICOM relationships, domestic factors are also to be considered. An examination of the current Caribbean political map raises questions related to governmental shifts from center-left to centre-right and the resultant change in the regional political tone. The Caribbean relations with Cuba are founded more on similar historical experiences based on the collective identity of societies born from slavery and colonization than on shared ideologies, but potential disruptions associated with dissimilar responses to political events should be contemplated.

In the case of Cuba, it must be noted that key political, economic, and social transformations such as the ongoing implementation of the 2011 Guidelines are under way. The election by the members of the National Assembly of People's Power of Miguel Díaz-Canel Bermúdez as the new President of Cuba's Council of State and Council of Ministers in April 2019 is also a change.[85] In April 2018, after the enforcement of the new Constitution voted on in February of that year, Díaz-Canel became Cuba's president. The Constitution was approved by 78.3 percent of Cuban citizens eligible to vote.[86]

In spite of key transformations taking place in Cuba, the new government has acknowledged its historic engagement with the rest of the Caribbean. In July 2018, President Díaz-Canel attended the 39th regular meeting of the Conference of Heads of Government of CARICOM. It was the first time that a Cuban President attended such a meeting. During the visit, President Díaz-Canel confirmed Cuba's commitment to sustain and enlarge cooperation initiatives with CARICOM. The Cuban President was one of the special guests at the meeting, along with Chilean president Sebastián Piñera.[87]

FINAL REMARKS

Since the 1959 Cuban Revolution, the country has taken a progressive approach to the Caribbean region. Navigating backdrops and challenges, Cuba–Caribbean relationships have progressed and today encompass economic, political, security, cultural, and social interactions in the spirit of cooperating to achieve sustainable development. Cuba is a Caribbean SIDS that shares with its neighboring islands the challenge of existing in a multi-polar and uncertain world menaced by the adverse effects of climate change. The biggest island in the Caribbean Sea has managed to establish and consolidate regional relations in spite of circumstances that often opposed the advancement of the Cuba–Caribbean relationship.

Besides strengthening bilateral relations with Caribbean states, Cuba has also advanced its regional links through its relation with CARICOM and across its membership in the ACS, ALBA-TCP, and CELAC. The relevance of the region for Cuba's foreign policy is explicitly recognized in the 2011 Guidelines, which established that Cuba aims to:

> [k]eep an active participation in the economic integration process with Latin America and the Caribbean as a strategic objective, and maintain Cuba's involvement in the regional trade economic arrangements to which Cuba has adhered, including but not limited to the Latin American Integration Association (LAIA), the Caribbean Community (CARICOM), the Association of Caribbean States (ACS) and PETROCARIBE, and continue to strengthen the unity among the members of these arrangements[88]

Currently, all Caribbean states have diplomatic missions in Havana and vice versa. Since 1966, the Puerto Rican Mission "Juan Mari Brás" has been established in Havana as a representation of the Pro Independence Movement. Caribbean countries and CARICOM have supported Cuban positions in international fora, particularly in condemning the U.S. embargo against the island. Cuba, as a Caribbean country, is part of the collective legacy of colonization and shares a dual Latin American and Caribbean identity that has been key in its role as mediator in matters between Latin America and the Caribbean.

Nevertheless, while the Cuba–Caribbean relationship shows significant advances on the diplomatic, political, and cooperation spheres, a major deficiency remains in the economic area. Trade and investment have not taken off in spite of the TECA and other initiatives: the advancement of intraregional trade is a pending subject.

It is precisely the economic dimension, which is the weakest link in Cuba's international relations. Havana needs to translate its political credit into tangible economic benefits. The economic reform the country advocates urge to diversify trade, investments, and tourism partners. Emphasis should be placed on encouraging non-traditional forms of economic links as a way to overcome the U.S. economic sanctions that prevent Cuba from accessing international credit mechanisms or using the U.S. dollar.

Caribbean states' relations with the United States are noteworthy elements of their foreign policy and international relations, and this fact hinders Cuba–Caribbean relations. The U.S.–Caribbean relationship influences Cuba–Caribbean relations and they may become an obstacle for the fluidity and progression of Cuba–Caribbean relations. In 2016, the United States resumed its strategy of obstructing Cuba's economic integration into regional and global markets. The goal is, again, to "keep the Cuban state isolated in the world, and punish the nation for supporting the Communist Party in power."[89] It is still unclear what the Biden's administration toward Cuba and the rest of the Caribbean will be.

The U.S. policy toward Cuba violates UN principles and declarations against the use of humanitarian arguments as weapons to resolve political differences. "These U.S. policies are a classic reminder of how the behaviour of a declining hegemon generally reflects an urge to violate world norms, bully allies, and oppress the weak and vulnerable in the name of freedom."[90] In the context of reinforced U.S. sanctions against Cuba, the island confers more relevance to a foreign policy strategy with Latin America and the Caribbean, regions that have periodically denounced the aggressive U.S. policy toward Cuba and argued for the normalization of Cuba–U.S. relations.

The Venezuela crisis poses difficulties for Cuba's international relations. It has adversely impacted the sustainability of the ALBA-TCP and the PetroCaribe agreement as well as the cementation of CELAC. The last Summit of CELAC was held in Punta Cana, Santo Domingo, in January 2017, and El Salvador continued to act as Pro-Tempore President of CELAC. The handing over of the Presidency is expected to happen in the 6th CELAC Summit meeting that has yet to be held although it was scheduled for January 2018. On September 29, 2019, Mexico announced it will assume as Pro-Tempore president for the period 2020–2021.[91]

It is fair to recognize that, even in the face of domestic challenges associated with the implementation of the economic reform approved in 2011, the intensification of the U.S. embargo, and the COVID-19 pandemic, the island has continued its wide-ranging cooperation with the Caribbean. However, changes to the cooperation mechanisms have been applied to ensure its continuity and sustainability. Wherever possible, some compensation is now being considered in order to alleviate the costs incurred by Cuban institutions. The conversion to "triangular cooperation" schemes, where a third actor provides the financial and material resources to support collaborative actions is another strategy for adapting cooperation delivery to pressing economic conditions.[92]

Finally, we must stress that it is mandatory for Cuba to achieve a comprehensive and up-to-date knowledge of all Caribbean territories and, at the same time, to fully assume its identity as a Caribbean SIDS. More efforts are needed to elaborate on earlier diagnoses of the economic, political, and social realities of Caribbean countries, including the non-independent territories. Such analyses are central not only for a better understanding of regional dynamics and for identifying opportunities for bilateral collaboration but also to foster regional institutions and mechanisms intended to work under the premises of cooperation and solidarity. A solid and wide-ranging Cuba–Caribbean relationship will definitively contribute to the goal of making the Caribbean a region of social justice, inclusion, and sustainable development.

NOTES

1. Carlos Andres Fabbri (1993). "La política exterior de Cuba hacia América Latina. Reflexiones en torno a la 'exportación del comunismo.'" *América latina hoy: Revista de Ciencias Sociales* 6: 39–44.

2. Andrés Serbín (2012). "La política exterior de Cuba en un mundo multipolar." *Anuario CEIPAZ 2012-2013*, No. 5: 187–219.

3. "(. . .) the Soviets exercise great influence on Cuban foreign policy in general and Cuban policy in the Third World in particular (. . .). But Cuba does provide limited inputs into Soviet foreign policy, most especially regarding Third World issues." (Valenta 1990, 6).

4. Carlos Andres Fabbri (1993). "La política exterior de Cuba hacia América Latina. Reflexiones en torno a la 'exportación del comunismo.'" *América latina hoy: Revista de Ciencias Sociales* 6: 39–44.

5. Carlos Alzugaray (2015). "Cuba's External Projection. The Interplay between International Relations Theory and Foreign Policy Analysis." In *Routledge Handbook of Latin America in the World*, edited by Jorge I. Dominguez and Ana Covarrubias, 180–196. New York and London: Routledge.

6. Republic of Cuba, (2019). *Constitución de la República de Cuba*. La Habana, Last modified April 10, 2019. http://media.cubadebate.cu/wp-content/uploads/2019/01/Constitucion-Cuba-2019.pdf.

7. Isabel Jaramillo Edwards (1999). *El multilateralismo en la política exterior de Cuba*. Santiago de Chile: FLACSO-Chile.

8. Jiri Valenta, (1990). "Cuba in the Soviet Alliance System." In *Cuba: The International Dimension*, edited by Georges Alfred Fauriol and Eva Loser, 3–39. New Brunswick and London: Transaction Publishers.

9. Jorge Dominguez, (2001). "Cuban Foreign Policy and the International System." In *Latin America in the New International System*, edited by Joseph and Ralph H. Espach Tulchin, 240. Boulder andLondon: Lynne Rienner Pub.

10. Carlos Alzugaray (2015). "Cuba's External Projection. The Interplay between International Relations Theory and Foreign Policy Analysis." In *Routledge Handbook*

of Latin America in the World, edited by Jorge I. Dominguez and Ana Covarrubias, 180–196. Ney York and London: Routledge.

11. Carlos Andres Fabbri (1993). "La política exterior de Cuba hacia América Latina. Reflexiones en torno a la "exportación del comunismo." *América latina hoy: Revista de Ciencias Sociales* 6: 39–44.

12. Juan Benemelis (1990). "Cuba's African Relation." In *Cuba: The International Dimension*, edited by Georges Alfred Fauriol and Eva Loser, 121–152. New Brunswick and London: Transaction Publishers.

13. Robert K. Furtak (1985). "Cuba: un cuarto de siglo de política exterior revolucionaria." *Foro Internacional (El Colegio de México)* 25, No. 4 (April–June): 343–361.

14. Andrés Serbín (2012). "La política exterior de Cuba en un mundo multipolar." *Anuario CEIPAZ 2012-2013*, No. 5: 187–219.

15. Carlos Alzugaray Treto (2014). "La actualización de la política exterior cubana." *Política Exterior*, September-October 2014: 70–82.

16. Gian Luca Gardini and Peter Lambert (2011). "Ideology and Pragmatism in Latin American Foreign Policy." In *Latin American Foreign Policies Between Ideology and Pragmatism*, edited by Gian Luca Gardini and Peter Lambert. London: Palgrave Macmillan, 1–33.

17. Costas Melakopides (2012). "Pragmatic Idealism Revisited: Russia's Post-1991 Cyprus Policy and Implications for Washington." *Mediterranean Quarterly* (Duke University Press) 23, No. 4: 107–134.

18. Costas Melakopides (2012). "Pragmatic Idealism Revisited: Russia's Post-1991 Cyprus Policy and Implications for Washington." *Mediterranean Quarterly* (Duke University Press) 23, No. 4: 107–134.

19. Costas Melakopides (2012). "Pragmatic Idealism Revisited: Russia's Post-1991 Cyprus Policy and Implications for Washington." *Mediterranean Quarterly* (Duke University Press) 23, No. 4: 107–134.

20. Petros Vamvakas (2017). "Russia-Cyprus Relations: A Pragmatic Idealist Perspective by Costas Melakopides (review)." *Mediterranean Quarterly* 28, No. 2: 146–148.

21. Carlos Alzugaray (2015). "Cuba's External Projection: The Interplay between International Relations Theory and Foreign Policy Analysis." In *Routledge Handbook of Latin America in the World*, edited by Jorge I. Dominguez and Ana Covarrubias, 180–196. Ney York and London: Routledge.

22. Prensa Latina (2021). "Economic and social results to focus PCC meeting in Cuba." *Prensa Latina*. Last modified March 15, 2021. https://www.plenglish .com/index.php?o=rn&id=65378&SEO=economic-and-social-results-to-focus-pcc-meeting-in-cuba.

23. Gerardo González Núñez (1991). *El Caribe en la política exterior de Cuba. Balance de 30 años: 1959-1989*. Santo Domingo: Ediciones CIPROS.

24. *New York Times* (1964). "Chile Breaks Cuban Ties, Carrying Out O.A.S. Ban; President Alessandri Severs Diplomatic Relations in the Face of Threats by Leftists of Street Violence." *New York Times*, Last modified August 12, 1964.

25. Granma (2014). "Nuestras aspiraciones son las mismas en toda América Latina." *Granma*, March 11, 2014.

26. Cheddi Jagan (1997). *Interview by Cuban journalist Ernesto Nustez Jimenez to the late President Cheddi Jagan.* Last modified January 22, 1997.

27. Fidel Castro (2002). "Discurso pronunciado por el Comandante en Jefe Fidel Castro Ruz con motivo del aniversario 30 de las relaciones diplomáticas con Barbados, Guyana, Jamaica y Trinidad y Tobago, en el Palacio de las Convenciones, el 8 de diciembre del 2002." *Fidel, Soldado de las Ideas.* Last modified December 8, 2002. http://www.fidelcastro.cu/es/discursos/discurso-con-motivo-del-30-aniversario -de-las-relaciones-diplomaticas-con-barbados-guyana.

28. Trinidad and Tobago and Barbados joined the OAS in 1967, while Jamaica did it in 1969.

29. Andrés Serbín (1987). *Etnicidad, clase y nación en la cultura política del Caribe de habla inglesa.* Caracas: Academia Nacional de la Historia.

30. David Binder (1975). "Cuba Sanctions, imposed in 1964, lifted by O.A.S." *New York Times,* July 30, 1975.

31. Odeen Ishmael (2015). *The Trail of Diplomacy: The Guyana-Venezuela Border Issue* (Volume Two). Bloomington: Xlibris Corporation.

32. Wendell Bell (2008). "The American invasion of Grenada: A note on false prophecy." *Foresight* 10, No. 3, May: 27–42.

33. Wendell Bell (2008). "The American invasion of Grenada: A note on false prophecy." *Foresight* 10, No. 3, May: 27–42.

34. Wendell Bell (2008). "The American invasion of Grenada: A note on false prophecy." *Foresight* 10, No. 3, May: 27–42.

35. Wendell Bell (2008). "The American invasion of Grenada: A note on false prophecy." *Foresight* 10, No. 3, May: 27–42.

36. Rafael Hernández (1997). "Cuba and Security in the Caribbean." In *Cuba and the Caribbean: Regional Issues and Trends in the Post-Cold War Era*, edited by Andrés Serbín and Rafael Hernández Joseph S. Tulchin, 275. Lanham: Rowman & Littlefield Publishers.

37. United Nations General Assembly (UNGA) (1983). "UNGA Resolution A/ RES/38/7." New York, Last modified November 2, 1983.

38. Office of the United States Trade Representative, (n.d.). "Caribbean Basin Initiative (CBI)." *Office of the United States Trade Representative. Executive Office of the President.* Last modified May 1, 2019. https://ustr.gov/issue-areas/trade-development/preference-programs/caribbean-basin-initiative-cbi.

39. Caribbean Community (CARICOM) (1993). "Agreement establishing the CARICOM - Cuba Joint Commission. Georgetown." Last modified December 13, 1993.

40. Michael H. Erisman, (1994). "Evolving Cuban-CARICOM Relations: A Comparative Cost/Benefit Analysis." paper presented at the Annual Conference of the Caribbean Studies Association (CSA). Mérida.

41. United Nations General Assembly (UNGA) (1993). *Yearbook of the United Nations 1992.* New York, Dordrecht: Martinu Nijhoff Publishers.

42. Michael H. Erisman (1994). "Evolving Cuban-CARICOM Relations: A Comparative Cost/Benefit Analysis." Paper presented at the Annual Conference of the Caribbean Studies Association (CSA). Mérida.

43. CARICOM and the Republic of Cuba (2000). "Trade and Economic Co-operation Agreement between CARICOM and the Republic of Cuba." Last modified July 5, 2000.

44. Caribbean Export Development Agency (CEDA) (2016). "TRADEWINS. Critical Issues for Business." *The CARICOM/Cuba Trade and Economic Co-Operation Agreement Explained* 2: 11.

45. Jamaica Observer (2019). "CARICOM, Cuba sign new trade agreement." *Jamaica Observer*. Las modified February 8, 2017. http://www.jamaicaobserver.com /news/CARICOM--Cuba-sign-new-trade-agreement.

46. Caribbean Community (CARICOM) (2017). "More opportunities provided for private sector as CARICOM, Cuba expand duty-free market access." Last modified November 10, 2017. https://caricom.org/media-center/communications/press-releas es/more-opportunities-provided-for-private-sector-as-caricom-cuba-expand-duty-fr ee-market-access.

47. Second Cuba-CARICOM summit in Bridgetown, 2005; Third Cuba-CARICOM Summit in Santiago de Cuba, 2008; Fourth Cuba-CARICOM Summit in Port of Spain, 2011; Fifth Cuba-CARICOM Summit in Havana, 2014; Sixth Cuba-CARICOM Summit in Saint Mary's, 2017, Seven Cuba-CARICOM Summit (online due to the COVID-19), 2020.

48. Association of Caribbean States (1994). "Convention Establishing the Association of Caribbean States." Last accessed February 5, 2019. http://www.acs -aec.org/index.php?q=about/convention-establishing-the-association-of-caribbean- states.

49. Association of Caribbean States (n.d.). "Maps of Maritime Routes of the Greater Caribbean." Last accessed February 5, 2019. http://www.acs-aec.org/index.p hp?q=transport/projects/maps-of-maritime-routes-of-the-greater-caribbean.

50. Dianet Doimeadios Guerrero and Irene Pérez (2017). "Inicia Conferencia de Cooperación de la Asociación de Estados del Caribe." *Cubadebate*. Last modified March 8, 2017. http://www.cubadebate.cu/noticias/2017/03/08/inicia-conferencia-de -cooperacion-de-la-asociacion-de-estados-del-caribe/#.XMz2_-hKg2w.

51. Harvey F. Kline, Christine J. Wade and Howard J. Wiarda (2017). *Latin American Politics and Development*. New York: Routledge.

52. Maribel Aponte Garcia, (2014). *El nuevo regionalismo estratégico: los primeros diez años del ALBA-TCP*. Ciudad Autónoma de Buenos Aires: CLACSO.

53. Caribbean Community (CARICOM) (2013). "PetroCaribe." Last modified September 9, 2013. https://caricom.org/projects/detail/petrocaribe.

54. Maribel Aponte Garcia (2014). *El nuevo regionalismo estratégico: los primeros diez años del ALBA-TCP*. Ciudad Autónoma de Buenos Aires: CLACSO.

55. Annita Montoute, Andy Knight, Jacqueline Laguardia Martínez, Debbie Mohammed and Dave Seerattan (2017). *The Caribbean in the European Union- Community of Latin American and Caribbean States Partnership*. Hamburg: EU-LAC Foundation.

56. Annita Montoute, Andy Knight, Jacqueline Laguardia Martínez, Debbie Mohammed and Dave Seerattan (2017). *The Caribbean in the European Union- Community of Latin American and Caribbean States Partnership*. Hamburg: EU-LAC Foundation.

57. Antonio Romero (2015). "Cuba, su política exterior y la nueva arquitectura de gobernanza regional en América Latina y el Caribe." *Pensamiento Propio. La arquitectura de gobernanza regional en América Latina* (Coordinadora Regional de Investigaciones Económicas y Sociales) 42, Año 20 (July–Decembe): 107–134.

58. Sheryl Gay Stolberg, and Alexei Barrionuevo (2009). "Obama Says U.S. Will Pursue Thaw With Cuba." *New York Times*, Last modified April 17, 2009.

59. Laura Dowrich-Phillips (2019). "President Trump to meet with five Caribbean leaders." *Loop*, Last modified March 20, 2019. https://www.looptt.com/content/pres ident-trump-meet-five-caribbean-leaders.

60. Antonio Romero (2015). "Cuba, su política exterior y la nueva arqui-tectura de gobernanza regional en América Latina y el Caribe." *Pensamiento Propio. La arquitectura de gobernanza regional en América Latina* (Coordinadora Regional de Investigaciones Económicas y Sociales) 42, Año 20 (July-Decembe): 107–134.

61. Elson Concepción Pérez (2018). "El Caribe que nos une y fortalece." *Cubadebate*. Last modified December 06, 2018. http://www.cubadebate.cu/opinion /2018/12/06/el-caribe-que-nos-une-y-fortalece/#.XMdKN-hKg2x.

62. Cuba's Representative Office Abroad (2017). "How does Cuba cooperate with the Caribbean?" *Cuba's Representative Office Abroad*. Last modified March 11, 2017. http://misiones.minrex.gob.cu/en/articulo/how-does-cuba-cooperate-caribbean.

63. Jessica Byron, Jacqueline Laguardia Martinez, Annita Montoute and Keron Niles (2021). "Impacts of COVID-19 in the Commonwealth Caribbean: key lessons." *The Round Table* 110, No. 1: 99–119. DOI: 10.1080/00358533.2021.1875694.

64. Julie M. Feinsilver (2010). "Fifty Years of Cuba's Medical Diplomacy: From Idealism to Pragmatism." *Cuban Studies* 41: 85–104.

65. Elson Concepción Pérez (2018). "El Caribe que nos une y fortalece." *Cubadebate*. Last modified December 06, 2018. http://www.cubadebate.cu/opinion /2018/12/06/el-caribe-que-nos-une-y-fortalece/#.XMdKN-hKg2x.

66. Jacqueline Laguardia Martinez, Georgina Chami, Annita Montoute and Debbie Mohammed (2019). *Changing Cuba-US Relations. Implications for CARICOM States*. London: Palgrave Macmillan.

67. Jacqueline Laguardia Martinez, Georgina Chami, Annita Montoute and Debbie Mohammed (2019). *Changing Cuba-US Relations. Implications for CARICOM States*. London: Palgrave Macmillan.

68. Jacqueline Laguardia Martinez, Georgina Chami, Annita Montoute and Debbie Mohammed (2019). *Changing Cuba-US Relations. Implications for CARICOM States*. London: Palgrave Macmillan.

69. Caribbean Community Climate Change Centre (CCCCC) (2012). *Delivering Transformational Change 2011–21. Implementing the CARICOM "Regional Framework for Achieving Development Resilient to Climate Change*. Technical Report 5C/CCCCC-12-03-01, Belmopan: Caribbean Community Climate Change Centre.

70. Opciones (2015). "Cooperación Sur-Sur, una baza contra el cambio climático." *Opciones. Seminario Económico y Financiero de Cuba*. http://www.opciones.cu/cuba /2015-08-06/cooperacion-sur-sur-una-baza-contra-el-cambio-climatico/.

71. Juventud Rebelde (2007). "Firmarán convenio de cooperación ambiental Cuba, Haití y Dominicana." *Juventud Rebelde*. Last modified July 9, 2007. http://www.juve ntudrebelde.cu/cuba/2007-07-09/firmaran-convenio-de-cooperacion-ambiental-cuba -haiti-y-dominicana.

72. Corredor Biológico en el Caribe (2018). "Corredor Biológico en el Caribe." Last modified June, 2018. https://cbcbio.org/2018/07/30/20-de-julio-de-2018-santo -domingo-republica-dominicana/.

73. Cuba's Representative Office Abroad (2017). "How does Cuba cooperate with the Caribbean?" *Cuba's Representative Office Abroad*. Last modified March 11, 2017. http://misiones.minrex.gob.cu/en/articulo/how-does-cuba-cooperate-caribbean.

74. CARICOM and the Republic of Cuba (2005). "Cultural Cooperation Agreement between the Caribbean Community (CARICOM) and the Republic of Cuba. Caribbean Community." Last modified December 8, 2005. https://caricom .org/communications/view/cultural-cooperation-agreement-between-the-caribbean -community-caricom-and-the-republic-of-cuba.

75. Prensa Latina (2018). "Firman acuerdo Ministerio de Cultura de Cuba y organización caribeña." *Cubasí*. Last modified July 19, 2018. http://cubasi.cu/cubasi- noticias-cuba-mundo-ultima-hora/item/82642-firman-acuerdo-ministerio-de-cultura -de-cuba-y-organizacion-caribena (accessed 04 29, 2019).

76. Rafael Hernández (1997). "Cuba and Security in the Caribbean." In *Cuba and the Caribbean: Regional Issues and Trends in the Post-Cold War Era*, edited by Andrés Serbín and Rafael Hernández Joseph S. Tulchin, 275. Lanham: Rowman & Littlefield Publishers.

77. Jacqueline Laguardia Martinez, Georgina Chami, Annita Montoute and Debbie Mohammed (2019). *Changing Cuba-US Relations. Implications for CARICOM States*. London: Palgrave Macmillan.

78. Davis Richardson (2019). "John Bolton Reaffirms America's Commitment to the Monroe Doctrine with New Sanctions." *Observer*. Last modified April 17, 2019. https://observer.com/2019/04/john-bolton-monroe-doctrine-sanctions-venezuela-nic aragua-cuba/.

79. Rafael Bernal (2018). "Bolton dubs Cuba, Venezuela and Nicaragua the 'Troika of Tyranny.'" *The Hill*. January 11, 2018. https://thehill.com/latino/414333- bolton-dubs-cuba-venezuela-and-nicaragua-the-troika-of-tyranny.

80. U.S. Citizenship and Immigration Services (USCIS) (2018). "USCIS Closes Havana Field Office on Dec. 10, 2018." *U.S. Citizenship and Immigration Services*. Last modified December 12, 2018. https://www.uscis.gov/news/alerts/uscis-closes -havana-field-office-dec-10-2018.

81. BBC News (2021). "Cuba placed back on US terrorism sponsor list." *BBC*, January 11, 2021. https://www.bbc.com/news/world-latin-america-55627032.

82. Zachary Cohen and Jennifer Hansler (2019). "Trump expected to become first President to target Cuba with this controversial policy." *CNN*. April 17, 2019. https:/ /edition.cnn.com/2019/04/16/politics/us-cuba-title-iii-venezuela/index.html.

83. Georgia Popplewell (2019). "Caribbean nations hesitate to recognise Venezuela's Guaidó." *Global Voices*. Last modified January 25, 2019. https://globalvoices .org/2019/01/25/caribbean-nations-hesitate-to-recognise-venezuelas-guaido/.

84. Caribbean Community (CARICOM) (2019). "Statement on escalating tensions in Venezuela issued by the Thirtieth Inter-Sessional Meeting of the Conference of Heads of Government of the Caribbean Community." Last modified February 27, 2019. https://today.caricom.org/2019/02/27/communique-issued-at-the-conclusion-of-the-thirtieth-intersessional-meeting-of-the-conference-of-heads-of-government-of-the-caribbean-community-frigate-bay-st-kitts-and-nevis-26-27-february-2019/.

85. Patrick Oppmann (2018). "Cuba's National Assembly announces Miguel Diaz-Canel as new president." *CNN*. Last modified April 19, 2018. https://edition.cnn.com/2018/04/18/americas/cuba-end-of-castro-era/index.html.

86. Cubadebate (2019a). "Comisión Electoral Nacional fija cifras definitivas: 90.15% de electores votaron en Referendo Constitucional." *Cubadebate*. Last modified March 1, 2019. http://www.cubadebate.cu/noticias/2019/03/01/comision-electoral-nacional-fija-cifras-definitivas-90-15-de-electores-votaron-en-referendo-constitucional/?fbclid=IwAR1oVv-eKNWTsoaz76fI_ee_FFyeZ5qfAru2mnZACzK qjoaFNBj14uvRpHw#.XMcUVOhKg2z.

87. Sputnik (2018). "Presidente cubano llega a Jamaica para asistir a 39 Reunión de Caricom." *Sputnik*. Last modified July 5, 2018. https://mundo.sputniknews.com/america-latina/201807051080179324-diaz-canel-en-jamaica-cumbre-caricom/.

88. Republic of Cuba. (2011). "Lineamientos de la política económica y social del partido y la revolución." *Cubadebate*. Last modified April 18, 2011. http://www.cubadebate.cu/wp-content/uploads/2011/05/folleto-lineamientos-vi-cong.pdf.

89. Hilbourne A. Watson, (1997). "The Techno-Paradigm Shift, Globalization, and Western Hemisphere Integration Trends and Tendencies: Mapping Issues in the Economic and Social Evolution of the Caribbean." In *Cuba and the Caribbean: Regional Issues and Trends in the Post-Cold War Era*, edited by Joseph S., Andrés Serbín and Rafael Hernández Rodríguez Tulchin, 275. Lanham: Rowman & Littlefield.

90. Hilbourne A. Watson (1997). "The Techno-Paradigm Shift, Globalization, and Western Hemisphere Integration Trends and Tendencies: Mapping Issues in the Economic and Social Evolution of the Caribbean." In *Cuba and the Caribbean: Regional Issues and Trends in the Post-Cold War Era*, edited by Joseph S., Andrés Serbín and Rafael Hernández Rodríguez Tulchin, 275. Lanham: Rowman & Littlefield.

91. Cubadebate (2019b). "México asumirá la presidencia pro tempore de la CELAC en 2020." *Cubadebate*. Last modified September 26, 2019. http://www.cubadebate.cu/noticias/2019/09/26/mexico-asumira-la-presidencia-pro-tempore-de-la-celac-en-2020/#.XY38KlVKjIU.

92. Antonio Romero (2015). "Cuba, su política exterior y la nueva arquitectura de gobernanza regional en América Latina y el Caribe." *Pensamiento Propio. La arquitectura de gobernanza regional en América Latina* (Coordinadora Regional de Investigaciones Económicas y Sociales) 42, Año 20 (July-December): 107–134.

REFERENCES

Association of Caribbean States (ACS). 1994. "Convention Establishing the Association of Caribbean States." Last accessed February 5, 2019. http://www.acs

-aec.org/index.php?q=about/convention-establishing-the-association-of-caribbean-states.

———. n.d. "Maps of Maritime Routes of the Greater Caribbean." Last accessed February 5, 2019. http://www.acs-aec.org/index.php?q=transport/projects/maps-of-maritime-routes-of-the-greater-caribbean.

Alzugaray Treto, Carlos. 2014. "La actualización de la política exterior cubana." *Política Exterior*, September–October 2014: 70–82.

———. 2015. "Cuba's External Projection. The Interplay between International Relations Theory and Foreign Policy Analysis." In *Routledge Handbook of Latin America in the World*, edited by Jorge I. Dominguez and Ana Covarrubias, 180–196. New York and London: Routledge.

Aponte Garcia, Maribel. 2014. *El nuevo regionalismo estratégico: los primeros diez años del ALBA-TCP*. Ciudad Autónoma de Buenos Aires: CLACSO.

Bell, Wendell. 2008. "The American invasion of Grenada: A note on false prophecy." *Foresight* 10, No. 3, May: 27–42.

BBC News. 2021. "Cuba placed back on US terrorism sponsor list." *BBC*, January 11, 2021. https://www.bbc.com/news/world-latin-america-55627032.

Benemelis, Juan. 1990. "Cuba's African Relation." In *Cuba: The International Dimension*, edited by Georges Alfred Fauriol and Eva Loser, 121–152. New Brunswick and London: Transaction Publishers.

Bernal, Rafael. 2018. "Bolton dubs Cuba, Venezuela and Nicaragua the 'Troika of Tyranny.'" *The Hill*. January 11, 2018. https://thehill.com/latino/414333-bolton-dubs-cuba-venezuela-and-nicaragua-the-troika-of-tyranny.

Binder, David. 1975. "Cuba Sanctions, imposed in 1964, lifted by O.A.S." *New York Times*, July 30, 1975.

Byron, Jessica, Jacqueline Laguardia Martinez, Annita Montoute and Keron Niles. 2021. "Impacts of COVID-19 in the Commonwealth Caribbean: key lessons." *The Round Table* 110, No. 1: 99–119. DOI: 10.1080/00358533.2021.1875694.

Caribbean Community Climate Change Centre (CCCCC). 2012. *Delivering Transformational Change 2011–21. Implementing the CARICOM "Regional Framework for Achieving Development Resilient to Climate Change."* Technical Report 5C/CCCCC-12-03-01, Belmopan: Caribbean Community Climate Change Centre.

Caribbean Export Development Agency (CEDA). 2016. "TRADEWINS. Critical Issues for Business." *The CARICOM/Cuba Trade and Economic Co-Operation Agreement Explained* 2: 11.

Caribbean Community (CARICOM). 1993. "Agreement establishing the CARICOM - Cuba Joint Commission. Georgetown." Last modified December 13, 1993.

———. 2013. "PetroCaribe." Last modified September 9, 2013. https://caricom.org/projects/detail/petrocaribe.

———. 2017. "More opportunities provided for private sector as CARICOM, Cuba expand duty-free market access." Last modified November 10, 2017. https://caricom.org/media-center/communications/press-releases/more-opportunities-provided-for-private-sector-as-caricom-cuba-expand-duty-free-market-access.

———. 2019. "Statement on escalating tensions in Venezuela issued by the Thirtieth Inter-Sessional Meeting of the Conference of Heads of Government of the Caribbean Community." Last modified February 27, 2019. https://today.caricom.org /2019/02/27/communique-issued-at-the-conclusion-of-the-thirtieth-intersessional-meeting-of-the-conference-of-heads-of-government-of-the-caribbean-community -frigate-bay-st-kitts-and-nevis-26-27-february-2019/.

CARICOM and the Republic of Cuba. 2005. "Cultural Cooperation Agreement between the Caribbean Community (CARICOM) and the Republic of Cuba. Caribbean Community." Last modified December 8, 2005. https://caricom.org/ communications/view/cultural-cooperation-agreement-between-the-caribbean-community-caricom-and-the-republic-of-cuba.

———. 2000. "Trade and Economic Co-operation Agreement between CARICOM and the Republic of Cuba." Last modified July 5, 2000.

Castro, Fidel. 2002. "Discurso pronunciado por el Comandante en Jefe Fidel Castro Ruz con motivo del aniversario 30 de las relaciones diplomáticas con Barbados, Guyana, Jamaica y Trinidad y Tobago, en el Palacio de las Convenciones, el 8 de diciembre del 2002." *Fidel, Soldado de las Ideas.* Last modified December 8, 2002. http://www.fidelcastro.cu/es/discursos/discurso-con-motivo-del-30-aniversario-de -las-relaciones-diplomaticas-con-barbados-guyana.

Cohen, Zachary and Jennifer Hansler. 2019. "Trump expected to become first President to target Cuba with this controversial policy." *CNN.* April 17, 2019. https ://edition.cnn.com/2019/04/16/politics/us-cuba-title-iii-venezuela/index.html.

Concepción Pérez, Elson. 2018. "El Caribe que nos une y fortalece." *Cubadebate.* Last modified December 06, 2018. http://www.cubadebate.cu/opinion/2018/12/06/ el-caribe-que-nos-une-y-fortalece/#.XMdKN-hKg2x.

Corredor Biológico en el Caribe. 2018. "Corredor Biológico en el Caribe." Last modified June, 2018. https://cbcbio.org/2018/07/30/20-de-julio-de-2018-santo-domingo -republica-dominicana/.

Cuba's Representative Office Abroad. 2017. "How does Cuba cooperate with the Caribbean?" *Cuba's Representative Office Abroad.* Last modified March 11, 2017. http://misiones.minrex.gob.cu/en/articulo/how-does-cuba-cooperate-caribbean.

Cubadebate. 2019a. "Comisión Electoral Nacional fija cifras definitivas: 90.15% de electores votaron en Referendo Constitucional." *Cubadebate.* Last modified March 1, 2019. http://www.cubadebate.cu/noticias/2019/03/01/comision-electoral-nacional -fija-cifras-definitivas-90-15-de-electores-votaron-en-referendo-constitucional/ ?fbclid=IwAR1oVv-eKNWTsoaz76fI_ee_FFyeZ5qfAru2mnZACzKqjoaFNBj14 uvRpHw#.XMcUVOhKg2z.

Cubadebate. 2019b. "México asumirá la presidencia pro tempore de la CELAC en 2020." *Cubadebate.* Last modified September 26, 2019. http://www.cubadebate .cu/noticias/2019/09/26/mexico-asumira-la-presidencia-pro-tempore-de-la-celac-en-2020/#.XY38KlVKjIU.

Doimeadios Guerrero, Dianet and Irene Pérez. 2017. "Inicia Conferencia de Cooperación de la Asociación de Estados del Caribe." *Cubadebate.* Last modified March 8, 2017. http://www.cubadebate.cu/noticias/2017/03/08/inicia-conferencia-de-cooperacion-de-la-asociacion-de-estados-del-caribe/#.XMz2_ -hKg2w.

Dowrich-Phillips, Laura. 2019. "President Trump to meet with five Caribbean leaders." *Loop*, Last modified March 20, 2019https://www.looptt.com/content/president-trump-meet-five-caribbean-leaders.

Dominguez, Jorge. 2001. "Cuban Foreign Policy and the International System." In *Latin America in the New International System*, edited by Joseph and Ralph H. Espach Tulchin, 240. Boulder-London: Lynne Rienner Pub.

Erisman, Michael H. 1994. "Evolving Cuban-CARICOM Relations: A Comparative Cost/Benefit Analysis." Paper presented at the Annual Conference of the Caribbean Studies Association (CSA). Mérida.

Fabbri, Carlos Andres. 1993. "La política exterior de Cuba hacia América Latina. Reflexiones en torno a la "exportación del comunismo." *América latina hoy: Revista de Ciencias Sociales* 6: 39–44.

Feinsilver, Julie M. 2010. "Fifty Years of Cuba's Medical Diplomacy: From Idealism to Pragmatism." *Cuban Studies* 41, 85–104.

Furtak, Robert K.1985. "Cuba: un cuarto de siglo de política exterior revolucionaria." *Foro Internacional (El Colegio de México)* 25, No. 4 (April–June): 343–361.

Gardini, Gian Luca and Peter Lambert. 2011. "Ideology and Pragmatism in Latin American Foreign Policy." In *Latin American Foreign Policies Between Ideology and Pragmatism*, edited by Gian Luca Gardini and Peter Lambert, London: Palgrave Macmillan, 1–33.

González Núñez, Gerardo. 1991. *El Caribe en la política exterior de Cuba. Balance de 30 años: 1959-1989*. Santo Domingo: Ediciones CIPROS.

Granma. 2014. "Nuestras aspiraciones son las mismas en toda América Latina." *Granma*, March 11, 2014.

Hernández, Rafael. 1997. "Cuba and Security in the Caribbean." In *Cuba and the Caribbean: Regional Issues and Trends in the Post-Cold War Era*, edited by Andrés Serbín and Rafael Hernández Joseph S. Tulchin, 275. Lanham: Rowman & Littlefield Publishers.

Ishmael, Odeen. 2015. *The Trail of Diplomacy: The Guyana-Venezuela Border Issue* (Volume Two). Bloomington: Xlibris Corporation.

Jagan, Cheddi. 1997. *Interview by Cuban journalist Ernesto Nustez Jimenez to the late President Cheddi Jagan*. Last modified January 22, 1997.

Jamaica Observer. 2019. "CARICOM, Cuba sign new trade agreement." *Jamaica Observer*. Las modified February 8, 2017. http://www.jamaicaobserver.com/news/CARICOM--Cuba-sign-new-trade-agreement.

Jaramillo Edwards, Isabel. 1999. *El multilateralismo en la política exterior de Cuba*. Santiago de Chile: FLACSO-Chile.

Juventud Rebelde. 2007. "Firmarán convenio de cooperación ambiental Cuba, Haití y Dominicana." *Juventud Rebelde*. Last modified July 9, 2007. http://www.juventud rebelde.cu/cuba/2007-07-09/firmaran-convenio-de-cooperacion-ambiental-cuba-haiti-y-dominicana.

Kline, Harvey F., Wade, Christine J. and Howard J. Wiarda. 2017. *Latin American Politics and Development*. New York: Routledge.

Laguardia Martinez, J., Chami, G., Montoute, A., Mohammed, D.A. 2019. *Changing Cuba-US Relations. Implications for CARICOM States*. London: Palgrave Macmillan.

Melakopides, Costas. 2012. "Pragmatic Idealism Revisited: Russia's Post-1991 Cyprus Policy and Implications for Washington." *Mediterranean Quarterly* (Duke University Press) 23, No. 4: 107–134.

Montoute, Annita and Andy Knight, Jacqueline Laguardia Martínez, Debbie Mohammed, Dave Seerattan. 2017. *The Caribbean in the European Union-Community of Latin American and Caribbean States Partnership*. Hamburg: EU-LAC Foundation.

Office of the United States Trade Representative. n.d. "Caribbean Basin Initiative (CBI)." *Office of the United States Trade Representative. Executive Office of the President*. Last modified May 1, 2019. https://ustr.gov/issue-areas/trade-development/preference-programs/caribbean-basin-initiative-cbi.

Opciones. 2015. "Cooperación Sur-Sur, una baza contra el cambio climático." *Opciones. Seminario Económico y Financiero de Cuba*. http://www.opciones.cu/cuba/2015-08-06/cooperacion-sur-sur-una-baza-contra-el-cambio-climatico/.

Oppmann, Patrick. 2018. "Cuba's National Assembly announces Miguel Diaz-Canel as new president." *CNN*. Last modified April 19, 2018. https://edition.cnn.com/2018/04/18/americas/cuba-end-of-castro-era/index.html.

Popplewell, Georgia. 2019. "Caribbean nations hesitate to recognise Venezuela's Guaidó." *Global Voices*. Last modified January 25, 2019. https://globalvoices.org/2019/01/25/caribbean-nations-hesitate-to-recognise-venezuelas-guaido/.

Prensa Latina. 2018. "Firman acuerdo Ministerio de Cultura de Cuba y organización caribeña." *Cubasí*. Last modified July 19, 2018. http://cubasi.cu/cubasi-noticias-cuba-mundo-ultima-hora/item/82642-firman-acuerdo-ministerio-de-cultura-de-cuba-y-organizacion-caribena (accessed 04 29, 2019).

———. 2021. "Economic and social results to focus PCC meeting in Cuba." *Prensa Latina*. Last modified March 15, 2021. https://www.plenglish.com/index.php?o=rn&id=65378&SEO=economic-and-social-results-to-focus-pcc-meeting-in-cuba.

Republic of Cuba. 2019. *Constitución de la República de Cuba*. La Habana, Last modified April 10, 2019. http://media.cubadebate.cu/wp-content/uploads/2019/01/Constitucion-Cuba-2019.pdf.

———. 2011. "Lineamientos de la política económica y social del partido y la revolución." *Cubadebate*. Last modified April 18, 2011. http://www.cubadebate.cu/wp-content/uploads/2011/05/folleto-lineamientos-vi-cong.pdf.

Richardson, Davis. 2019. "John Bolton Reaffirms America's Commitment to the Monroe Doctrine with New Sanctions." *Observer*. Last modified April 17, 2019. https://observer.com/2019/04/john-bolton-monroe-doctrine-sanctions-venezuela-nicaragua-cuba/.

Romero, Antonio. 2015. "Cuba, su política exterior y la nueva arquitectura de gobernanza regional en América Latina y el Caribe." *Pensamiento Propio. La arquitectura de gobernanza regional en América Latina*. (Coordinadora Regional de Investigaciones Económicas y Sociales) 42, Año 20 (July-Decembe): 107–134.

Serbín, Andrés. 1987. *Etnicidad, clase y nación en la cultura política del Caribe de habla inglesa*. Caracas: Academia Nacional de la Historia.

———. 2012. "La política exterior de Cuba en un mundo multipolar." *Anuario CEIPAZ* 2012–2013, No. 5: 187–219.

Sputnik. 2018. "Presidente cubano llega a Jamaica para asistir a 39 Reunión de Caricom." *Sputnik*. Last modified July 5, 2018. https://mundo.sputniknews.com/america-latina/201807051080179324-diaz-canel-en-jamaica-cumbre-caricom/.

Stolberg, Sheryl Gay and Alexei Barrionuevo. 2009. "Obama Says U.S. Will Pursue Thaw with Cuba." *New York Times*, Last modified April 17, 2009.

New York Times. 1964. "Chile Breaks Cuban Ties, Carrying Out O.A.S. Ban; President Alessandri Severs Diplomatic Relations in the Face of Threats by Leftists of Street Violence." *New York Times*, Last modified August 12, 1964.

U.S. Citizenship and Immigration Services (USCIS). 2018. "USCIS Closes Havana Field Office on Dec. 10, 2018." *U.S. Citizenship and Immigration Services*. Last modified December 12, 2018. https://www.uscis.gov/news/alerts/uscis-closes-havana-field-office-dec-10-2018.

United Nations General Assembly (UNGA). 1983. "UNGA Resolution A/RES/38/7." New York, Last modified November 2, 1983.

———. 1992. *Yearbook of the United Nations 1992*. New York, Dordrecht: Martinu Nijhoff Publishers.

Valenta, Jiri. 1990. "Cuba in the Soviet Alliance System." In *Cuba: The International Dimension*, edited by Georges Alfred Fauriol and Eva Loser, 3–39. New Brunswick and London: Transaction Publishers.

Vamvakas, Petros. 2017. "Russia-Cyprus Relations: A Pragmatic Idealist Perspective by Costas Melakopides (review)." *Mediterranean Quarterly* 28, No. 2: 146–148.

Watson, Hilbourne A. 1997. "The Techno-Paradigm Shift, Globalization, and Western Hemisphere Integration Trends and Tendencies: Mapping Issues in the Economic and Social Evolution of the Caribbean." In *Cuba and the Caribbean: Regional Issues and Trends in the Post-Cold War Era*, edited by Joseph S., Andrés Serbín and Rafael Hernández Rodríguez Tulchin, 275. Lanham: Rowman & Littlefield.

Chapter 6

Reflections on the Socially Responsive Regional Integration Process of UNASUR

A Small State Perspective

Ruben Martoredjo

INTRODUCTION

Colombia's president, Iván Duque, and Chile's president, Sebastián Piñera, spearheaded the launch of what they hope will be an important new initiative in South American politics: the Progress of South America (PROSUR). In the presence of seven "right-wing" presidents, PROSUR was announced in Chile's capital, Santiago, on Friday, March 22, 2019.[1] Brazil, Argentina, Chile, Paraguay, Colombia, Ecuador, Peru, and Guyana signed on to PROSUR while Bolivia, Uruguay, and Suriname did not join the bloc. PROSUR's proponents argue that it will serve as a pragmatic replacement to the nearly extinct Union of South American Nations (UNASUR), promoting economic integration and political coordination in the region without the latter's bureaucratic and ideological excesses.[2]

According to President Pinera, the new bloc would function without ideology and bureaucracy, and in total commitment to freedom, democracy, and human rights.[3] PROSUR reflects a new platform for South American states to exchange ideas, work together, make their voices heard, and together achieve more freedom, integration, and development. PROSUR would also allow member states to discuss infrastructure, energy, security, health, defense, crime, and response to natural disasters.[4] It was also announced that PROSUR embodies "a regional space of coordination and cooperation, without exclusion of ideologies," yet we witness that Venezuela with its twenty-first-century socialism was not invited to join. Venezuela in its post-Chavez era, characterized by economic collapse and political instability, seems to have a dividing effect on the South American region.

It is too early to reach conclusions as to whether PROSUR marks the birth of a genuine regional integration process or of an opportunistic attempt to contradict the more socialist-leaning movement embodied by UNASUR. Some argue that with the political shift in Latin America, we are witnessing the demise of socially responsive regionalism spearheaded by UNASUR and Bolivarian Alliance for the Peoples of Our America (ALBA TCP). In fact, the region is again engaged in an attempt at regional grouping in addition to those groups already in existence, without structural alignment and/or efforts at resurgence.

The region should take stock of and reflect on what previous attempts have yielded for member states and their citizens in regard to their development and well-being, articulated by the impact on social issues, cooperation, political dialogue, the environment, energy, and food safety and security.

Small states, such as Suriname and Guyana, already have difficulties in simultaneously actively engaging with multiple regional initiatives such as Caribbean Community (CARICOM), UNASUR, ALBA TCP, and Community of Latin American and Caribbean States (CELAC).

Written from a small state perspective, this article reflects on the key "social" elements mainstreamed in UNASUR's regional integration process which has dominated South America in the last decade, and which PROSUR claims to replace.

SOUTH AMERICAN REGIONALISM IN CONTEXT

South American regionalism is exemplary of the definition of regionalism, which notes that it has a complex history because of its essentially contested and flexible nature, and because of a divergence of views as to whether or not regionalism is an effective or desirable organizing mechanism in international politics.[5] According to Farrell, the very nature of regionalism is one of great diversity, and contemporary regionalism actually comprises many different regionalisms, reflecting different conditions, values, and even ideological positions across the global arena; it is a product of the historical, social and political conditions, and of the strengths and weaknesses of any particular region.[6]

The terms of regionalism can be defined not simply by visions of how collective action in a specific geographic area responds to challenges and needs from external actors (or from other regions), but also by perceptions, motivations, and norms based on interaction. This notion was captured by constructivist approaches which claim that regions are social constructions.[7] From this perspective, regionalism can take a variety of paths and paces, and overlapping and even competing projects may manifest within one region as specific practices and different narratives in different domains.[8] In South America this situation is embodied by the prominent simultaneous active presence of Mercado Común del Sur (MERCOSUR), UNASUR, Pacific Alliance, and CELAC.

At least in theory, regional integration offers a number of possibilities for the development of social regulation, rights, and redistribution schemes. These occur in the forms of regional social, health, and labor regulations; regional mechanisms which give citizens a voice to challenge their governments in terms of social rights; regional intergovernmental forms of cooperation in social policy; regional cross-border investments in the area of social policy; regional coordination of economic and developmental policies; regional initiatives in capacity-building and innovation; and inter-regional agreements and arrangements related to social issues.[9]

We have witnessed the increase in prominence that social development and social policy considerations have gained in the debate about regionalism as countries have attempted to address increasing poverty, unemployment, and social inequality in past decades.

In South America, since the 1960s there has been very little dialogue about trade policies, issues of poverty and inclusion, and collective action in relation to social policy goals. Delivering social protection and human development in South America was firmly assigned to the sphere of domestic spending choices, where it was designed to mitigate the effects of market reforms or to secure political and electoral support.[10] The rise of New Leftist governments across the region, in Venezuela (1998), Brazil (2002), Argentina (2003), Uruguay (2004), Bolivia (2005), Ecuador (2006), Paraguay (2008), and Peru (2011), was argued to be a profound acknowledgment that economic governance could not be delinked from the responsibilities of the state to deliver inclusive democracy and socially responsive political economies.[11]

Particularly since the 1990s, there has been a growing consensus that, in an increasingly globalized world, new political thinking and new kinds of policies are necessary to achieve socially equitable development.[12]

Pero and Szerman (2010) note that new regionalism, particularly that of South America, has as a common denominator, the aim of reaching beyond the traditional approach of strictly commercial and economic integration based on the need of nations, toward a broad multidisciplinary agenda that addresses not only economic themes but social issues, cooperation, political dialogue, the environment, energy, and food, and which calls upon direct societal actors and the responsible authorities whose power is sustained by a participative democracy. [13]

A process of political renewal has emerged in Latin America, and largely in South America, since the early 2000s, which means that regionalism may

be in the process of "catching up" with social concerns. Loosening the con-
strictions of the neoliberal myth as an organizing principle of national and
regional political economy has allowed for new governing arrangements and
practices across South America.[14]

Monica Hirst argues that this new period of Latin American regionalism is
characterized by complexity and some degree of anarchy, leading to her use
of the term "anarchical regionalism."[15] Initiatives such as ALBA, UNASUR,
and the so-called "new MERCOSUR' encourage a regional agenda beyond
free trade, while other initiatives such as the Andean Community or the
Central American Integration System are still committed to free trade and
open regionalism. Meanwhile, Mexico, Colombia, Peru, and Chile have
established the Pacific Alliance, a new regional body that subscribes entirely
to the ideas of an open regional economic integration. Neoliberal and post-
liberal initiatives coexist, creating a complex network of overlapping mem-
berships and regional approaches, and new framings of regionalism have
emerged and seem set to continue to emerge.

García (2015) presents the view that the emergence of a New Strategic
Regionalism, embodied by the ALBA-TCP at the beginning of the twenty-
first century, presents regional action around sovereignty, not from the scope
of traditional international relations, but from the scope of public policy
responses to the contradictions of the international political economy.[16] The
possible outcomes of the project therefore lie in two paths that converge: on
the one hand, strengthening an alternative regional integration model that
transcends the characteristics of the New Regionalism and the problems it
creates, and on the other hand, creating a new vision for a socialism of the
twenty-first century that allows it to surpass all the limitations of the existing
socialism that characterized the twentieth century, and to promote diversity
and democracy.[17]

At present, a shift in the direction of the regional political economy as a
consequence of electoral defeat of "left-leaning" governments is exemplified
by the establishment of PROSUR. Combined with a regained interest of the
U.S. hegemon, which seems to manipulate the region under the umbrella of
safeguarding political and democratic freedom, we may witness the emergence of a new form of regionalism on the South American continent.

THE "SOCIAL" IN REGIONALISM
OF SOUTH AMERICA

Although South American countries have been hailed for their progress in
addressing longstanding social ills in the last decade, according to the Social
Panorama 2017 of the Economic Commission for Latin America and the

Caribbean (ECLAC)[18], it now seems that citizens who climbed out of poverty and inequality have been sliding back in the past few years.

ECLAC's Social Panorama 2017 reports that the regional average of poverty and extreme poverty levels rose in Latin America in 2015 and 2016, after more than a decade of declines in the majority of countries. In 2014, 28.5 percent of the region's population (168 million people) were in situations of poverty, a percentage that increased to 29.8 percent (178 million) in 2015 and to 30.7 percent (186 million people) in 2016. Extreme poverty, meanwhile, rose from 8.2 percent (48 million people) in 2014 to 10 percent (61 million people) in 2016.[19]

Despite considerable spending since 2000, the very poor still lack the income and capital that would enable them to be resilient in more difficult times. As such, there are real concerns that a ceiling has been reached in terms of reducing poverty and inequality, and even doubts about whether the current levels of social protection can be maintained for much longer.[20]

These experiences indicate that the success achieved by the region in addressing social ills has not been sustained. Strengthened by the current situation in Venezuela with the collapse of the Petro economy, by decreasing commodity prices (oil) and by the tightening of the U.S. embargo, there are emerging views that left-oriented regimes have had their time as they are unable to sustain the improved social conditions of their citizens.

With all the geopolitical rhetoric and criticism currently propagated about the failure of UNASUR, and in light of the efforts to justify the emergence of PROSUR, it may be prudent to question the extent to which UNASUR's stand in regard to social development in a post-neoliberal era is understood.

In the analysis of social policy at the regional tier of governance, a relevant factor is that of scope conditions which can determine in which ways and to what extent regional organizations can play a positive role in regional social governance. When investigating the implications of international agreements on foreign investment on governments' ability to regulate and implement social policy reforms, Clarkson and Hindelag (2016) underscore the intersectionality between governance systems of foreign investment protection and social policy.[21]

Their main contention is that certain kinds of international agreements on foreign investment protection can hinder the capacity of governments to regulate and implement social policies. This assertion implies that specific types of foreign investment agreements and the resulting governance system should be seen as scope conditions for the formulation and implementation of effective social policy at all levels, and also, of regional social norms, instruments, and policies. Yeates (2014) and Deacon et al. (2010), identify four main types of instruments: forums, standard-setting activities, resources, and regulation, as well as selected instances of their existence in practice.

The effectiveness of social policies is intrinsically related to the availability of resources. The availability of resources also influences the capacity of regional organizations to perform social distribution. Latin American countries are historically known for their constrained budgets for social protection spending, which worsens in times of fiscal adjustment and financial crisis.

Medeiros et al. (2016) argue that in the context of financial crises, regional funds can play a central role in guaranteeing the continuity of social policies in poor countries by performing countercyclical investments in areas affected by a significant and unexpected decrease in external funding or domestic budgetary cuts.

Langenhove and Kingah (2016) argue that the effectiveness of regional social policy depends on the willingness, acceptance, and capacity of these

Table 6.1   Regional Policy Instruments and Examples for LAC Region

1. Instrument	2. Functions to.	3. Instances
Regional forum	Share information for mutual education, analysis, and debate; promote shared analyses and create epistemic communities and networks that can inform policy debate and provide a platform for collaboration	CARICOM: capacity building and communicable diseases UNASUR: ISAGS regional think tank
Social standard-setting	Define international social standards and common frameworks for social policy (e.g., human rights charters, labor, social protection, and health conventions)	UNASUR: Constitutional Treaty enshrines common normative framework
Resource mobilization and allocation	Provide resources, supporting policy development and provision (e.g., stimulus finance, technical assistance, policy advice, and expertise)	Andean Community (CAN): Social Humanitarian Fund ALBA: anti-poverty projects, trading schemes; UNASUR: regionally-funded think tank ISAGS delivers programs of institutional reform, professionalization, and capacity-building
Regulation	Regulatory instruments and reform affects entitlements and access to social provision	MS: Removal of work visa requirements for migrant workers; CARICOM: Mutual recognition agreements in education; MERCOSUR, CAN: Social security portability

Source: Developed by Author...and adapted from Yeates (2014); Deacon et al. (2010); Yeates and Riggirozzi (2015).

organizations to act. Visionary leaders with a regional appreciation of social problems are invaluable for policy effectiveness in this respect: leaders at regional institutions and in local governments who are able to define common problems. Such leaders must be willing to commit to regional disciplines once these are negotiated and accepted at the regional level. At the heart of an effective social policy is the willingness of national and local focal points and officials to learn.

UNASUR SOCIAL

As Riggirozzi and Grugel(2015) posit, UNASUR has been a new experience for South America. It is a regional governance project based not on economic integration but on social policies, political cooperation, and a defense of democracy; its aspirations are limited, but there are realistic plans in place for delivery; and it appears to prefer to create a team of professional specialists to take charge of a policy area rather than have politicians make grand (and unrealistic) statements of policy intent.

UNASUR's objectives indicate a new agenda of integration that goes far beyond trade facilitation, reflecting a new concept of common interests in the region and entailing the provision of regional goods, exemplified by the case of health care. UNASUR also embodies a new kind of regionalism, with the ability and flexibility to not only overcome some of the region's most enduring disagreements, but to develop a common voice for the continent in key areas, which would help to achieve the regions' goals and increase its international insertion.

Riggirozzi and Grugel (2016) advance that UNASUR is developing policies and a normative structure in support of broader equity and social development, and the legitimacy of UNASUR is based on a combination of the promotion of welfare and public good in the region, and a defense of minimum standards of regional democracy.

The Constitutive Treaty of UNASUR stipulates that UNASUR will promote dialogue initiatives on regional or international topics of interest, and will seek to consolidate cooperation mechanisms with other regional groups, states, and other entities with international legal status, prioritizing projects in the areas of energy, financing, infrastructure, social policies, and education.

UNASUR has a very ambitious agenda in the area of social policy and this indicates that "regionalism may be in the process of 'catching up' with social concerns."[22] This was clearly acknowledged in the UNASUR Treaty, which outlines one of the specific aims of the regional group as the promotion of social and human development and the eradication of poverty and inequalities.

A focus on social development within UNASUR was institutionalized in 2009 with the formation of the South American Council on Social
Development (CSDS) also known as UNASUR-Social. The work of the
CSDS is carried out by the Ministers of Social Development of member
countries organized into four working groups, each of which deals with a
different social issue: food security and the fight against hunger and mal-
nutrition; social and solidarity economy; protection and promotion of social
security; and instruments of cooperation.

UNASUR emerges as a standard-bearer in the advocacy of social development, revealing "Southern origins of norms" that are central to contemporary
regional and global governance. The organization already supports a rights-
based social policy delivered through member states as a "regional" responsibility, and its Constitutive Treaty explicitly declares the need to foster
integration that would support social inclusion and poverty eradication based
on the realization of rights. Its member states need, however, to work toward
a common approach to social policy.

UNASUR consists of twelve countries with different objectives, which
inevitably causes political or economic conflicts. One of their shared objectives is, however, as the Constitutive Treaty preamble states, "to develop an
integrated regional space in the political, economic, social, cultural, environmental, energy and infrastructure areas in order to strengthen the unity
of Latin America and the Caribbean." The development of this integration
mechanism must "contribute to solve problems that still affect the region such
as poverty, exclusion and persisting social inequality."[23]

UNASUR's support of a rights-based social policy delivered through member states came to be framed as a "regional" responsibility. Its Constitutive
Treaty explicitly declares the need—based on the realization of rights—to
foster integration that would support social inclusion and poverty eradication.[24] The treaty indicates that it is "convinced that the South American
integration and South American unity are necessary to promote the sustainable development and well-being of its peoples, and to contribute to the solu-
tion of the problems which still affect the region, such as persistent poverty,
social exclusion, and inequality." It also acknowledges that "fully functioning democratic institutions and the unrestricted respect for human rights are
essential conditions for building a common future of peace, economic and
social prosperity and for the development of integration processes among the
Member States."

The social agenda of UNASUR focuses on three main themes, namely:
Social (with a main focus on social inclusion); Economic (with a main focus
on competitiveness); and Political (with a main focus on defending democracy). Three underlying ideas are also identified, these are: General Rights,
Environmental Rights, and Human Rights.[25]

UNASUR's social agenda concentrates on the areas of health, education, and social development; thus, there are three corresponding councils of importance, namely Education, Social Development, and Health councils.

In general, it is easy to find common ground and areas of mutual interest among the twelve member states in the area of Education—for instance, the creation of common conditions for students, and in Health—such as best practices of the member states. Driven by the need for mutual recognition of professional and educational qualifications and educational institutions, countries are more open to uniformity and to regionally coordinated education policies. However, the biggest challenge for the councils is to find a common concept which represents the views and strategies of all twelve member states.

The Conditional Cash Transfer (CCT) program, for instance, is one area where there are twelve visions and methods of implementation. Some of the programs are more services-based, while others are focused on opportunity-creation and innovation. It is also challenging to reach a common view regarding the roles of the state and that of the regional organization in relation to social policy.[26] Under the social development agenda, CCT is featured by the CSDS as a means of elevating citizens out of poverty and of addressing inequality.

It is difficult to establish a generic social development strategy as demands differ among countries. However, consensus has been reached by the twelve member countries on the concept of social development. It captures the social actions of the member states and is aligned with the post-2015 Development Agenda (Sustainable Development Goals (SDGs)), specifically, translation of the UN development goals in South America (localizing SDGs). UNASUR has taken a unique position in the negotiations regarding the adoption of the SDGs.[27]

The CSDS (South American Council on Social Development) aims to contribute to the establishment of conditions for the development of fairer, more participative, solidary and democratic societies, as well as to promote mechanisms of solidarity cooperation in social policies for the reduction of asymmetries and the deepening of integration processes. Their action plan proposes a series of activities and products in terms of strategic planning which integrate progressive levels of complementarity in the joint work between countries.[28] These include, among others: compilation and system-atization of experiences and/or national conceptualizations; identification of best practices and design and implementation of regional pilot experiences; and regional cooperation in social policy.

UNASUR, in its efforts to achieve its social development objectives, has established mechanisms which facilitate the exchange of knowledge and experiences in social policies among the member states. Also, a funding facility has been created to finance intergovernmental collaboration in the area of social development.

The Observatory for Human Social Development and Inclusion

The member states agreed upon the establishment of the Observatory for Human Social Development and Inclusion (OBSERVASUR). OBSERVASUR was instituted on the Biennial Plan 2009–2011 and began operations in 2010.[29] OBSERVASUR is a platform where best practices in the area of social development are shared with other member countries—this includes information on the program or project, lessons learned, and contact details of the responsible authorities and officers. Requests for technical assistance can also be obtained through the platform. The establishment of OBSERVASUR is funded by FIC (Fondo de Iniciativas Comunes—Common Initiative Fund), which has a budget of approximately US$1,000,000 per year allocated for UNASUR's development projects. FIC is financed with resources from the annual budget (annual contribution from member states), and contributions may also be made through a voluntary pledge.[30] The establishments of OBSERVASUR and a micro-financing mechanism for livelihood development of the socially weak segment of the population are seen as UNASUR's strategic achievements in social development.

Progress is also expected from pilots in three countries in the areas of nutrition and childhood assistance, and from the sharing of statistical data among countries. A positive outcome of which member states are proud is the synchronization of social programs and status, where these countries are making efforts to improve and sustain their policies by sharing practices and experiences. Another positive aspect is that UNASUR observes the principle of equal membership. Aspiration for the future is to reach regional complementarity and convergence between UNASUR, MERCOSUR, CELAC, and ALBA, where UNASUR functions as the regional institution which sets the norms in the area of social policies.[31]

The Common Initiatives Fund

The aforementioned Common Initiatives Fund (FIC) aims to support intergovernmental programs and projects in order to contribute to the UNASUR objectives set out in Articles 2 and 3 of the Treaty. According to article 44 of the General Regulation of UNASUR, "The financing of common initiatives will be defined by the Council of Ministers of Foreign Affairs, on the basis of proposals submitted to the General Secretariat for the different bodies of UNASUR."[32] The Constitutive Treaty of UNASUR captures through its objective (Article 2) the prioritization of social policies, and lists among its specific objectives; Social and human development with equity and inclusion to eradicate poverty and overcome inequalities and universal access to social security and health services (Article 3 c, k).[33] Article 2 indicates that

> the objective is to build, in a participatory and consensual manner, an integration and union among its peoples in the cultural, social, economic and political fields, prioritizing political dialogue, social policies, education, energy, infrastructure, financing, and the environment, among others, with a view to eliminating socioeconomic inequality, in order to achieve social inclusion and participation of civil society, to strengthen democracy and reduce asymmetries within the framework of strengthening the sovereignty and independence of the States.

Further, Article 3 includes the following UNASUR objectives: cc) "The inclusive and equitable social and human development in order to eradicate poverty and overcome inequalities in the region"; and kk) "Universal access to social security and health services."

Member states like Suriname could have benefited from these two initiatives, namely the OBSERVASUR and FIC, for their social development initiatives. Already, through OBSERVASUR, information on the cash transfer initiatives of all member states is mapped and stored, and is available to all members. Further, technical assistance can be facilitated through OBSERVASUR. In tandem with the availability of information, funding can be accessed through FIC for joint social development initiatives among countries or institutions, so that collaborations between member countries could be submitted to FIC for funding.

OBSERVASUR may be the first broad and purely South American attempt to amalgamate knowledge and could be have been upgraded to a Comprehensive Regional Online Social Development Platform, structured to capture all experiences, knowledge, and technical information on the various social programs of the twelve member states of UNASUR. Thus, Suriname could have benefited from the process of knowledge/experience sharing and technical assistance to develop its social sector.

UNASUR HEALTH

The emergence of UNASUR as an actor in Global Health marked a milestone in diplomacy. The countries of South America united in an unprecedented way to influence issues of common interest. Despite the previous existence of other regional and sub-regional blocs and organizations in the Americas, it is evident that social and economic circumstances, as well as issues of geographic contiguity, often create interests and goals that differ from those of developed countries. The area of Health has been a significant area of consensus among the member countries of UNASUR, and it has the potential to be an important integrating axis in the region. Circumstantial dissimilarities or ideological disagreements will always be present as long as democracy and diversity are respected, but it is argued that achieving the social development goals embodied in the Constitutive Treaty of UNASUR and the Plans agreed upon in the Health Council reflects the existing aspirations in each of the constitutional texts of the member states.[34]

The South American Institute of Government in Health (ISAGS) of UNASUR has implemented two successful projects. One of them, the Drug Price Bank (DPB), is regarded as the instrument of UNASUR's with the most practical and continuous effects in the area of Health. It consists of a database of drug prices with comparable information from the twelve- member states on pharmacological and economic aspects: this serves as a powerful tool for setting reference prices, establishing drug price ceilings, and negotiating prices with the pharmaceutical industry. It is thus a very important base from which to mitigate discrepancies, but is also valuable for negotiations or even joint purchases.

Another initiative is the Mapping of Drug Production Capacities (MDPC) which has the potential to foster regional production and facilitate the creation of a regional policy. As a collaborative effort, ISAGS and the CSDS conducted a mapping exercise, and the results highlight the need to reflect on and inquire about the social determinants of health.[35]

As a member state, Suriname could turn to UNASUR or its members for health-related cooperation and assistance. Surely DPB and MDPC could provide solutions in the supply of medication at affordable prices. It is important to have a professional executive institution to lead and champion work in the area of health sector development, specifically to facilitate knowledge exchange and experience sharing—for instance, on the social determinants of health. This should be accompanied by promotion of the use of the OBSERVASUR platform, advance research in the areas of social development, and regular publication of the progress and results of the work done by UNASUR.[36] Cuba is well known for its South–South Cooperation (SSC) in the areas of health and education, and Suriname cooperates with Cuba in the area of health, specifically in strengthening its health system and improving its coverage of health services[37] as is the case with larger nations such as Venezuela and Brazil. A triangular cooperation between UNASUR, Cuba, and Suriname may be an avenue through which to solidify region-wide efforts to improve health situations.

RELEVANCE FOR SURINAME

Cavlak(2016) noted that the integration of Guyana and Suriname in the South American context is understudied and that one of the reasons is that these countries do not fit into the classical chronology of other South American countries. For these countries, which historically have been in closer contact with their ex-metropoles (the United Kingdom and the Netherlands, respectively) and with other European countries, UNASUR is an avenue toward integration with the continent.[38]

The Caribbean region, of which both these states are also members, has recognized the importance of emerging markets, and there is a mutuality of interest among Caribbean and South American states. Among the emerging markets, Caribbean countries have turned especially to Brazil, Venezuela, and China. Brazil and Venezuela are active in the region and to some extent rival each other for influence. Brazil has opened a number of diplomatic missions throughout the region and has offered financial and technical assistance to Caribbean states over the last two decades—a significant part of this assistance has been focused on Guyana and Suriname.

Guyana and Suriname have ratified the UNASUR Treaty and stand to benefit from assistance with regard to trans-national crime, climate change, and energy security, provided that CARICOM appropriately reforms its governance structure and develops a strategic agenda. The potential of Guyana and Suriname to act as bridges between UNASUR and CARICOM depends upon the evolution of geopolitical dynamics in the region and on the role of other groupings, including the Community of Latin American and Caribbean States (CELAC).

Political perceptions are that Suriname's participation in regional "blocs" may be a win-win situation, since Guyana and Suriname are able to both defend the interests of relatively small Caribbean economies and bring CARICOM and UNASUR closer together. Lima (2017) observes Suriname's propensity to advance in the processes of regional integration even while identifying more closely with the Caribbean. Regional integration is a priority of Suriname's foreign policy agenda; the Surinamese government believes that a successful approach to contemporary issues must include cooperation in a wider context. Regional integration is thus seen as active participation in a forum from which answers can be found for issues that cross boundaries and require common interest, and where concerted efforts may result in actions that have broad support. As such, regional integration is an instrument for national development, which thrives best in its own environment and can take place in various ways, including political, economic, cultural, and technical.[39]

As for the region, particular thought must be given to the roles of small countries such as Suriname, and the opportunities available to acknowledge their status as small and vulnerable states. Suriname, like many countries in the region, has a small and open economy, and will, in its pursuit of economies of scale, initiate strategic associations in order to increase access to export markets, technological innovation, external financing, and the provision of special and differential treatment. Partly in the light of this, further diversification of bilateral/regional relations and/or rationalization of existing relationships, has become an imperative aspect of foreign policy. Research points to the need to include the social element in the regional integration agenda of Suriname since some social ills are inherently cross-border challenges, and are exacerbated or facilitated by regional developments. Regional rules can improve collective management, while pulling together knowledge and material resources reduces transaction costs. One aspect of this is that domestic politics has become more closely interrelated to regional normative and policy outcomes.[40]

As continental countries, Guyana and Suriname can potentially benefit from improved regional infrastructure, environmental management, and human security, as well as gain from access to much of the larger market for goods, services, and investment that UNASUR offers. As the north-eastern part of Brazil develops and attempts to forge new links with Guyana and Suriname, there is every incentive for these two countries to participate in UNASUR.[41] Although physically part of South America, Suriname lacks significant infrastructural links to its neighbors. Surrounded by dense rainforest, it is accessible only by ferry from either Guyana on one side, or French Guiana on the other, while its border with Brazil remains virtually undeveloped.[42] Suriname is the country with the lowest number of projects in the Initiative for the Integration of Regional Infrastructure in South America (IIRSA) portfolio, followed by Guyana, although it forms part of the interconnection of the eastern part of Venezuela with the Northern part of Brazil.[43]

During its chairmanship of UNASUR, Suriname placed issues related to young people in South America on the agenda of the Heads of State, and more attention was paid to the establishment of consultative bodies of young people in the member countries. In August 2014 a declaration was adopted by the twelve member countries under the leadership of Suriname: this resulted in, among other things, the establishment of a working group on youth, the appointment of a permanent representative of youth/young people within the UNASUR Secretariat; and creation of a strategic action plan on youth policy.[44] The establishment of the Working Group of UNASUR High Youth Authorities can be regarded as a contribution of Suriname toward regional social policy. The working group leads the process of the youth policy formulation at UNASUR and also has influence in social development policy formulation, especially in the area of social security, health, and education.

The Proposal from Suriname on establishing a permanent UNASUR Youth Body was formally presented to the secretary general during his official visit to Suriname in 2015,[45] and the ultimate goal was the creation of a Youth Council in UNASUR. Although Suriname's minister of social affairs and public housing chaired the CSDS during the period of Suriname's pro tempore chairmanship, Suriname's government felt that the UNASUR decision-making process was slow, resulting in delays in the implementation of its social agenda. Suriname was dissatisfied with UNASUR's effectiveness and advocated for more diligence, while stressing that a change of attitude is needed in the organization. That change, it was argued, should result in member countries providing more impetus for the implementation of social programs.[46]

Suriname's Development Plan 2012–2016 (Ontwikkelingsplan (OP) 2012–2016), includes the following main goals on social development: poverty and access to public services, health care, and social security.[47] The Development Plan places emphasis on building national capabilities in achieving national development goals. It also indicates that social development and social inclusion will be achieved through a "social agreement" with all social partners and the people of Suriname, based on solidarity, mutual respect, and understanding.[48] Suriname's membership in UNASUR may provide avenues through which to achieve these national development goals.

It must be noted, however, that limited capacity and resources have constrained the country in participating fully in all the activities of the UNASUR. Suriname has not yet filled the post of permanent representative at UNASUR, and this limits engagement with the substantive work being conducted by the organization, as each permanent representative is assigned a portfolio, and leads and coordinates the efforts of the organization in the designated area. Another consequence for the country is that it faces challenges in keeping pace with the processes taking place in the organization, and as such, often does not contribute fully in the strategic decision-making process. Bearing in mind that Suriname has limited financial and human resources, it faces challenges in participating in technical working groups and committee meetings, which prohibits the country from benefiting from all the opportunities that the organization offers.

The eradication of poverty at national levels demands an integrated approach and should be a joint effort between government, civil society, and the private sector, while curbing inequality requires the development of a fully comprehensive public policy aimed at bridging the huge gaps between the different strata within societies.[49] UNASUR has no regional legal system which enables individuals to claim social rights. Neither are there regional mechanisms that give citizens a voice with which to challenge their governments in terms of social rights. Thus far, UNASUR remains largely an intergovernmental organization, and social policy is delivered through intergovernmental cooperation.

Although the treaty gives UNASUR legal personality and the capacity to adopt binding measures, a consensus must always be reached before they do so. This is often a challenging task given the intergovernmental nature of the organization, which prescribes that all decisions taken by its governing bodies are obligatory only after being passed by each member's internal legislative body.[50] The principles of national sovereignty, non-interference in internal affairs, and self-determination of the people are guaranteed, and Suriname is strongly ascribed to these principles, as clearly confirmed by its Minister of Foreign Affairs.[51]

Through the Council of Head of States, the Council of Ministry of Foreign Affairs, the Council of Delegates, and specifically, via representatives at the CSDS, members states could influence and direct UNASUR's social agenda and advocate for social policy to receive the highest political attention. In the current political climate with the emergence of new political leadership with right-leaning orientation in countries such as Brazil and Argentina, which are the main financial contributors of UNASUR, it will be a significant challenge to sustain social policy as a key element of the regional agenda.

CONCLUDING NOTES

"Integration has costs, and demands compromises (thus losers and winners) that make it very difficult."[52] President Morales of Bolivia, as pro tempore chair of UNASUR, argued that all countries should, despite differences of ideological nature put "integration first" while echoing that the best contribution leaders could give is to "integrate with social policies, not only by respecting human rights and collective rights, but also by working for South American and universal citizenship."[53] UNASUR's social integration process has a short history but demonstrates clear intentions in addressing social issues with the involvement of all member countries. It is important to note that this is done in the absence of a permanent executive capacity and structure, with the exception of ISAGS in the case of health.

The former secretary general of UNASUR, Samper, has stated that in the social area the basic problems are not only the reduction of poverty, but also the reduction of inequalities, given that South America "is an unequal region"; therefore, the task remains to find concrete formulas for reducing that inequality which manifests itself among different social classes, between urban and rural, and in matters of race and gender.[54]

Social development and social policy considerations have gained attention and will remain prominent in the debate about regionalism as countries attempt to address increasing poverty, unemployment, and social inequality. Particularly since the 1990s, there has been a growing consensus that, in an increasingly globalized world, new political thinking and new kinds of policies are necessary to achieve socially equitable development. Contemporary forms of regionalism have been linked to the issue of the extent to which regional integration can promote social development. In South America, regionalism may be in the process of "catching up" with social concerns and represents a comprehensive process which includes "trade and economic integration, but also addresses the environment, social policy, security and democracy, including the whole issue of accountability and legitimacy."[55] According to Da Motta Veiga and Rios (2007) and Sanahuja (2010), regional agreement should be used to further endogenous economic development and should be committed to fostering agreements cantered on development and equity issues.

UNASUR has been seen as a catalyst for social mobilization, activism of civil society actors, and the promotion of a process of regional integration in South America.[56] However, as UNASUR remains largely an intergovernmental organization, social policy is delivered through a full consensus-based decision-making process which is an impediment of the aspired efficiency and progress.

The change in power in Brazil and Argentina as main sponsors of UNASUR, with the elections of President Bolsanaro and President Macri, clearly has its impact on the future of the organization and its social policy. Both Brazil and Argentina are experiencing challenges regarding their economies, and this combined with their political ideologies has a bearing on their regional orientation.

It remains to be seen if, given the lack of resources, but with willingness and capacities, UNASUR—at least what remains of it—will succeed in keeping the social agenda high on its list of priorities for regional cooperation.[57]

The fact that social ills are still widely present on the South American continent lends some weight to the idea that at a regional level the focus will not be easily diverted from addressing poverty and inequality: hopefully these issues will continue to receive the highest political attention in the regional integration process.

NOTES

1. DW. "South America leaders form Prosur to replace defunct Unasur bloc." *DW*, March 23, 2019. Accessed May 1, 2019. https://www.dw.com/en/south-america -leaders-form-prosur-to replace-defunct-unasur-bloc/a-48034988.

2. Americas Quarterly. "South America's Prosur: The Answer to a Question Nobody Asked." *Americas Quarterly,* February 26, 2009. Assessed May 2, 2019. https://www.americasquarterly.org/content/south-americas-prosur-answer-question-nobody-asked.

3. Latin America Reports. "Chilean president proposes Venezuela-less alternative to UNASUR: Piñera cites excessive ideology as the reason why Latin America needs a new union." *Latin America Reports,* February 21, 2019. Accessed May 15, 2019. https://latinamericareports.com/pinera-proposes-venezuela-less-prosur-as-alternative-to-unasur-failure/1192/.

4. DW. "South America leaders form Prosur to replace defunct Unasur bloc." *DW,* March 23, 2019. Accessed May 1, 2019. https://www.dw.com/en/south-america-leaders-form-prosur-to-replace-defunct-unasur-bloc/a-48034988.

5. Luk van Langenhove. *Building Regions. The Regionalisation of World Order.* London: Routledge, 2011.

6. Soren Dosenrode. "On Regional Integration." In *Limits to Regional Integration,* edited by Soren Dosenrode, 1–16. United Kingdom: Taylor & Francis Ltd, 2015.

7. Emanuel Adler, and Michael Barnett. "Framework for the Study of Security Communities ." In *Security Communities,* edited by E. Adler and M. Barnett, 29–66. Cambridge: Cambridge University Press, 1998; Katzenstein, Peter. *A World of Regions: Asia and Europe in the American Imperium .* Cornell: Cornell University Press, 2005; Hurrell, Andrew. "Regionalism in Theoretical Perspective." In *Regionalism in World Politics: Regional Organisation and International Order,* edited by Andrew L. Fawcett and A. Hurrell, 37–73. Oxford: Oxford University Press, 1995.

8. Pia Riggirozzi. "Region, Regionnnes and Regionalism in Latin America: Towards a New Synthesis." Domumento de Trabajo #54, Area de Relaciones Internationalis, FLASCO, Buenos Aires, Argentina, 2010.

9. UNU-CRIS. "Deepening the Social Dimension of Regional Integration: An Overview of Recent Trends and Future Challenges in the Light of the World Commission on the Social Dimension of Globalisation." Ills Discussion Paper, ILO, Geneva, 2008.

10. C. Lewis, and P. Lloyd-Sherlock. "Social Policy and Economic Development in South America: An Historical Approach to Social Insurance." *Economy and Society* 38 (2009): 109–131.

11. Jean Grugel, and Pia Riggirozzi. "Post-neoliberalism in Latin America: rebuilding and reclaiming the state after crisis." *Development and Change* 43 (1) (2012): 1–21.

12. Pia Riggirozzi. "Regionalism through Social Policy: Collective Action and Health Diplomacy in South America." *Economy and Society.* University of Southampton, 2014: 432–454. Accessed 18 January, 2014.; Yeates, Nicola. "Globalisation and Social Policy: From Global Neoliberal Hegemony to Global Political Pluralism." *Global Social Policy* 2 (1) (2002): 69–91.

13. Valéria Pero, and Dimitri Szerman. "The New Generation of Social Programs in Brazil." In *Conditional Cash Transfers in Latin America,,* edited by Michelle Adato and John Hoddinott, 78–100. Baltimore: The Johns Hopkins University Press, 2010.

14. Pia Riggirozzi. "Regionalism through Social Policy: Collective Action and Health Diplomacy in South America." *Economy and Society.* University of Southampton, 2014: 432–454. Accessed 18 January, 2014.

15. Mónica Hirst. "América Latina: Méritos del Regionalismo Anárquico." 2009. Accessed October 19, 2016. http://edant.clarin.com/diario/2009/10/05/opinion/o-020 12303.htm.

16. Maribel Aponte García. "La Teorización del Nuevo Regionalismo Estratégico en el ALBA-TCP." In *El ALBA-TCP Origen y Fruto del Noevo Regionalismo Latinoamericano y Caribeno*, edited by Maribel Aponte García and Gloria Amézquita Puntiel, 25–68. Buenos Aires: CLACSO, 2015.

17. Maribel Aponte García. "La Alianza Bolivariana como Modelo Alternativo de Producción y Empresas, Integración Regional y Desarrollo Endógeno con Inclusión Social: El Caso de la Integración Petrolera." In *Los Retos de la Integración y América del Sur*, edited by Carlos Eduardo Martins, 253–282. Buenos Aires: CLACSO, 2013.

18. CEPAL. "Social Panorama of Latin America 2017," 2017. Accessed April 10, 2019. URL: https://repositorio.cepal.org/bitstream/handle/11362/42717/6/S1800001e n.pdf.

19. CEPAL. "Poverty Increased in 2016 in Latin America and Reached 30.7% of the Population, a Percentage Seen Holding Steady in 2017." *CEPAL*, December 20, 2017 (b). Accessed April 25, 2019. https://www.cepal.org/en/pressreleases/poverty -increased-2016-latin-america-and-reached-307-population-percentage-seen.

20. Alicia Barcena. *Estancada: la Reduccion de la Pobreza e Indigencia en America Latina*. Santiago de Chile: CEPAL, 2016.

21. Stephan Clarkson, and Steffen Hindelang. "How Parallel Lines Intersect: Investor-State Dispute Settlement and Regional Social Policies." In *Regional Organisations and Social Policy in Europe and Latin America*, edited by Andrea C. Bianculli and Andrea Ribeiro Hoffmann, 25–45. London, UK: Palgrave Macmillan, 2016.

22. Pía Riggirozzi. "Regionalism through Social Policy: Collective Action and Health Diplomacy in South America." *Economy and Society*. University of Southampton, 2014: 432–454. Accessed 18 January, 2014; Nicola Yeates. "Globalisation and Social Policy: From Global Neoliberal Hegemony to Global Political Pluralism." *Global Social Policy* 2 (1) (2002): 69–91.

23. Javier Fernando Luchetti. "Political Dialogue in South America: The Role of South American Nations Union." In *Limits to Regional Integration*, edited by Soren Dosenrode, 95–108. United Kingdom: Taylor & Francis Ltd, 2015.

24. UNASUR."Documentos Normativos UNASUR." 2016. Accessed August 28, 2016. http://www.unasursg.org/documentos-normativos-unasur; UNASUR. "Tratado Constitutivo." 2014. Accessed January 20, 2014. http://www.unasursg.org/uploads/0c/ c7/0cc721468628d65c3c510a577e54519d/Tratado-constitutivo-english-version.pdf.

25. Ruben S. Martoredjo. "Regionalism and social policy in UNASUR: Widening the application of the Latin American model of Conditional Cash Transfer: A case of Suriname." PhD diss., University of the West Indies, 2017.

26. Ruben S. Martoredjo. "Regionalism and social policy in UNASUR: Widening the application of the Latin American model of Conditional Cash Transfer: A case of Suriname." PhD diss., University of the West Indies, 2017.

27. Ruben S. Martoredjo. "Regionalism and social policy in UNASUR: Widening the application of the Latin American model of Conditional Cash Transfer: A case of Suriname." PhD diss., University of the West Indies, 2017.

28. UNASUR. *South American Council of Social Development Action Plan 2015-2017.* Quito, Ecuador: UNASUR, 2015.

29. ISAGS (Instituto Suramericano de Gobierno en Salud). "South American Council on Social Development." 2013. Accessed November 30, 2013. http://www .isags-unasursalud.org/interna.asp?lang=2&idArea=38.

30. Ruben S. Martoredjo. "Regionalism and social policy in UNASUR: Widening the application of the Latin American model of Conditional Cash Transfer: A case of Suriname." PhD diss., University of the West Indies, 2017.

31. Ruben S. Martoredjo. "Regionalism and social policy in UNASUR: Widening the application of the Latin American model of Conditional Cash Transfer: A case of Suriname." PhD diss., University of the West Indies, 2017.

32. UNASUR. "UNASUR Common Initiatives Fund." 2016. Accessed October 16, 2016. http://www.unasursg.org/en/unasur-common-initiatives-fund.

33. UNASUR. "Tratado Constitutivo." 2014. Accessed January 20, 2014. http:// www.unasursg.org/uploads/0c/c7/0cc721468628d65c3c510a577e54519d/Tratado-constitutivo-english-version.pdf.

34. UNASUR-ISAGS. "UNASUR and regional integration in Health." *UNASUR-ISAGS,* May 23, 2018. Accessed April 23, 2019. http://isags-unasur.org/en/unasur-and-regional-integration-in-health/.

35. UNASUR, CSDS-ISAGS. *Mapping of Conditional Cash Transfer Policies in Member States of the Union of South American Nations (UNASUR).* Assessment Report, Rio de Janeiro: South American Health Council, 2016.

36. Ruben S. Martoredjo. "Regionalism and social policy in UNASUR: Widening the application of the Latin American model of Conditional Cash Transfer: A case of Suriname." PhD diss., University of the West Indies, 2017.

37. Ruben S. Martoredjo, Jennifer Olivieira, and Youandi Berrenstein. "Las relaciones entre Cuba y Surinam: dimensión política y cooperación Sur-Sur." In *Cuba en sus relaciones con el resto del Caribe: Continuidades y rupturas tras el restablecimiento de las relaciones diplomáticas entre Cuba y los Estados Unidos,* edited by Jaqueline Laguardia Martínez, 161–182. Buenos Aires, CLACSO, 2017.

38. Javier Fernando Luchetti. "Political Dialogue in South America: The Role of South American Nations Union." In *Limits to Regional Integration,* edited by Soren Dosenrode, 95–108. United Kingdom: Taylor & Francis Ltd, 2015.

39. Government of Suriname. "Integratie in de Regio." 2014. Accessed June 21, 2014. http://gov.sr/sr/ministerie-van-buza/onderwerpen/onderwerp.aspx? subjectId=10060&subject=Integratie%20in%20de%20regio.; Suriname. Government. "President Bouterse Doet Verslag Over UNASUR Voorzitterschap Suriname." 2014. Accessed December 12, 2014. http://gov.sr/sr/actueel/president-bouterse-doet-verslag-over-unasur-voorzitterschap-suriname-(1).aspx.

40. Ruben S. Martoredjo. "Regionalism and social policy in UNASUR: Widening the application of the Latin American model of Conditional Cash Transfer: A case of Suriname." PhD diss., University of the West Indies, 2017.

41. Ralph Henry. "Caribbean Development Report: Macroeconomic Policy for Structural Transformation and Social Protection in Small States." Caribbean Development Report LC/CAR/L.411, UNECLAC, Port of Spain, 2013.

42. Anneke Jessen, and Andrew Katona. *Breaking from Isolation: Suriname's Participation in Regional Integration Initiatives.* Intal ITD-STA, Occasional Paper 10, Washington: IDB, 2001.

43. Suely A. De Lima. "Guiana e Suriname na integracao da America Do Sul." *RELEA* 2 (1) (2017): 51–74.

44. Government of Suriname. "Suriname Langer Voorzitter van Unie van Zuid-Amerikaanse Naties (UNASUR)." 2014. Accessed December 22, 2014. http://gov.sr/sr/ministerie-van-buza/actueel/suriname-langer-voorzitter-van-unie-van-zuid-amerikaanse-naties-(unasur).aspx.

45. De West. "UNASUR Jeugdraad krijgt Meer Gestalte." *De West*, January 19, 2015.

46. Suriname Times. "Amafo Geeft UNASUR Sneer Voor Slappe Afhandeling Sociale Agenda" *Suriname Times,* Augustus 14, 2014. Accessed October 6, 2016. http://www.surinametimes.com/amafo-geeft-unasur-sneer-voor-slappe-afhandeling-sociale-agenda/.

47. IDB (Inter-American Development Bank). *Country Programme Evaluation—Suriname—2011-2015.* Washington: IDB, 2016.

48. Government of Suriname. "Statement by The Outgoing Chairman of The Caribbean Community H.E. Desire D. Bouterse, President of The Republic of Suriname." Statement on The Occasion of the 33rd Regular Meeting of The Conference of The Heads of Government, Castries, St. Lucia, July 4, 2012.

49. Ruben S. Martoredjo. "Regionalism and Social Policy in UNASUR: Addressing Inequality." Paper presented at Seminar: Analysing Current Issues in the Changing Hemispheric Environment. LIRDS Think Tank and UWI IIR. Georgetown, Guyana, 11 April, 2014.; Martoredjo, Ruben S. "Regionalism and social policy in UNASUR: Widening the application of the Latin American model of Conditional Cash Transfer: A case of Suriname." PhD diss., University of the West Indies, 2017.

50. José Antonio Sanahuja. "Post-Liberal Regionalism in South America: The Case of UNASUR." EUI Working Papers, RSCAS 2012/05, Robert Schuman Centre For Advanced Studies, 2012. http://hdl.handle.net/1814/20394.

51. De Waretijd Online. "Suriname tegen militaire invasie Venezuela." *De Waretijd Online,* September 18, 2018. Accessed May 21, 2019. http://www.dwtonline.com/laatste-nieuws/2018/09/18/suriname-tegen-militaire-invasie-venezuela/.

52. Latin American Post. "Unasur is in crisis: why are their projects stagnating?" *Latin American Post*, November 03, 2018. Accessed May 1, 2019. https://latinamericanpost.com/24363-unasur-is-in-crisis-why-are-their-projects-stagnating.

53. Colombia Reports. Colombia to withdraw from Unasur; South America split over Venezuela. *Colombia Reports*, August 10, 2018. Accessed April 1, 2019. https://colombiareports.com/colombia-to-withdraw-from-unasur-south-america-split-over-venezuela/.

54. Latino Foxnews. "Rousseff and Samper want UNASUR to be More Active in Social Sector." *Latino Foxnews.* November 10, 2014. Accessed August twelve, 2015.

55. Mark Kirton. "UNASUR in the Context of a Changing Regional Environment: Prospects and Challenges." In *Comparative Regionalisms for Development in the 21st Century—Insights from the Global South,* edited by Timothy M. Shaw, Vanessa T. Tang, and Emmanuel Fanta, 57–69. Farnham: Ashgate Publishing Limited, 2013.

56. Bob Deacon, Maria Cristina Macovei, Luk van Langenhove and Nicola Yeates. *World-Regional Social Policy and Global Governance: New Research and Policy Agendas in Africa, Asia, Europe and Latin America.* Oxon: Routledge, 2010; Deacon, Bob, Isabel Ortiz, and Sergey Zelenev. "Regional Social Policy." Working Paper No. 37., UNDESA, New York, 2007.

57. Bob Deacon, Maria Cristina Macovei, Luk van Langenhove and Nicola Yeates. *World-Regional Social Policy and Global Governance: New Research and Policy Agendas in Africa, Asia, Europe and Latin America.* Oxon: Routledge, 2010; Deacon, Bob, Isabel Ortiz, and Sergey Zelenev. "Regional Social Policy." Working Paper No. 37., UNDESA, New York, 2007; Bianculli, Andrea C., and Andrea Ribeiro Hoffmann. "Regional Organisations and Social Policy in Comparative Perspective." In *Regional Organisations and Social Policy in Europe and Latin America*, edited by Andrea C. Bianculli and Andrea Ribeiro Hoffmann, 291–307. London, UK: Palgrave Macmillan, 2016.

REFERENCES

Adler, Emanuel, and Michael Barnett. "Framework for the Study of Security Communities." In *Security Communities*, edited by E. Adler and M. Barnett, 29–66. Cambridge: Cambridge University Press, 1998.

Americas Quarterly. "South America's Prosur: The Answer to a Question Nobody Asked." *Americas Quarterly,* February 26, 2009. Assessed May 2, 2019. https ://www.americasquarterly.org/content/south-americas-prosur-answer-question-nobody-asked.

Barcena Alicia. *Estancada: la Reduccion de la Pobreza e Indigencia en America Latina.* Santiago de Chile: CEPAL, 2016.

Bianculli, Andrea C., and Andrea Ribeiro Hoffmann. "Regional Organisations and Social Policy in Comparative Perspective." In *Regional Organisations and Social Policy in Europe and Latin America*, edited by Andrea C. Bianculli and Andrea Ribeiro Hoffmann, 291–307. London, UK: Palgrave Macmillan, 2016.

Cavlak, Iuri. *Breve História da Guiana.* Rio de Janeiro: Autografia; Macapá: UNIFAP, 2016.

CEPAL. "Social Panorama of Latin America 2017." 2017 (a). Accessed April 10, 2019. URL: https://repositorio.cepal.org/bitstream/handle/11362/42717/6/S180 0001_en.pdf.

———. "Poverty Increased in 2016 in Latin America and Reached 30.7% of the Population, a Percentage Seen Holding Steady in 2017." *CEPAL*, December 20, 2017 (b). Accessed April 25, 2019. https://www.cepal.org/en/pressreleases/povert y-increased-2016-latin-america-and-reached-307-population-percentage-seen.

Clarkson, Stephan, and Steffen Hindelang. "How Parallel Lines Intersect: Investor-State Dispute Settlement and Regional Social Policies." In *Regional Organisations and Social Policy in Europe and Latin America*, edited by Andrea C. Bianculli and Andrea Ribeiro Hoffmann, 25–45. London, UK: Palgrave Macmillan, 2016.

Colombia Reports. Colombia to withdraw from Unasur; South America split over Venezuela. *Colombia Reports*, August 10, 2018. Accessed April 1, 2019. https

://colombiareports.com/colombia-to-withdraw-from-unasur-south-america-split
-over-venezuela/.

Comunidad Andina. "Tratado Constitutivo de la Union de Naciones Sudamericanas."
2013. Accessed December 20, 2013. http://www.comunidadandina.org/unasur/
tratado_constitutivo.htm.

Da Motta Veiga, P., and S. Rios. *O Regionalismo Pos-Liberal, na America do Sul:
Origens, Iniciativas e Dilemas.* Santiago de Chile: CEPAL, 2007.

Deacon, Bob, Maria Cristina Macovei, Luk van Langenhove and Nicola Yeates.
*World-Regional Social Policy and Global Governance: New Research and Policy
Agendas in Africa, Asia, Europe and Latin America.* Oxon: Routledge, 2010.

Deacon, Bob, Isabel Ortiz, and Sergey Zelenev. "Regional Social Policy." Working
Paper No. 37., UNDESA, New York, 2007.

De Waretijd Online. "Suriname tegen militaire invasie Venezuela." *De Waretijd
Online,* September 18, 2018. Accessed May 21, 2019. http://www.dwtonline.com/
laatste-nieuws/2018/09/18/suriname-tegen-militaire-invasie-venezuela/.

De West. "UNASUR Jeugdraad krijgt Meer Gestalte." *De West,* January 19, 2015.

Dosenrode, Soren. "On Regional Integration." In *Limits to Regional Integration,*
edited by Soren Dosenrode, 1–16. United Kingdom: Taylor & Francis Ltd, 2015.

DW. "South America leaders form Prosur to replace defunct Unasur bloc." *DW,*
March 23, 2019. Accessed May 1, 2019. https://www.dw.com/en/south-america
-leaders-form-prosur-to-replace-defunct-unasur-bloc/a-48034988.

Fawcett, Louise. "The History and Concept of Regionalism." Conference Paper Series,
No. 4/2012 Florence, Italy: European Society of International Law (ESIL), 2012.

García, Maribel Aponte. "La Alianza Bolivariana como Modelo Alternativo de
Producción y Empresas, Integración Regional y Desarrollo Endógeno con Inclusión
Social: El Caso de la Integración Petrolera." In *Los Retos de la Integración y
América del Sur,* edited by Carlos Eduardo Martins, 253–282. Buenos Aires:
CLACSO, 2013.

———. "La Teorización del Nuevo Regionalismo Estratégico en el ALBA-TCP."
In *El ALBA-TCP Origen y Fruto del Noevo Regionalismo Latinoamericano y
Caribeno,* edited by Maribel Aponte García and Gloria Amézquita Puntiel, 25–68.
Buenos Aires: CLACSO, 2015.

Grugel, Jean, and Pia Riggirozzi. "Post-neoliberalism in Latin America: Rebuilding
and Reclaiming the State after Crisis." *Development and Change* 43 (1) (2012):
1–21.

Henry, Ralph. "Caribbean Development Report: Macroeconomic Policy for Structural
Transformation and Social Protection in Small States." Caribbean Development
Report LC/CAR/L.411, UNECLAC, Port of Spain, 2013.

Hirst, Mónica. "América Latina: Méritos del Regionalismo Anárquico." 2009.
Accessed October 19, 2016. http://edant.clarin.com/diario/2009/10/05/opinion/
o-02012303.htm.

Hurrell, Andrew. "Regionalism in Theoretical Perspective." In *Regionalism in World
Politics: Regional Organisation and International Order,* edited by Andrew L.
Fawcett and A. Hurrell, 37–73. Oxford: Oxford University Press, 1995.

IDB (Inter-American Development Bank). *Country Programme Evaluation—
Suriname—2011-2015.* Washington: IDB, 2016.

ISAGS (Instituto Suramericano de Gobierno en Salud). "South American Council on Social Development." 2013. Accessed November 30, 2013. http://www.isags-unasursalud.org/interna.asp?lang=2&idArea=38.

Jamaica Observer. "Countries protest appointment of new Venezuelan representative at OAS." *Jamaica Observer* April 25, 2019. Accessed May 1, 2019. https://www.jamaicaobserver.com/news/countries-protest-appointment-of-new-venezuelan-representative-at-oas_163073?profile=1373.

Jessen, Anneke, and Andrew Katona. *Breaking from Isolation: Suriname's Participation in Regional Integration Initiatives.* Intal ITD-STA, Occasional Paper 10, Washington: IDB, 2001.

Katzenstein, Peter. *A World of Regions: Asia and Europe in the American Imperium.* Cornell: Cornell University Press, 2005.

Kirton, Mark. "UNASUR in the Context of a Changing Regional Environment: Prospects and Challenges." In *Comparative Regionalisms for Development in the 21st Century - Insights from the Global South*, edited by Timothy M. Shaw, Vanessa T. Tang, and Emmanuel Fanta, 57–69. Farnham: Ashgate Publishing Limited, 2013.

Langenhove, Luk van. *Building Regions. The Regionalisation of World Order.* London: Routledge, 2011.

Langenhove, Luk van, and Stephen Kingah. "Conditions for Effective Regional Social (Health) Policies: The EU and Unasur Compared." In *In Regional Organisations and Social Policy in Europe and Latin America*, edited by Andrea C. Bianculli and Andrea Ribeiro Hoffmann, 231–250. London, UK: Palgrave Macmillan, 2016.

Latin American Post. "Unasur is in crisis: why are their projects stagnating?" *Latin American Post*, November 03, 2018. Accessed May 1, 2019. https://latinamericanpost.com/24363-unasur-is-in-crisis-why-are-their-projects-stagnating.

Latin America Reports. "Chilean president proposes Venezuela-less alternative to UNASUR: Piñera cites excessive ideology as the reason why Latin America needs a new union." *Latin America Reports,* February 21, 2019. Accessed May 15, 2019. https://latinamericareports.com/pinera-proposes-venezuela-less-prosur-as-alternative-to-unasur-failure/1192/.

Latino Foxnews. "Rousseff and Samper want UNASUR to be More Active in Social Sector." *Latino Foxnews.* November 10, 2014. Accessed August twelve, 2015. http://latino.foxnews.com/latino/politics/2014/11/10/rousseff-samper-want-unasur-to-be-more-active-in-social-sector/.

Lewis, C., and P. Lloyd-Sherlock. "Social Policy and Economic Development in South America: An Historical Approach to Social Insurance." *Economy and Society* 38 (2009): 109–131.

Lima, Suely A. De. "Guiana e Suriname na integracao da America Do Sul." *RELEA* 2 (1) (2017): 51–74.

Luchetti, Javier Fernando. "Political Dialogue in South America: The Role of South American Nations Union." In *Limits to Regional Integration*, edited by Soren Dosenrode, 95–108. United Kingdom: Taylor & Francis Ltd, 2015.

Martoredjo, Ruben S. "Regionalism and Social Policy in UNASUR: Addressing Inequality." Paper presented at Seminar: Analysing Current Issues in the Changing Hemispheric Environment. LIRDS Think Tank and UWI IIR. Georgetown, Guyana, 11 April 2014.

Martoredjo, Ruben S. "Regionalism and social policy in UNASUR: Widening the application of the Latin American model of Conditional Cash Transfer: A case of Suriname." PhD diss., University of the West Indies, 2017.

Martoredjo, Ruben S., Jennifer Olivieira, and Youandi Berrenstein. "Las relaciones entre Cuba y Surinam: dimensión política y cooperación Sur-Sur." In *Cuba en sus relaciones con el resto del Caribe: Continuidades y rupturas tras el restablecimiento de las relaciones diplomáticas entre Cuba y los Estados Unidos,* edited by Jaqueline Laguardia Martínez, 161–182. Buenos Aires, CLACSO, 2017.

Medeiros, Marcelo de Almeida, Ella Elisa Cia Alves, Ivan Filipe Fernandes, and Marcelo Eduardo Alves da Silva. "Funding Social Policy at the Regional Level: The Development Bank of Latin America (CAF) and Social Policy in Bolivia." In *Regional Organisations and Social Policy in Europe and Latin America*, edited by Andrea C. Bianculli and Andrea Ribeiro Hoffmann, 46–71. London, UK: Palgrave Macmillan, 2016.

OAS. "Special Meeting of the Permanent Council. April 9th, 2019." *OAS Videos— Events* April 9, 2019. Accessed April 10, 2019. https://www.youtube.com/watch? v=hxDBBWJaNjk&feature=youtu.be.

Pero, Valéria, and Dimitri Szerman. "The New Generation of Social Programs in Brazil." In *Conditional Cash Transfers in Latin America,*, edited by Michelle Adato and John Hoddinott, 78–100. Baltimore: The Johns Hopkins University Press, 2010.

Riggirozzi, Pia. "Region, Regionnnes and Regionalism in Latin America: Towards a New Synthysis." Domumento de Trabajo #54, Area de Relaciones Internationalis, FLASCO, Buenos Aires, Argentina, 2010.

———. "Regionalism through Social Policy: Collective Action and Health Diplomacy in South America." *Economy and Society*. University of Southampton, 2014: 432–454. Accessed 18 January 2014.

———. http://www.southampton.ac.uk/C2G2/media/2012%20Discussion%20Papers /Riggirozzi%20(2012).pdf.

Riggirozzi, Pía, and Jean Grugel. "Regional Governance and Legitimacy in South America: the meaning of UNASUR." *International Affairs* 91 (4) (2015): 781–797.

———. "Políticas de Salud en UNASUR: Legitimidad, Democracia y Legitimidad de Resultado." *Pensamiento Propio* 43 (2016): 173–200.

Sanahuja, José Antonio. "Del Regionalismo Abierto' al 'Regionalismo Post-Liberal.' Crisis y Cambio en La Integracion Latinoamericana." *Anuario de la Integracion Regional en America Latina y el Gran Caribe* 7 (2010): 11–53.

———. "Post-Liberal Regionalism in South America: The Case of UNASUR." EUI Working Papers, RSCAS 2012/05, Robert Schuman Centre For Advanced Studies, 2012. http://hdl.handle.net/1814/20394.

Suriname. Government. "Statement by The Outgoing Chairman of The Caribbean Community H.E. Desire D. Bouterse, President of The Republic of Suriname." Statement on The Occasion of the 33rd Regular Meeting of The Conference of The Heads of Government, Castries, St. Lucia, July 4, 2012.

———. "Integratie in de Regio." 2014. Accessed June 21, 2014. http://gov.sr/ sr/ministerie-van-buza/onderwerpen/onderwerp.aspx?subjectId=10060&subject= Integratie%20in% 20de%20regio.

————. "President Bouterse Doet Verslag Over UNASUR Voorzitterschap Suriname." 2014. Accessed December 12, 2014. http://gov.sr/sr/actueel/president-bouterse-doet-verslag-over-unasur-voorzitterschap-suriname-(1).aspx.

————. "Suriname Langer Voorzitter van Unie van Zuid-Amerikaanse Naties (UNASUR)." 2014. Accessed December 22, 2014. http://gov.sr/sr/ministerie-van -buza/actueel/suriname-langer-voorzitter-van-unie-van-zuid-amerikaanse-naties-(unasur).aspx.

Suriname Times. "Amafo Geeft UNASUR Sneer Voor Slappe Afhandeling Sociale Agenda" *Suriname Times,* Augustus 14, 2014. Accessed October 6, 2016. http: //www.surinametimes.com/amafo-geeft-unasur-sneer-voor-slappe-afhandeling-sociale-agenda/.

UNASUR. "Documentos Normativos UNASUR." 2016. Accessed August 28, 2016. http://www.unasursg.org/documentos-normativos-unasur.

————. *South American Council of Social Development Action Plan 2015-2017.* Quito, Ecuador: UNASUR, 2015.

————. "Tratado Constitutivo." 2014. Accessed January 20, 2014. http://www.unasursg. org/uploads/0c/c7/0cc721468628d65c3c510a577e54519d/Tratado-constitutivo-english-version.pdf.

————. "UNASUR Common Initiatives Fund." 2016. Accessed October 16, 2016. http://www.unasursg.org/en/unasur-common-initiatives-fund.

UNASUR, CSDS-ISAGS. *Mapping of Conditional Cash Transfer Policies in Member States of the Union of South American Nations (UNASUR).* Assessment Report, Rio de Janeiro: South American Health Council, 2016.

UNASUR-ISAGS. "UNASUR and regional integration in Health." *UNASUR-ISAGS,* May 23, 2018. Accessed April 23, 2019. http://isags-unasur.org/en/unasur-and-regional-integration-in-health/.

UNU-CRIS. "Deepening the Social Dimension of Regional Integration: An Overview of Recent Trends and Future Challenges in the Light of the World Commission on the Social Dimension of Globalisation." Ills Discussion Paper, ILO, Geneva, 2008.

Yeates, Nicola. "Globalisation and Social Policy: From Global Neoliberal Hegemony to Global Political Pluralism." *Global Social Policy* 2 (1) (2002): 69–91.

————. "The Socialisation of Regionalism and Regionalism of Social Policy: Contexts, Imperatives, and Challenges." In *Transformations in Global and Regional Social Policies*, by editors Alexandra Kaash and Paul Stubbs, 17–43. Basingstoke: Palgrave Macmillan, 2014.

Yeates, Nicola, and Pia Riggirozzi. "Global Social Regionalism: Regional Organisations as Social Policy Actors." Paper presented at the Annual Conference of Research Committee 19, International Sociological Association, University of Bath, London, UK, August 26–28, 2015.

Chapter 7

Validating the Dimensions of Human Security Using a Factor-Analytic Procedure

Clement Henry

INTRODUCTION

Traditional security studies have directed significant attention to inter-state conflict and national security with little reflection on security issues related to sub-state actors. National security interests of the state, politico-strategic concerns, diplomacy, military capabilities of states, territorial integrity, and sovereignty are the principal issues to traditional security thinking.[1] Talukder Maniruzzaman, for example, defines security as "protection and preservation of the minimum core values of any nation: political independence and territorial integrity."[2] Bellamy presents security as "relative freedom from war, coupled with a relatively high expectation that defeat will not be a consequence of any war that should occur,"[3] and Giacomo Luciani sees security as the ability of the state to withstand aggression from abroad.[4] This narrow politico-military motif among traditionalists presents misleading and false images of reality.[5] Accordingly, there is a compelling motive for analysts to embrace security concepts that factor in other variables and actors.

An important issue in this analysis is whether the conceptualization of security should be restricted to that of national security. Taylor Owen advances that current and past global realities indicate that state security does not always correlate with security of citizens as there are numerous instances where people have suffered horribly and died because of poverty, hunger, diseases, criminal violence, and environmental disasters even as state structures remain intact.[6] Dominant security knowledge has not only completely neglected non-military threats to human survival but has failed to accommodate changing international contexts in its theorizing; consequently, there is a chasm between conventional understanding of security

131

and existing forms of insecurity. It is now difficult to ignore the heavy toll that non-traditional security challenges[7] have inflicted on human survival prospects. Because non-traditional security challenges have caused so much death, suffering, fear, and immiseration far beyond that associated with inter-state war, scholars have begun to question the utility of a strictly state-centric approach to security analysis and practice. In fact, the conceptualization of security is undergoing a metamorphosis with emerging paradigms analyzing security of the state and its citizens as two distinct, albeit related, phenomena.[8]

Transnational terrorist networks and transnational criminal organizations, for instance, both of which pose grave threats to the security of states and people, cannot be properly analyzed from a narrow state-centric perspective. Thus, a convincing case can be made for security scholars to broaden the range of agents and issues they study under the rubric of security in the light of changing domestic and international security environments. Michael Klare is in-step with this emerging reality as he asserts:

> A fresh assessment of the world security environment suggests that the major international schisms of the twenty-first century will not always be definable in geographic terms. Many of the most severe and persistent threats to global peace and stability are arising not from conflicts between major political entities but from increased discord within states, societies, and civilizations along ethnic, racial, religious, linguistic, caste, or class lines.[9]

It is against this background that the concept of human security—a construct arising out of the United Nations Development Programme (UNDP) and highlighting various vulnerabilities and insecurities that people face in their everyday lives—has emerged. This concept, in giving primacy to individuals and not states, quintessentially represents a fundamental departure from orthodoxy in international relations security analysis, which exclusively positions states as the primary security referent and fundamental unit of analysis.[10]

Predictably, the attempt to introduce a new security referent has resulted in a highly animated debate. Three distinct and seemingly antagonistic schools of thought have emerged. 1: The argument that human security is not a concept that should engage international relations academics because it is too broad, vague, and lacks analytical utility.[11] 2: A minimalist conception of human security focusing on the prevention and protection of individuals from organized violence.[12] 3: A maximalist view of human security encompassing economic security, food security, health security, personal security from violence, societal security, environmental security, and security of political freedoms.[13]

It stands to reason that empirical validation undertaken in this study can potentially provide answers to the current debate. This will be done using confirmatory factor analysis; a procedure that takes a hypothesis-testing approach to the analysis of the underlying structural theory of a phenomenon under study. Utilizing this technique facilitates statistical testing of a hypothesized model to determine the extent to which it is consistent with the data. This determination is made by assessing the adequacy of the goodness-of-fit statistics. Where the goodness-of-fit statistics are adequate, the model affirms the plausibility of the hypothesized relations among variables; if the goodness-of-fit statistics are inadequate, the tenability of such relations is not accepted.[14]

JUSTIFICATION AND SIGNIFICANCE
OF THIS RESEARCH

There are some compelling reasons for undertaking this research on human security. Researching and testing the dimensions of human security are important steps in determining the scope of the concept, facilitating the formulation of a precise definition of the concept, and achieving a more coherent human security practice. The acknowledgment and treatment of human security as a latent construct along with the application of latent variable techniques in validating its multidimensional nature has thus far been absent from research. Instead, researchers have arbitrarily selected and aggregated numerous indicators at the level of the state without robust testing and validation. This research seeks to correct this omission by establishing the multidimensional nature of human security utilizing confirmatory factor analysis, which has been used extensively in social sciences to validate and measure latent constructs using manifest or observable proxies.[15]

As a people-centered approach, the study of human security requires inquiry at the individual level of analysis. Previous researchers of human security have not paid enough attention to testing their views on the dimensionality of human security using data gathered from individuals—the postulated referent object of the concept. What is ironic about customary approaches to measuring human security using national aggregates is that they reinforce the primacy of the state as the unit of analysis. Human security research must therefore assess the concept using the experiences and perceptions of individuals rather than national level aggregates. This will be achieved using survey sampling among the Guyanese population. The possibility of massive natural disasters arising from the effects of climate change, entrenched socio-political issues, political exploitation of ethnic linkages, lack of trust between the major ethnic groups, social and economic exclusion of youths from low-income communities, and crime and insecurity are some of the main issues in Guyana that facilitated the testing of a comprehensive human security concept.

A further justification for undertaking this research is the increasing recognition that the diverse range of security threats facing people, particularly in underdeveloped and developing countries, requires new and innovative analytical instruments given that the solutions to mitigating these threats lie outside the realm of traditional approaches in security and development thinking. It is pertinent at this time to recall Jolly's and Basu Ray's noteworthy observation that human security, when applied within states, is robust in identifying policy measures and actions to tackle serious problems of insecurity of people within the country concerned.[16] It is also important to note Gasper's enlightened outlook that human security is becoming a global language that plays an important role in directing attention to survival challenges individuals face and in problem diagnosis, recognition, response, and evaluation.[17]

The clarification of issues related to the concept of human security requires rigorous empirical testing since it is an effective way of assessing propositional claims and theoretical constructs.[18] Helga Haftendorn proposes that clarification of emerging concepts is subject to critical criteria:

> To clarify our concept of security and to construct an empirically testable paradigm, we must define the "set of observable hypotheses," the "hard core of irrefutable assumptions," and the "set of scope conditions" that according to Lakatos, are required for a progressive research programme that will lead to new facts and explanations.[19]

Hughes, Price, and Marrs[20] concur with this prescription, arguing that a key condition for the advancement of theoretical constructs and the resulting research program is that they survive empirical testing. Braumoelle and Sartori,[21] too, emphasize that quantitative statistical approaches allow researchers to make inferences about reality based on the data and this is immensely useful in evaluating the extent to which the empirical expectations generated by theories are consistent with reality. Indeed, an important utility of quantitative methods is their ability to test two explanations against each other with remarkable precision.

SURVEY OF EMPIRICAL STUDIES

Measurement studies on human security suffer from several shortcomings; four prominent studies highlight this point. Taylor Owen[22] used subnational data to map and spatially analyze human security threats in Cambodia utilizing involved focus interviews with regional and local experts along with secondary data from a range of other sources. Owen's efforts, however, are flawed by the heterogeneous nature of the data used in the analysis raising questions over the consistency of estimates; the issue of selection effect in the choice of experts; and the possibility of experts being deliberately biased in their responses.

Research by James Michel[23] is a second case in point. Michel attempted to create an index of human security using published national-level quantitative data from sources such as the World Bank and the United Nations. He also used community-level data collected through focus interviews, workshops, and observations to get a qualitative grasp of the impact of threats to human security in disadvantaged and marginalized segments of the population. His aggregate index comprised twelve indicators categorized under three broad headings: survival indicators (access to food, access to water, vulnerability to violent conflict, and access to health services), livelihood indicators (access to education, access to income, vulnerability to poverty, and access to electricity), and dignity indicators (voice and accountability, vulnerability to corruption, access to justice, and gender integration). Michel's emphasis on national-level aggregates does little to promote human security scholarship; to the contrary, it reinforces state-centrism. Further, his qualitative inputs into the study limit the comparability of the estimates.

David Hastings,[24] too, created a human security index, which included *inter alia*: societal fairness, physical, social and environmental harmony, individual empowerment based on knowledge, access to trustworthy and supportive information, financial benefits and opportunities, and resources to support a long and healthy life. Hastings' proxy indicators range from gender equality to prison population to fixed telephone lines, and it would be difficult for analysts to find relevance in, for example, fixed telephone lines in light of the ubiquity of mobile phones. When improving the human security score under this approach could mean supplying more landlines or developing a system for alternative sentencing, developing policy approaches to enhance human security based on this computation, would, in many instances, border on the absurd.

Ronald Inglehart and Pippa Norris[25] measured subjective perceptions of human security among "ordinary people" in order to compare perceptions among and within diverse societies worldwide. They reasoned that security perceptions are predicated and shaped by a wide range of cultural values including feelings of well-being and happiness, social trust and tolerance, the strength of religiosity and political orientations, attitudes toward gender equality, and sexual liberalization values. Evidence is drawn from a new battery of survey items designed to monitor perceptions of human security which were included for the first time in the 6th wave of the World Values Survey.

The authors use factor analysis to analyze the data. Constructively, this study offers a valuable foundation for cross-comparability at local, national, and regional levels. However, their adoption of factor analysis as the analytical technique does not facilitate theory testing and measurement.[26]

Considering these gaps and shortcomings, this study seeks to advance the human security research program by adopting confirmatory the factor analysis technique, which is capable of incorporating conceptual and theoretical underpinnings of human security in modeling and estimation. Confirmatory factor analysis offers four distinct advantages.

(i) It provides a mechanism for taking into account measurement errors in indicator variables, since variables in the social sciences are generally known to contain sizable measurement errors, which if disregarded can result in biased parameter estimates and incorrect conclusions.[27]
(ii) Unlike other techniques that can only utilize observed variables and measurements, it is able to model both observed and latent variables.[28] This is a very relevant feature because the dimensions of human security are all latent variables.
(iii) It can facilitate the estimation and subsequent measurement of multidimensional concepts such as human security where no operational method for direct measurement exists.[29]
(iv) It incorporates the theoretical framework on which the latent construct is based.[30]

CONCEPTUAL ISSUES: DEFINING SECURITY

A thorough perusal of the literature on security reveals that there is little agreement on the meaning and content of the term. For example, Post and Kingsbury point out that

> security is often used loosely and in different contexts. For example, national security, international security, internal security, private security, retail security, physical security, and industrial security are all used in daily conversations. The definitions of these terms are not often clear and are often used interchangeably.[31]

Buchan, as well, states that "security is a word with many meanings,"[32] and Helga Haftendorn[33] opines that "security is as ambiguous in content as in format." She further contends that academic pursuit on the subject of security "suffers from the absence of a common understanding of what security is, how it can be conceptualized, and what its most relevant research questions are." Wolfers counsels that the term security, when used without specification, leads to more confusion than scientific usage can afford.[34]

Nevertheless, Paul Williams[35] proposes an effective approach for conducting the essential specification to derive a useful meaning of the word "security." He suggests four critical actions:

 (i)   identifying the object being secured;
 (ii) determining the values worth securing;
 (iii) identifying the threats to the meaningful values; and
 (iv) determining the agent providing the protection.

According to Williams, the specification of security should include a referent, something valuable/asset to be protected, threat(s) to the asset, and agent(s) of protection. Based on the preceding, a function (f) can be deduced for security:

$$S = f\{R, V, T, P\}$$

Where S is the security status, R is the object being secured or security referent, V is the value worth protecting, T is the threat, danger, and/or risk, and P is the actor involved in protection and/or mitigation. Based on the functional relationship, security in this study is defined as protection from or mitigation (P) of threats (T) to the survival prospects and core functioning (V) of a specific referent object (R).

Drawing on the foregoing, human security is defined as protection (P) of individuals (R) from threats (T) to their survival and core functioning (V). It involves protection from and/or mitigation of threats to seven critical value dimensions, viz.: economic, food, health, physical, environmental, societal, and political. The dimensions are considered critical because they are inescapably linked to human survival and core functioning.

A discussion on the various elements of the definition is obligatory at this stage. The security referent is any object that has a legitimate claim to survival that is existentially threatened.[36] States and individuals are the most common referents of security.[37]

Three theoretical perspectives dominate international relations, namely: realism, constructivism, and liberalism. Realist scholars theorize that the study of international relations is principally concerned with states and their interests. As Fred Chernoff[38] explains, realists point out that state-centrism is an inflexible imperative in international relations theory largely because theorists aim for parsimony in theory development, and in part because of the perception that leaders' behavior under similar circumstances does not vary greatly. Furthermore, state-centrism has now become a deeply entrenched position because of the recognition both in international law and

by governments that states have final authority over the territory and populations they control.[39] In realist analysis, the state's dominance in theorizing is
reinforced by the sovereignty concept. Sovereignty as defined by Dunne and
Schmidt "means that the state has supreme authority to make and enforce
laws."[40] Consequently, realists assert that the presence of a sovereign authority implies individuals should not be too overly concerned as to their own
security since it is provided through state institutions. Because state-centrism
is a fundamental assumption of realist theory, analysts are no longer operat-
ing within the realist paradigm if they embrace other referents other than the
state.

Constructivist thought in international relations is not a unified movement.
In fact, there are differences among constructivists concerning the choice
of referent object in security analysis.[41] Constructivist scholars who emphasize states in security analysis are referred to as conventional or systemic
constructivists as opposed to critical or holistic constructivists who adopt a
perspective that include other actors and integrate domestic and international
structures. Critical constructivists, by accommodating other actors and referents along with states, have opened the way for deepening of security thinking to incorporate individuals in the analysis. Notwithstanding, constructivist
researchers reject any notion that seeks to falsify hypothesis. In fact, based on
constructivists' emphasis on the intersubjective nature of reality and the dia-
logical aspects of its knowledge claims, it is suggested by Klotz and Lynch[42]
that participant observation and ethnography are more useful methods than
the hypothesis-testing approach adopted in this study.

The liberalist image of the world is a pluralist one. The milieu in which
liberalism was born was characterized by extremely violent and widespread
civil and religious wars which threatened the lives, liberties, livelihood, and
economic interests of populations in Europe. As such early liberalism placed
a high priority on the protection of individuals in their social, political, and
economic life.[43] As is gleaned from Chernoff,[44] liberalists are known to focus
their analyses at the individual, state, system, and global levels, contending
that all actors including those at the sub-state and international levels are
important in international relations. Their attention to the freedom of individuals from repression either from states or other actors has made liberalism
a powerful influence on the international discourse on human security and
rights. Francheschet[45] explains that human security is a liberalist notion that
articulates the need for individuals to be protected from wide-ranging threats
in domains such as personal safety, hunger, health, and political freedoms.

Andrew Moravcsik's[46] paradigmatic recasting of liberal international relations theory holds firm to liberal tenets while employing scientific epistemol-
ogy. Labeled positive liberalism, this theory positions state-society relation
at the center of global politics. Moravcsik states that rational individuals and

private groups are fundamental actors in international politics. Because a state comprises numerous individuals and groups representing multitudes of competing preferences, a state's preferences generally represent a subset of society: the dominant social group. Once a dominant group captures the state, it subverts the welfare of other groups in the quest of its own interests and preferences in the domestic and international arenas. This means that governments do not equally represent the interests of all people that live within its borders. However, de facto political power is wielded by subordinate groups even though they are not allocated power by political institutions in that they can engage in costly civil war or in peaceful but economically costly protest to impose their wishes on society.[47] In light of this, it is difficult not to impute referent status to individuals since they face the brunt of the consequences arising out of domestic political rivalry.

A key feature of many definitions of security is the protection and preservation of cherished values or assets.[48] In realist explanations, the cherished value protected is preservation of territorial integrity and political independence when the state is the referent. When humans are the referent, human security is a concept that proposes seven dimensions linked to the survival and functioning of individuals: food and health security; personal security from physical violence; environmental, societal, and political security. These value dimensions have their legitimacy enshrined in a time-proven and internationally accepted list of norms and values.

A security threat is defined as an action or a sequence of actions that affects the survival chances of a referent or drastically narrows the real opportunities to realize its core functioning. Sources of threats can be internal actors, external actors, or environmental phenomena. When assessing threat intensity, Buzan[49] suggests three considerations: the range of the threat in terms of its temporal and spatial characteristics; the probability of it occurring; and the consequences.

Security also involves protection. The protector is linked to the nature of the referent and the typology of the threat. Actors are involved in protection function at the international, regional, national, and subnational levels. For example, civil society organizations and local NGOs operate at the subnational levels; the police and social services arm of the state function at the national level; and intergovernmental organizations and international NGOs, and multilateral development agencies work at the regional and international levels. The state, though, is perhaps the most important provider of security. It is important to note that protection requires strategies that both shield individuals from threats and enable them to develop resilience against threats. Prevention and resilience-building are mutually reinforcing and should not be approached in isolation since both are required in addressing human security issues.

Approaches to achieving and sustaining human security include economic development through rules-based trade; economic insertion projects; poverty reduction; agriculture diversification; disaster mitigation and management; climate change mitigation and adaptation; promotion of citizen security and peaceful coexistence; peacekeeping; disarmament, including the elimination of anti-personnel landmines; and safeguarding the rights of children.[50]

STUDY DESIGN

A first-order confirmatory factor analysis (CFA) model was designed to test the multidimensionality of the theoretical construct human security. Below is the seven-factor confirmatory factor analysis (CFA) model in the format of seventeen structural equation model (SEM) basic equations. In the SEM basic equations, each observed indicator (X_1, X_2, X_3 … X_{17}) is presented as a linear function of one of the latent factors (ξ) and a random error (δ). The various factor loads are represented by λ. The subscript of a factor load refers to the indicator number and its corresponding factor number.

$$X_1 = \xi_1 + \delta_1 \qquad X_2 = \lambda_{21}\xi_1 + \delta_2$$
$$X_3 = \xi_2 + \delta_3 \qquad X_4 = \lambda_{42}\xi_2 + \delta_4$$
$$X_6 = \xi_3 + \delta_6 \qquad X_7 = \lambda_{73}\xi_3 + \delta_7 \qquad X_5 = \lambda_{52}\xi_2 + \delta_5$$
$$X_9 = \xi_4 + \delta_9 \qquad X_{10} = \lambda_{104}\xi_4 + \delta_{10} \qquad X_8 = \lambda_{83}\xi_3 + \delta_8$$
$$X_{11} = \xi_5 + \delta_{11} \qquad X_{12} = \lambda_{125}\xi_5 + \delta_{12}$$
$$X_{13} = \xi_6 + \delta_{13} \qquad X_{14} = \lambda_{146}\xi_6 + \delta_{14}$$
$$X_{15} = \xi_7 + \delta_{15} \qquad X_{16} = \lambda_{167}\xi_7 + \delta_{16} \qquad X_{17} = \lambda_{177}\xi_7 + \delta_{17}$$

A 17-item instrument, each structured on a 5-point Likert-type scale ranging from 1 for low ratings to 5 for higher ratings was designed (table 7.2 and appendix A for questionnaire items). Higher scores represented higher human security and, correspondingly, lower values represented lower human security. The instrument comprises seven subscales based on the seven dimensions of human security. Pre-survey evaluation of the instrument included:

Table 7.1: Indicator Variables and Corresponding Factors

Indicator Variables (X)	Corresponding Factors (ξ)	Indicator Variables (X)	Corresponding Factors (ξ)
X_{1-2}	Economic Security	X_{11-12}	Environmental Security
X_{3-5}	Food Security	X_{13-14}	Societal Security
X_{6-8}	Health Security	X_{15-17}	Political Security
X_{9-10}	Personal Security		

"*Source*: Data compiled from author research."

Table 7.2   Summary Table on the 17-Indicator Instrument

Indicator Variables	Corresponding Factor	Indicators
X_1	Economic Security	Access to resources/income
X_2	Economic Security	Income adequacy
X_3	Food Security	Capability to access/purchase food
X_4	Food Security	Adequacy of Food Resources
X_5	Food Security	Worry over access to food
X_6	Health Security	Access to Health Care
X_7	Health Security	Satisfaction with health care services
X_8	Health Security	Satisfaction with communicable diseases prevention
X_9	Personal Security	Experience with crime/violence victimization
X_{10}	Personal Security	Fear of crime and violence
X_{11}	Environmental Security	Perception on the severity of environmental problems
X_{12}	Environmental Security	Fear of impact of future environmental disasters
X_{13}	Societal Security	Perception on citizens' access to fair justice
X_{14}	Societal Security	Perception on the level of respect for citizens' rights in the country
X_{15}	Political Security	Freedom of expression
X_{16}	Political Security	Trust in State Institutions
X_{17}	Political Security	Freedom to exercise political choices

Source: Data compiled from author research.

focus group discussions, intensive individual interviews, and field pretesting. These approaches have been deemed effective in improving the reliability and validity of survey instruments.[51]

Economic security refers to assured basic income through productive and remunerative work, or in the last resort from some publicly financed safety net.[52] Two indicators are used to capture economic security: access to income/financial resources; and perception on the adequacy of monthly household income, and Taylor Owen confirms that these are adequate proxies for assessing economic security for individuals.[53] Owen adds safety nets—welfare systems—to his list of proxies for economic security; however, these are generally minimal or non-existent in developing countries.[54] In the context of Guyana, access to income covers pensions, stable public welfare programs, and regular remittances as well as income received from involvement in productive activities. Adequacy of income relates to respondents' perception on whether current income is able to cover necessities such as food, shelter, clothing, and medicine.

The 1994 *Human Development Report*[55] defines food security as peoples' physical and economic access to basic food. The three indicators for food security are resources to purchase food or access to food produce; perception on the adequacy of food a respondent can access; and frequency of worry over the availability of enough food during the past four weeks. Questions on the capability to purchase food for the household and the adequacy of food purchased and/or cultivated are adopted from the U.S. Household Food Security Survey Module: Six-Item Short Form.[56] The third indicator, worry associated with food access and availability, captures respondents' anxieties regarding the possibility of future food shortages.

Health security refers to access to essential health care and prevention of the spread of communicable diseases.[57] Underlying determinants of health security are access to health care; satisfaction with the quality of health care; and perception of the efficacy of national efforts in preventing communicable diseases. Access to health care is people's ability to get effective curative care, treatment, and medicine at affordable costs. Satisfaction with the quality of health care captures respondents' assessment of the quality of care, treatment, or the efficacy of medicine they received. The final health security indicator seeks to garner respondents' satisfaction on the effectiveness of national efforts in communicable diseases prevention.

Jon Barnett[58] states that environmental security refers to the protection of individuals from environmental hazards. The first indicator of environmental security relates to respondents' perception on how severely they were affected by environmental events over the last five years. The second indicator assesses individuals' anxieties on the likelihood of environmental events destroying their lives and livelihoods.

The personal security dimension of human security refers to protection from physical violence associated with events such as war, crime, torture, and civil strife.[59] Indicators of personal security used in the research are individual experiences with crime and/or violence, and prevalence of fear of crime and violence. Questions on fear of crime and perception of insecurity are adapted from the Safe Neighborhood Survey. The first indicator for personal security, individuals' experiences with crime and violence, captures how often an individual was a victim of crimes such as murder, assault, robbery, kidnapping, rape, or burglary in the past 12 months. The second indicator of personal security, fear of crime, assesses individuals' perceptions on their likelihood of becoming a victim of crime within their communities after dark.[60]

Paul Roe[61] explains that the term societal "is used for communities in which one identifies." Societal security therefore refers to protection from discriminatory practices based on ethnicity, cultural practices, and religion.[62] In this study, societal security is captured by the following indicators: fair treatment in matters before the law; and perception of respect for citizens' rights. The indicator "fair treatment in matters before the law" refers to whether people from every group in the society are treated equally in matters of justice. The indicator "respect for citizens" rights' captures whether people are protected from inhumane treatment and torture, arbitrary search or entry, exploitation or forced labor or slavery, and granted freedom of association and movement.

Political security refers to protection from political or state repression and detention and prevention of military abuse and ill-treatment.[63] Political security indicators are perception of individual freedom of expression; level of trust in state institutions; and perception of individual freedom to exercise political choices.

Perception of individual freedom of expression examines how free people feel to express themselves without fear of government reprisal. The second indicator—level of trust in state institutions—is an assessment of the level of trust citizens have in the military arm of the state. The third indicator—individual freedom to express political choices—represents individuals' perceptions and experiences on the following issues: freedom to exercise political choices and fair electoral processes.

Data was collected via a quantitative study conducted utilizing a multistage proportional probability sampling design. Multistage sampling is used when it is impractical to compile an exhaustive list of members comprising the target population owing to the size of the population under study.[64] In this type of sampling the natural segments/clusters of the population are utilized, and the variations in population size are accounted for by using proportional sampling, since in this technique the probability of selection into the survey sample for each sample unit is directly proportional to the number of elements in the unit.[65] The application of proportionality was done only at the regional level. At the village/ward level twenty interviews were conducted in each village/ward selected at random. All ten administrative regions were sampled, with one respondent from each household randomly selected through the "last birthday" method. Face-to-face interviews were conducted using the pre-designed questionnaire.

FINDINGS AND DISCUSSION

The indicators of goodness of fit for the model were all supportive of the hypothesized structure for human security comprising seven dimensions.[66] The fact that this study was able to utilize a complex multivariate statistical method to confirm the dimensions of human security reverses criticisms of the analytical strand that claims that it is impossible to conduct hypothesis-testing with human security. Latent variable methods, which have been used extensively in social sciences, are effective in analyzing abstract multidimensional concepts: previous failures in determining the contours of human security were the results of misspecification. Threat-based approaches have forced analysts to consider a multitude of threats, whereas the value-dimension approach adopted in this study facilitates parsimonious specification of human security along with putting attention only on what is essential for human survival and core functioning.

Validation of the seven human security dimensions along with the 17-indicator variables offer a simple human security evaluative tool, the strength of which is that it captures individuals' perceptions and experiences in assessing human security. Previous security assessment approaches did not incorporate the perceptions and experiences of the referent of human security; this study has gone some way in addressing this omission.

CONCLUSION

Recognition that current and past global realities were inevitably leading to a new organizing principle in international relations prompted an examination of an emerging paradigm that is focused on the security of individuals apart from the state. Undeniably, global trends have impacted security thinking by instigating discontent with international relations paradigms that failed to address the differentiated experiences of people. Moreover, horrendous atrocities committed by both state and non-state conflict actors over the past three decades have contributed to a metamorphosis in security thinking. The overwhelming view arising from these global realities was that there was a need for security paradigms to address the security of the state and the security of its citizens as two distinct but related phenomena.

The results of this study have implications for human security policymaking. Confirmation of the value dimensions along with indicators means that analysts can identify challenges and prioritize response based on the evidence obtained. Further, the evaluative instrument validated in this study can serve as a simple early-warning mechanism to identify and react to challenges to any of the value dimensions. The validated instrument can also be used as a human security assessment tool and be applied periodically to provide evidence for the design of human security actions and to monitor trends in the quality of human security. Moreover, incorporating individuals' experiences and perceptions allows for bottom-up and participative approaches to tackling human security.

The study reaches three salient conclusions. One; it is important to assess human security knowledge claims in the field of international relations utilizing rigorous methodologies so as to fully comprehend the nature of concepts and eliminate erroneous propositions. The study resolutely defends the notion that scientific knowledge must be founded on, tested by, and grounded on observations. The adoption of a quantitative approach facilitates data-based discussion and conclusions about reality, and this is immensely useful in evaluating the extent to which the empirical expectations generated by human security perspectives are consistent with reality.

Two; human security is analyzable in its maximalist form. The view of some scholars is that the concept defies methodical examination. The successful application of confirmatory factor analysis falsifies this notion. The major challenge with previous human security studies was that all efforts were placed in the direction of arriving at a manageable number of threats to define the scope of human security. Threat-based analysis of human security misses the mark: the protection of an asset or something of value is inherent to security practice and therefore definition and specification based on human security value dimensions will bring parsimony, precision, and clarity to explanations of human security.

Three; values worth protecting must be categorized under two headings—survival and core functioning. The term "core functioning" refers to the ability to carry out basic functions or the minimum set of accomplishments that any referent must attain for existence to be deemed fulfilling, and existence is often considered paltry in the absence of "core functioning." When human security is defined as protection of individuals from threats and dangers to their survival and core functioning, this allows for meaningful model-building. The seven value dimensions—economic, food, health, physical, environmental, societal, and political—are enshrined in time proven and internationally accepted lists of norms and values: The Universal Declaration on Human Rights, the Covenant on Economic, Social and Cultural Rights, and the Covenant on Civil and Political Rights. These conditions can only be achieved in the context of individual freedoms, which explains why human security is broadly seen as freedom from fear and freedom from want.

A confirmatory factor analysis approach, even though it is incredibly useful in hypothesis-testing and theory validation, often requires multiple studies and the use of several samples taken in different contexts before research findings can be more definitively confirmed. A limitation of this research, therefore, is that at this stage the findings and conclusions are only suggestive, which leads to the recommendation for more studies of this nature in different settings.

Finally, it is important to note that human security is not a substitute for state security. In fact, there is no need for human security to address all the issues related to national security. In the case of Guyana, for example, it is clear that the considerable territorial challenges facing the country, which arise from disputes with more than one neighboring state, are not amenable to analysis using the human security approach. Analyzing security in this context requires analyzing security of the state and its citizens as two distinct albeit related phenomena. As such, despite the study acknowledging the

Clement Henry

explanatory value of the human security approach, it cannot credibly concede to its application in evaluating the totality of a country's multidimensional security landscape.

NOTES

1. Stephen Walt. 1991. "The Renaissance of Security Studies." *International Studies Quarterly* 35 (2), p. 212. Alan Collins. 2010. *Contemporary Security Studies.* Oxford: Oxford University Press, p. 2.

2. Talukder Maniruzzaman. 1982. The Security of Small States in the Third World. Canberra Papers on Strategy and Defence, No. 25, Strategic and Defence Studies Centre, Australian National University, p. 15.

3. Ian Bellamy. 1981. "Towards a Theory of International Security." *Political Studies* 29 (1), p. 102.

4. Giacomo Luciani. 1989. "The Economic Content of Security." *Journal of Public Policy* 8 (2), p. 151.

5. Richard Ullman. 1983. "Redefining Security." *International Security* 8 (1), p. 129.

Ron Walker. 1990. "Security, Sovereignty, and the Challenge of World Politics." *Alternatives: Global, Local, Political* 15 (1), p. 24.

6. Taylor Owen. 2013. "Editor's Introduction: Human Security." Vol. 1, in *Human Security: Concept and Critique*, edited by Taylor Owen, xxv–li. London: Sage.

7. Non-traditional threats include crippling social and economic exclusion, hunger, increasing environmental vulnerability, high levels of crime and violence, human trafficking, malaria, HIV/AIDS, and political repression.

8. Navnita Chadha Behera. 2008. "The Security Problematique in South Asia: Alternative Conceptualizations." In *Globalization and Environmental Challenges: Reconceptualising Security in the 21st Century*, edited by Hans Günter Brauch, Úrsula Spring, Czeslaw Mesjasz, John Grin, Pál Dunay, Navnita Chadha Behera, Béchir Chourou, Patricia Kameri-Mbote and P. H. Liotta, 819–828. New York: Springer Berlin Heidelberg, p. 819.

9. Michael Klare. 1996. Redefining Security: The New Global Schisms. http://www.u.arizona.edu/~volgy/klare.htm, p. 1.

10. Des Gasper and Oscar Gómez. 2014. "Evolution of Thinking and Research on Human and Personal Security 1994-2013." UNDP Human Development Report Office, Occasional Paper. http://hdr.undp.org/sites/default/files/ gomez_hdr14.pdf.

Pauline Ewan. 2007. "Deepening the Human Security Debate: Beyond the Politics of Conceptual Clarification." *Politics* 27 (3).

Caroline Thomas. 2001. "Global Governance, Development and Human Security: Exploring the Links." *Third World Quarterly* 22 (2), p. 161.

Stephen Walt. 1991. "The Renaissance of Security Studies," p. 212.

11. Barry Buzan. 2004. "A Reductionist, Idealistic Notion that Adds Little Analytical Value." *Security Dialogue* 35 (3). Buzan argues that if academics and practitioners label all potential harm to individuals as security threats it is virtually

impractical to identify priorities for political action.Roland Paris. 2001. "Human Security: Paradigm Shift or Hot Air?" *International Security* 26 (2). Paris contends that human security is Characterized by definitional elasticity and lacking analytical utility Yuen Foong Khong. 2001. "Human Security: A Shotgun Approach to Alleviating Human Misery?" *Global Governance* 7 (3). Khong warns against the potential pitfalls associated with the methodological and conceptual reorientation of security to recognize human beings as a referent claiming that it will only give citizens false hopes premised on false priorities and causal assumptions.

12. Andrew Mack. 2004. "The Concept of Human Security." In Promoting Human Security: But How and for Whom-- Contributions to BICC Ten-year Anniversary Conference, edited by Michael Brzoska and Peter Croll, 47–50. Bonn: Bonn International Centre for Conversion (BICC).

Keith Krause. 2004. "The Key to a Powerful Agenda if Properly Defined." *Security Dialogue* 35 (3). Both Krause and Mack insist that human security should only be concerned with threats originating from war and other forms of violence, since going beyond these will only come at the expense of analytical rigor.

13. United Nations Development Programme (UNDP). 1994. *Human Development Report 1994: New Dimensions of Human Security.* New York: United Nations Development Programme. Fen Hampson, Jean Daudelin, John Hay, Todd Martin, and Holly Reid. 2002. *Madness in the Multitude: Human Security and World Disorder.* Toronto: Oxford University Press. Taylor Owen. 2004. "Human Security—Conflict, Critique and Consensus: Colloquium Remarks and a Proposal for a Threshold-Based Definition." *Security Dialogue* 35 (3).

Shahrbanou Tadjbaksh and Anuradha Chenoy. 2007. *Human Security: Concepts and Implications.* Routledge: New York.

14. Barbara Byrne. 2010. *Structural Equation Modelling with Amos: Basic Concepts, Applications, and Programming.* New York: Routledge, p. 3.

15. Marie Hughes, Leon Price and Daniel Marrs. 1986. "Linking Theory Construction and Theory Testing: Models with Multiple Indicators of Latent Variables." *The Academy of Management Review* 11 (1). Patricia Cohen, Jacob Cohen, Jeanne Teresi, Margaret Marchi and Noemi Velez. 1990. "Problems with Measurement of Latent variables in Structural Equations Causal Models." *Applied Psychological Measurement* 14 (2). Kenneth Bollen. 2002. "Latent Variables in Psychology and Social Sciences." *Annual Review of Psychology* 53.

16. Richard Jolly and Deepayan Basu Ray. 2007. "Human Security—National Perspectives and Global Agendas: Insights from National Human Development Reports." *Journal of International Development* 19, p. 459.

17. Des Gasper. 2008. The Idea of Human Security. GARNET Working Paper: No 28/08, The Hague: Institute for Social Studies, p. 2.

18. Carl Hempel. 1965. *Aspects of Scientific Explanation: And Other Essays in the Philosophy of Science.* New York: The Free Press, p. 101.

Adrienne Heritier. 2008. "Causal Explanation." In *Approaches and Methodologies in the Social Sciences: A Pluralist Perspective*, edited by Donatella della Porta and Michael Keating, 61–79. Cambridge, p. 62.

19. Helga Haftendorn. 1991. "The Security Puzzle: Theory-Building and Discipline Building in International security." *International Studies Quarterly* 35 (1), p. 12.

20. Marie Hughes, Leon Price and Daniel Marrs. 1986. "Linking Theory Construction and Theory Testing," p. 128.

21. Bear Braumoelle and Anne Sartori. 2002. "Empirical-Quantitative Approaches to the Study of International Relations." In *Cases, Numbers, Models: International Relations Research Methods*, edited by Detlef Sprinz and Yael Wolinsky, 139–163. http://www.sscnet.ucla.edu/polisci/faculty/trachtenberg/syllabi,lists/harvard/moravcsik%20 (sprinz%20wolinsky).pdf, p. 139.

22. Taylor Owen. 2003. "Measuring Human Security: Overcoming the Paradox." *Human Security Bulletin* 2 (3).

23. James Michel. 2005. "Human Security and Social development: Comparative Research in Four Asian Countries." Arusha Conference, New Frontiers of Social Policy. http://siteresources.worldbank.org/intranetsocialdevelopment/Resources/Michel.rev.pdf.

24. David Hastings. 2009. "From Human Development to Human Security: A Prototype Human Security Index." UNESCAP WORKING PAPER. http://www.unescap.org/sites/default /files/wp-09-03_0.pdf.

25. Ronald Inglehart and Pippa Norris. 2012. "The Four Horsemen of the Apocalypse: Understanding Human Security." *Scandinavian Political Studies* 35 (1).

26. Ian Jolliffe. 2002. *Principal Component Analysis*. New York: Springer-Verlag.
    Nicolás Sánchez and Miles Cahil. 1998. "The Strengths and Weaknesses of Factor Analysis in Predicting Cuban GDP in Cuba." *Cuba in Transition* 8.

27. Jichuan Wang and Xiaoqian Wang. 2012. *Structural Equation Modelling: Applications Using Mplus*. Sussex: John Wiley & Sons, p. 1.

28. Barbara Byrne. 2010. *Structural Equation Modelling with Amos*, pp. 3–4.

29. Jichuan Wang and Xiaoqian Wang. 2012. *Structural Equation Modelling*, p. 1.

30. Myint Swe Khine. 2013. *Application of Structural Equation Modelling in Educational Research and Practice*. Rotterdam: Sense Publishers, p. 3.

31. Richard Post and Arthur Kingsbury. 1991. *Security Administration: An Introduction to the Protective Services*. Stoneham: Butterworth-Heinemann, p. 1.

32. Alistair Buchan. 1966. *War in Modern Society*. London: Collins, p. 24.

33. Helga Haftendorn. 1991. "The Security Puzzle," p. 3.

34. Arnold Wolfers.1952. "'National Security' as an Ambiguous Symbol." *Political Science Quarterly* 67 (4), 483.

35. Paul Williams. 2013. *Security Studies: An Introduction*. 2nd. New York: Routledge.

36. Barry Buzan, Ole Wæver, and Jaap de Wilde. 1998. *Security: A New Framework for Analysis*. Boulder: Lynne Rienner Publishers, p. 36.

37. Walter Lippmann. 1943. *US Foreign Policy: Shield of the Republic*. Boston: Little, Brown and Co. Shahrbanou Tadjbaksh and Anuradha Chenoy. 2007. Human Security.

38. Fred Chernoff. 2007. *Theory and Metatheory in International Relations: Concepts and Contending Accounts*. New York: Palgrave Macmillan, p. 46.

39. Edward Kolodziej. 2005. *Security and International Relations*. Cambridge: Cambridge University Press, p. 128.

40. Tim Dunne and Brian Schmidt. 2011. "Realism." In *The Globalisation of World Politics: An Introduction to International Relations*, edited by John Baylis, Steve Smith and Patricia Owens, 84–99. Oxford: Oxford University Press, p. 172.

41. Leading constructivist scholar Alexander Wendt has focused on interaction between states in the international system. He along with a group of constructivist scholars hold a state-centric view of security but explain security/insecurity from the perspective of ideational factors as apart from material factors. This type of constructivist viewpoint is focused on explaining state behavior and is largely conducted in line with positivist research methodologies.

42. Audie Klotz and Cecelia Lynch. 2007. *Strategies for Research in Constructivist International Relations*. Armonk: M.E. Sharpe, pp. 106–107.

43. Paul Viotti and Mark Kauppi. 2012. *International Relations Theory*. New York: Longman, p. 132.

44. Fred Chernoff. 2007. *Theory and Metatheory in International Relations*.

45. Antonio Franceschet. 2006. "Global Legalism and Human Security." In *A Decade of Human Security: Global Governance and New Multilateralisms*, edited by Sandra Maclean, David Black and Timothy Shaw, 31–37. Aldershot: Ashgate Publishing Limited, pp. 31–33.

46. Andrew Moravcsik. 2003. "Liberal International Relations Theory: A Scientific Assessment." In *Progress in International Relations Theory: Appraising the Field*, edited by Colin Elman and Miriam Elman, 159–204. Cambridge: MIT Press.

47. Daron Acemoglu, Simon Johnson, and James Robinson. 2004. "Institutions as the Fundamental Cause of Long-Run Growth," p. 4.

48. Ivelaw Griffith. 2004. *Caribbean Security in the Age of Terror: Challenge and Change*. Kingston: Ian Randle Publishers, p. 10.

Paul Williams. 2013. *Security Studies*, p. 6.

49. Barry Buzan. 1991. People, States, and Fear, 2nd ed.: *An Agenda for International Security in the Post-ColdWar Era*. Hertfordshire: Harvester Wheatsheaf.

50. Lloyd Axworthy. 1997. "Canada and Human Security: The Need for Leadership." *International Journal* 52 (2), pp. 185–196.

51. Floyd Fowler. 1995. *Improving Survey Questions: Design and Evaluation*. London: Sage, p. 104.

52. United Nations Development Programme (UNDP). 1994. Human Development Report 1994. Jorge Nef. 1999. *Human Security and Mutual Vulnerability: The Global Political Economy of Development and Underdevelopment*. Ottawa: International Development Research Centre.

53. Taylor Owen. 2008. "Measuring Human Security: Methodological Challenges and the Importance of Geographically Referenced Determinants." In *Environmental Change and Human Security: Recognizing and Acting on Hazard Impacts*, edited by P. H. Liotta, David Mouat, William Kepner and Judith Lancaster, 35–64. Dordrecht: Springer Netherlands.

54. Tara McCormack. 2011. "Human Security and the Separation of Security and Development." *Conflict Security and Development* 11 (2), p. 243.

55. United Nations Development Programme (UNDP). 1994. Human Development Report 1994, p. 26.

56. United States Department of Agriculture. 2012. "U.S. Household Food Security Survey Module: Six-Item Short Form." http://www.ers.usda.gov/datafiles/Food_ Security_in_the_United_States/Food_Security_Survey_Modules /short2012.pdf.

57. William Aldis. 2008. "Health Security as a Public Health Concept: A Critical Analysis." *Health Policy and Planning*, p. 370.

58. Jon Barnett. 2010. "Environmental Security." In *Contemporary Security Studies*, edited by Alan Collins, 218–238. Oxford: Oxford University Press, p. 232.

59. United Nations Development Programme (UNDP). 1994. Human Development Report 1994, pp. 30–31.

60. Crime and Social Observatory. 2014. Report of the 2014 Safe Neighbourhood Survey. Georgetown: Ministry of Home Affairs, Government of Guyana.

61. Paul Roe Roe, Paul. 2010. "Societal Security." In *Contemporary Security Studies*, edited by Alan Collins, 202–217. Oxford: Oxford University Press, p. 205.

62. Jorge Nef. 1999. *Human Security and Mutual Vulnerability.*
Shahrbanou Tadjbaksh and Anuradha Chenoy. 2007. *Human Security*, p. 16.

63. Jorge Nef. 1999. *Human Security and Mutual Vulnerability.*

64. Earl Babbie. 2010. *The Practice of Social Research.* Belmont: Wadsworth, p. 219.
Alan Bryman and Emma Bell. 2007. *Business Research Methods.* Oxford: Oxford University Press, p. 188.

65. William Crano and Marilynn Brewer. 2002. *Principles and Methods of Social Research*, p. 179. Sharon Lohr. 2010. *Sampling: Design and Analysis.* Boston: Brooks/Cole Cengage Learning, 266.

66. All the goodness-of-fit statistics suggest that it is plausible to accept the null hypothesis (H0) that the data support the hypothesized relationship among the variables. The $\chi2$ to degrees of freedom ratio is 2.205 to 1; the Root Mean Square Error of Approximation (RMSEA) is 0.038 with 90 percent confidence interval ranging from 0.031 to 0.046; the probability of RMSEA $\leq$ 0.05 is 0.996; the Comparative Fit Index and the Tucker Lewis Index are 0.967 and 0.952 respectively; and the Standardized Root Mean Square Residual (SRMR) is 0.034.

REFERENCES

Acemoglu, Daron, Simon Johnson, and James Robinson. 2004. "Institutions as the Fundamental Cause of Long-Run Growth." *NBER Working Paper* 10481. Accessed December 21, 2016. http://www. nber.org/papers/w10481.

Aldis, William. 2008. "Health Security as a Public Health Concept: A Critical Analysis." *Health Policy and Planning*, 369–375.

Axworthy, Lloyd. 1997. "Canada and Human Security: The Need for Leadership." *International Journal* 52 (2): 183–196.

Babbie, Earl. 2010. *The Practice of Social Research.* Belmont: Wadsworth.

Barnett, Jon. 2010. "Environmental Security." In *Contemporary Security Studies*, edited by Alan Collins, 218–238. Oxford: Oxford University Press.

Behera, Navnita Chadha. 2008. "The Security Problematique in South Asia: Alternative Conceptualizations." In *Globalization and Environmental Challenges: Reconceptualizing Security in the 21st Century*, edited by Hans Günter Brauch, Úrsula Spring, Czeslaw Mesjasz, John Grin, Pál Dunay, Navnita Chadha Behera, Béchir Chourou, Patricia Kameri-Mbote and P. H. Liotta, 819–828. New York: Springer Berlin Heidelberg.

Bellamy, Ian. 1981. "Towards a Theory of International Security." *Political Studies* 29 (1): 100–105.

Bollen, Kenneth. 2002. "Latent Variables in Psychology and Social Sciences." *Annual Review of Psychology* 53: 605–634.

Braumoelle, Bear and Anne Sartori. 2002. "Empirical-Quantitative Approaches to the Study of International Relations." In *Cases, Numbers, Models: International Relations Research Methods*, edited by Detlef Sprinz and Yael Wolinsky, 139–163. Accessed May 24, 2014. http://www. sscnet.ucla.edu/polisci/faculty/trachtenberg/syllabilists/harvard/moravcsik%20(sprinz%20wolinsky).pdf.

Bryman, Alan, and Emma Bell. 2007. *Business Research Methods*. Oxford: Oxford University Press.

Buchan, Alistair. 1966. *War in Modern Society*. London: Collins.

Buzan, Barry. 2004. "A Reductionist, Idealistic Notion that Adds Little Analytical Value." *Security Dialogue* 35 (3): 369–370.

———. 1991. *People, States, and Fear: An Agenda for International Security in the Post-Cold War Era*. Hertfordshire: Harvester Wheatsheaf.

Buzan, Barry, Ole Wæver, and Jaap de Wilde. 1998. *Security: A New Framework for Analysis*. Boulder: Lynne Rienner.

Byrne, Barbara. 2010. *Structural Equation Modelling with Amos: Basic Concepts, Applications, and Programming*. New York: Routledge.

Chernoff, Fred. 2007. *Theory and Metatheory in International Relations: Concepts and Contending Accounts*. New York: Palgrave Macmillan.

Cohen, Patricia, Jacob Cohen, Jeanne Teresi, Margaret Marchi and Noemi Velez. 1990. "Problems with Measurement of Latent variables in Structural Equations Causal Models." *Applied Psychological Measurement* 14 (2): 183–196.

Crano, William, and Marilynn Brewer. 2002. *Principles and Methods of Social Research*. Mahwah: Lawrence Erlbaum Associates.

Crime Observatory. 2013. *Report of the 2013 Safe Neighbourhood Survey: Citizen Security Survey*. Georgetown: Ministry of Home Affairs, Government of Guyana.

Dunne, Tim, and Brian Schmidt. 2011. "Realism." In *The Globalisation of World Politics: An Introduction to International Relations*, edited by John Baylis, Steve Smith and Patricia Owens, 84–99. Oxford: Oxford University Press.

Ewan, Pauline. 2007. "Deepening the Human Security Debate: Beyond the Politics of Conceptual Clarification." *Politics* 27 (3): 182–189.

Fowler, Floyd. 1995. *Improving Survey Questions: Design and Evaluation*. London: Sage.

Franceschet, Antonio. 2006. "Global Legalism and Human Security." In *A decade of Human Security: Global Governance and New Multilateralisms*, edited by Sandra Maclean, David Black and Timothy Shaw, 31–37. Aldershot: Ashgate.

Gasper, Des and Oscar Gómez. 2014. "Evolution of Thinking and Research on Human and Personal Security 1994-2013." UNDP Human Development Report Office, Occasional Paper. Accessed February 22, 2015. http://hdr.undp.org/sites/default/files/gomez_hdr14.pdf.

Gasper, Des. 2008. The Idea of Human Security. *GARNET Working Paper,* No 28/08, The Hague: Institute for Social Studies.

Ivelaw Griffith. 2004. *Caribbean Security in the Age of Terror: Challenge and Change*. Kingston: Ian Randle.

Haftendorn, Helga. 1991. "The Security Puzzle: Theory-Building and Discipline Building in International security." *International Studies Quarterly* 35 (1): 3–17.

Hampson, Fen, Jean Daudelin, John Hay, Todd Martin, and Holly Reid. 2002. *Madness in the Multitude: Human Security and World Disorder*. Toronto: Oxford University Press.

Hastings, David. 2009. "From Human Development to Human Security: A Prototype Human Security Index." *UNESCAP WORKING PAPER*. Accessed January 15, 2014. http://www.unescap.org/ sites/default/files/wp-09-03_0.pdf.

Hempel, Carl. 1965. *Aspects of Scientific Explanation: And Other Essays in the Philosophy of Science*. New York: The Free Press.

Heritier, Adrienne. 2008. "Causal Explanation." In *Approaches and Methodologies in the Social Sciences: A Pluralist Perspective*, edited by Donatella della Porta and Michael Keating, 61–79. Cambridge.

Hughes, Marie, Leon Price and Daniel Marrs. 1986. "Linking Theory Construction and Theory Testing: Models with Multiple Indicators of Latent Variables." *The Academy of Management Review* 11 (1): 128–144.

Inglehart, Ronald, and Pippa Norris. 2012. "The Four Horsemen of the Apocalypse: Understanding Human Security." *Scandinavian Political Studies* 35 (1): 71–96.

Jolliffe, Ian. 2002. *Principal Component Analysis*. New York: Springer-Verlag.

Jolly, Richard and Deepayan Basu Ray. 2007. "Human Security—National Perspectives and Global Agendas: Insights from National Human Development Reports." *Journal of International Development* 19: 457–472.

Khine, Myint Swe. 2013. *Application of Structural Equation Modelling in Educational Research and Practice*. Rotterdam: Sense Publishers.

Khong, Yuen Foong. 2001. "Human Security: A Shotgun Approach to Alleviating Human Misery?" *Global Governance* 7 (3): 231–236.

Klare, Michael. 1996. *Redefining Security: The New Global Schisms*. Accessed February 24, 2015. http://www.u.arizona.edu/~volgy/klare.htm.

Klotz, Audie, and Cecelia Lynch. 2007. *Strategies for Research in Constructivist International Relations*. Armonk: M.E. Sharpe.

Kolodziej, Edward. 2005. *Security and International Relations*. Cambridge: Cambridge University Press.

Krause, Keith. 2004. "The Key to a Powerful Agenda if Properly Defined." *Security Dialogue* 35 (3): 367–368.

Lippmann, Walter. 1943. *US Foreign Policy: Shield of the Republic*. Boston: Little, Brown and Co.

Lohr, Sharon. 2010. *Sampling: Design and Analysis*. Boston: Brooks/Cole Cengage Learning.

Luciani, Giacomo. 1989. "The Economic Content of Security." *Journal of Public Policy* 8 (2): 151–173.

Mack, Andrew. 2004. "The Concept of Human Security." In *Promoting Human security: But How and for Whom?* edited by Michael Brzoska and Peter Croll, 47–50. Bonn: Bonn International Centre for Conversion (BICC).

Maniruzzaman, Talukder. 1982. *The Security of Small States in the Third World*. Canberra: Strategic and Defence Studies Centre.

McCormack, Tara. 2011. "Human Security and the Separation of Security and Development." *Conflict Security and Development* 11 (2): 235–260.

Michel, James. 2005. "Human Security and Social development: Comparative Research in Four Asian Countries." *Arusha Conference, New Frontiers of Social Policy*. Accessed January 23, 2014. http://siteresources.worldbank.org/INTRA NETSOCIALDEVELOPMENT/Resources/Michel.rev.pdf.

Moravcsik, Andrew. 2003. "Liberal International Relations Theory: A Scientific Assessment." In *Progress in International Relations Theory: Appraising the field*, edited by Colin Elman and Miriam Elman, 159–204. Cambridge: MIT Press.

Nef, Jorge. 1999. *Human Security and Mutual Vulnerability: The Global Political Economy of Development and Underdevelopment*. Ottawa: International Development Research Centre.

Owen, Taylor. 2013. "Editor's Introduction: Human Security." In *Human Security: Concept and Critique*, edited by Taylor Owen, xxv- li. London: Sage.

———. 2008. "Measuring Human Security: Methodological Challenges and the Importance of Geographically Referenced Determinants." In *Environmental Change and Human Security: Recognizing and Acting on Hazard Impacts*, edited by P. H. Liotta, David Mouat, William Kepner and Judith Lancaster, 35–64. Dordrecht: Springer Netherlands.

———. 2004. "Human Security—Conflict, Critique and Consensus: Colloquium Remarks and a Proposal for a Threshold-Based Definition." *Security Dialogue* 35 (3): 373–387.

———. 2003. "Measuring Human Security: Overcoming the Paradox." *Human Security Bulletin* 2 (3). http://www.prio.no/publications/archive/2003/to002.pdf.

Paris, Roland. 2001. "Human Security: Paradigm Shift or Hot Air?" *International Security* 26 (2): 87–102.

Post, Richard, and Arthur Kingsbury. 1991. *Security Administration: An Introduction to the Protective Services*. Stoneham: Butterworth-Heinemann.

Roe, Paul. 2010. "Societal Security." In *Contemporary Security Studies*, edited by Alan Collins, 202–217. Oxford: Oxford University Press.

Sánchez, Nicolás, and Miles Cahil. 1998. "The Strengths and Weaknesses of Factor Analysis in Predicting Cuban GDP in Cuba." *Cuba in Transition* 8: 273–288.

Tadjbaksh, Shahrbanou and Anuradha Chenoy. 2007. *Human Security: Concepts and Implications*. New York: Routledge.

Thomas, Caroline. 2001. "Global Governance, Development and Human Security: Exploring the Links." *Third World Quarterly* 22 (2): 159–175.

Ullman, Richard. 1983. "Redefining Security." *International Security* 8 (1): 129–153.

United Nations Development Programme (UNDP). 1994. *Human Development Report 1994: New Dimensions of Human Security.* New York: United Nations Development Programme.

United States Department of Agriculture. 2012. *U.S. Household Food Security Survey Module: Six-Item Short Form.* Accessed June 15, 2013. http://www.ers.usda.gov /datafiles/Food_Security_in_the_United_States/Food_Security_Survey_Modules/ short2012.pdf.

Viotti, Paul and Mark Kauppi. 2012. *International Relations Theory.* New York: Longman.

Walt, Stephen. June 1991. "The Renaissance of Security Studies." *International Studies Quarterly* 35 (2): 211–239.

Wang, Jichuan and Xiaoqian Wang. 2012. *Structural Equation Modelling: Applications Using Mplus.* Sussex: John Wiley & Sons.

Williams, Paul. 2013. *Security Studies: An Introduction.* 2nd. New York: Routledge.

Wolfers, Arnold. 1952. "'National Security' as an Ambiguous Symbol." *Political Science Quarterly* 67 (4): 481–502.

Appendix A

Questionnaire

Appendix A Questionnaire

Item	Summary Variable	Indicator Name	Questionnaire Statement
X_1	Economic Security	Access to financial resources/income	In the past 12 months, how many months have you gone without a cash income? 1 Often (10 or more times) 2 Fairly Often (5–9 times) 3 Sometimes (3–4 times) 4 Rarely (1–2 times) 5 Never
X_2	Economic Security	Perception on household income adequacy	Considering food, shelter, clothing, and medicine: how often in the past 12 months, because of your household income level, was your family unable to cover any of these basic necessities? 1 Often (10 or more times) 2 Fairly Often (5–9 times) 3 Sometimes (3–4 times) 4 Rarely (1–2 times) 5 Never
X_3	Food Security	Access to food produce/resources to purchase food	In the past four weeks, how often did the food that you bought/grew just didn't last, and you didn't have money to get more? 1 Often (10 or more times) 2 Fairly Often (5–9 times) 3 Sometimes (3–4 times) 4 Rarely (1–2 times) 5 Never
X_4	Food Security	Adequacy of Food Resources	Sometimes people eat less, miss meals, or go hungry because there are not enough resources to get food. In the past four weeks, how often did this happen to you or to a household member? 1 Often (10 or more times) 2 Fairly Often (5–9 times) 3 Sometimes (3–4 times) 4 Rarely (1–2 times) 5 Never
X_5	Food Security	Worry associated with food access and availability	In the past four weeks, how often did you worry that your household would not have enough food? 1 Often (10 or more times) 2 Fairly Often (5–9 times) 3 Sometimes (3–4 times) 4 Rarely (1–2 times) 5 Never
X_6	Health Security	Perception on access to Health Care	How difficult would you say it is to get good health care and medicine at an affordable cost when someone in your household is sick or in an emergency? 1 Very Difficult 2 Difficult 3 Not too difficult 4 Easy 5 Very easy

(Continued)

Appendix A Questionnaire (*Continued*)

Item	Summary Variable	Indicator Name	Questionnaire Statement
X_7	Health Security	Level of satisfaction with health care services	Thinking about the last time you or someone you know were in need of medical attention and visited a public or private health care facility, how satisfied were/was you/he/she with the quality of health care you/he/she received? 1 very dissatisfied 2 fairly dissatisfied 3 neither satisfied nor dissatisfied 4 fairly satisfied 5 Very satisfied
X_8	Health Security	Level of satisfaction with communicable disease prevention	In general, would you say that you are very satisfied, fairly satisfied, neither satisfied nor dissatisfied, fairly dissatisfied, or very dissatisfied with the quality of public services available to prevent communicable diseases. 1 very dissatisfied 2 fairly dissatisfied 3 neither satisfied nor dissatisfied 4 fairly satisfied 5 Very satisfied
X_9	Personal Security	Experience with crime/violence victimisation	In the past 12 months, how often have you or anyone in your household been the victim of a violent crime such as murder, assault, robbery, kidnapping, or rape? 1 Often (6 or more times) 2 Fairly Often (4–5 times) 3 Sometimes (2–3 times) 4 Rarely (once) 5 Never
X_{10}	Personal Security	Fear of crime and violence	In general, how safe from crime and violence do you feel when you are walking on the streets of your community at nights? 1 Not safe at all 2 Slightly safe 3 Moderately Safe 4 Safe 5 Completely safe
X_{11}	Environmental Security	Where people live and the nature of environmental challenges	Please rate how these problems [environmental] have affected your household over the past 5 years using a five-point scale corresponding to very severe, severe, slightly severe, not severe, and not at all affected. 1 Very Severe 2 Severe 3 Slightly Severe 4 Not Severe 5 Not affected at all

(*Continued*)

Appendix A Questionnaire (*Continued*)

Item	Summary Variable	Indicator Name	Questionnaire Statement
X_{12}	Environmental Security	People's susceptibility to environmental threats	How worried are you about environmental/ natural disasters taking your life and livelihood? 1 Extremely worried 2 Worried 3 Moderately worried 4 Not worried 5 Not at all worried
X_{13}	Societal Security	Perception of whether there is equality before the law	In relation to police matters and justice, is every group in society (including different ethnic groups) treated equally? 1 Completely disagree 2 disagree 3 Neither agree nor disagree 4 Agree 5 Completely Agree
X_{14}	Societal Security	Perception on the level of respect for citizens' rights	Kindly indicate your view on the level of respect for citizens' rights in the country. Consider rights such as protection from inhuman treatment & torture, protection against arbitrary search or entry, protection against forced labour or slavery, freedom of association and movement and equality of persons before the law. Would you say that there is _____ for citizens' rights nowadays in this country? 1 No respect at all 2 Not much respect 3 Neutral 4 Fairly much respect 5 A great deal of respect
X_{15}	Political Security	Perception of individual freedom to express oneself on political matters	How free do you think you are to express yourself without fear of government reprisal? 1 Not free at all 2 Not free 3 Slightly free 4 free 5 Completely free
X_{16}	Political Security	Level of trust in state institutions	Using a 5-point scale with each point indicating a score that goes from 1 meaning NOT AT ALL to 5, meaning A LOT, kindly state how much you trust the following state institutions. (A) The Guyana Defence Force 1 Not at all 2 3 4 5 A lot (B) The Guyana Police Force 1 Not at all 2 3 4 5 A lot

(*Continued*)

Appendix A Questionnaire (*Continued*)

Item	Summary Variable	Indicator Name	Questionnaire Statement
X_{17}	Political Security	Perception of individual freedom to exercise political choices	(A) Freedom of voting is secured in this country. 1 Completely disagree 2 disagree 3 Neither agree nor disagree 4 Agree 5 Completely Agree (B) Votes are counted fairly in this country. 1 Completely disagree 2 disagree 3 Neither agree nor disagree 4 Agree 5 Completely Agree (C) Voters are threatened with violence at the polls. 1 Completely Agree 2 Agree 3 Neither agree nor disagree 4 disagree 5 Completely disagree

Source: Data compiled from author research.

Appendix B
Sample Size Selection

In determining the size of the sample Cochran's formula for computing sample size was applied. This method is ideally suited for categorical data collection. Cochran's formula is presented below:

$$N_0 = Z^2 *_{E^2} pq$$

Where N_0 is the sample size, Z^2 is the value for the selected alpha level based on the confidence level (e.g., 1.96 for 95 percent confidence level), E is the desired level of precision or the amount of error the researcher is willing to accept, p is the estimated proportion of an attribute that is present in the population, and q is $1 - p$.

Since there was no knowledge of the variability in the proportion of human insecurities, it is customary, in similar instances, to adopt the maximum variability option of $p = 0.5$. The research aims for 95 percent confidence and ±3 percent precision. Taking these figures into consideration, the sample size was computed as:

$$N_o = (1.96)^2 \times .5 \times .5$$

$$(0.03)^2$$

This gives us a sample size of 1,067.

Index

Italicized pages refer to tables.

About the Editors and Contributors

Dr. Raymond Mark Kirton is a citizen of Guyana, who is the holder of the Bachelor of Arts (with distinction) from the University of Guyana, Master of Science (M.Sc) from Georgetown University, Washington DC, and a PhD from the University of Texas at Austin. His professional career includes senior lecturer and head of the Department of Government and International Affairs as well as dean of the Faculty of Social Sciences at University of Guyana. Most recently, he served as the director of the Institute of International Relations at the University of the West Indies, St. Augustin, Trinidad, from where he retired. He also served as the Special Political Advisor to the President of Guyana until August 2020. He has published numerous articles in journals and chapters in books and has coedited two books: *Governance, Conflict Analysis and Conflict Resolution* with the late Cedric Grant, and *Selected Essays on Contemporary Caribbean Issues: An International Relations Perspective* with Marlon Anatol.

Dr. Marlon Anatol is senior fellow at the Cipriani College of Labour and Cooperative Studies, and has taught at the Institute of International Relations at the University of the West Indies for many years. He is the director of Research at TAIRASS, a research consultancy, and holds an Honours Degree in Applied Sociology and a PhD in international relations, specializing in research, with expertise in the areas of security, migration, trade, and development. He was the director of Project R.E.A.S.O.N., the most successful crime-prevention initiative undertaken in Trinidad and Tobago, which led to a 45 percent reduction in shootings and woundings between 2015 and 2017 in the East Port of Spain areas of Laventille, Morvant, Sea Lots, and Beetham Gardens.

Amanda Anatol has focused on the delivery of life skills to students of the University of Trinidad and Tobago for over a decade, and before returning to Trinidad and Tobago she taught in the UK and in the Middle East for several years. In each of these countries she has participated in community outreach programs, and she has held a variety of positions during all of the aforementioned posts, ranging from curriculum leader to head of Key Stage to vice principal, and has wide-ranging experience of dealing with people across various communities.

Dr. Ashaki L. Dore, is a member of the Trinidad and Tobago Regiment and has been in the military service for fifteen years. Dr. Dore is currently attached to the Trinidad and Tobago Defence Force's Military Community Support System (MCSS). She holds a PhD in international relations, with a focus on citizen security and citizen participation. Her PhD thesis is titled "Conceptualizing the Notion of Citizen Participation in the Citizen Security Framework of Countries Facing High Levels of Crime and Violence: The Cases of Trinidad and Tobago and El Salvador." She also holds a Master of Science degree in global studies and a Bachelor of Arts in Latin American Studies and Spanish (First Class Honours) from the University of the West Indies.

Dr. Clement Henry is a policy research consultant. His earlier positions include manager of the Government of Guyana/Inter-American Development Bank's *Citizen Security Strengthening Programme*, chairman of the Guyana National Data Management Authority, and head of the Policy Research Unit in the Ministry of Home Affairs. Dr. Henry is a graduate of the University of the West Indies, St. Augustine-Doctor of Philosophy; the University of Guyana, Turkeyen-Master of Social Science; and a bachelor of arts from Andrews University, Michigan. His publications include *Poverty and Human Security in Guyana* and *An Analysis of the Effectiveness of Foreign Aid Flows to Guyana*. His research interests include citizen and human security, international regimes, inclusive growth, and business cycle analysis.

Dr. Sacha Joseph-Mathews is associate professor of marketing in the Eberhardt School of Business at the University of the Pacific. She obtained both her master's in tourism and hospitality management and her PhD in business administration degrees from Florida State University. Professor Joseph-Mathews has been working and teaching in marketing, customer service, and international business for almost twenty years. In addition to teaching, Dr. Joseph-Mathews is an avid researcher, consultant, and advisor.

Dr. Jacqueline Laguardia Martinez holds a PhD in economics from the University of Havana. She is Lecturer at the Institute of International Relations at the University of the West Indies, St. Augustine campus. Previously, she was lecturer and researcher at the University of Havana. She is member of the Cátedra de Estudios del Caribe "Norman Girvan" at the University of Havana and a coordinator of the CLACSO Working Group on "Crisis, respuestas y alternativas en el Gran Caribe."

Milagros Martinez Reinosa holds an MSc degree in Caribbean Studies from the University of Havana. She was assistant professor at the University of Havana (UH) between 2002 and 2016. Previously, she worked in the Ministry of Foreign Affairs of Cuba and was executive secretary of the Cátedra de Estudios del Caribe "Norman Girvan" at the University of Havana. She is a member of the Union of Writers and Artists of Cuba (UNEAC) and of the Cuban Association of United Nations (ACNU). She is also a member of the CLACSO Working Group on "Crisis, respuestas y alternativas en el Gran Caribe."

Dr. Ruben Martoredjo holds a PhD (2018) in international relations from the Institute of International Relations, University of the West Indies. He also holds a Master of Science degree in international relations from the University of the West Indies (St. Augustine Campus) (2009, graduated as top of class with distinction), and a Doctorandus degree (candidate to doctorate's degree) in commercial economics from the Anton de Kom University of Suriname (1992). His research interests include the areas of globalization, regionalism, regional integration, Latin America and the Caribbean, Suriname, social development, and social and economic dimension of climate change.

Dr. Kai-Ann D. Skeete is the Trade Research Fellow at the University of the West Indies, Cave Hill Campus, Barbados. Dr. Skeete lectures research methods for trade, trade aspects of regional integration as well as CARICOM and the CSME. Her research interests include CARICOM's forward trade agenda, Caribbean Regional Integration, geopolitics, security studies and regional governance systems. Dr. Skeete is the co-author of a Commonwealth Secretariat Small States Digest (2015) titled *Regionalism among Small States—Challenges & Prospects: The Case of the Caribbean Community (CARICOM)*. She has worked across the Caribbean region as a Trade Consultant since 2009.

www.ingramcontent.com/pod-product-compliance
Lightning Source LLC
Chambersburg PA
CBHW022319280326
41932CB00010B/1154